yes please

yes please

AMY POEHLER

DEY ST.
AN IMPRINT OF WILLIAM MORROW PUBLISHERS

All photographs are courtesy of the author, except pages
xx, 14, 50, 104, 183: © Liezl Estipona; pages 28, 33, 134, 244, 268:
© NBC/Getty Images; page 106: © Jeff Clampitt; page 141: courtesy
of Broadway Video Enterprises and NBC Studios, LLC; page 295: ©
Stephen Lovekin/Getty Images; page 310: © Kelly Campbell, WWO.

Chapter "Don't Forget to Tip Your Waitresses" contains content
first published by *The New Yorker* in "Take Your Licks,"
October 14, 2013.

HarperCollins books may be purchased for educational, business,
or sales promotional use. For information please e-mail the
Special Markets Department at SPsales@harpercollins.com.

A hardcover edition of this book was published in 2014 by Dey
Street Books, an imprint of William Morrow Publishers.

FIRST DEY STREET BOOKS PAPERBACK EDITION PUBLISHED 2015.

Designed by Headcase Design, headcasedesign.com

Library of Congress Cataloging-in-Publication Data
has been applied for.

ISBN 978-0-06-226835-8

15 16 17 18 19   ID6s/RRD   10 9 8 7 6 5 4 3 2 1

For my bold and beautiful boys.

contents

Writing Is Hard: A Preface ix

Instructions for How to Use This Book xvii

PART ONE:

SAY

WHATEVER YOU WANT

How I Fell in Love with Improv: Boston 3

Plain Girl vs. the Demon 15

Laughing to Crying to Laughing 29

The Day I Was Born 57

Sorry, Sorry, Sorry 65

My Books on Divorce 87

Talk to Yourself Like You're Ninety 97

PART TWO:

DO

WHATEVER YOU LIKE

How I Fell in Love with Improv: Chicago 107

The Russians Are Coming 121

Humping Justin Timberlake 135

Every Mother Needs a Wife 149

My World-Famous Sex Advice 153

Gimme That Pudding 157

Bad Sleeper 171

PART THREE:

BE

WHOEVER YOU ARE

How I Fell in Love with Improv: New York 185

Parents Just Do Understand 201

Don't Forget to Tip Your Waitresses 207

Treat Your Career Like a Bad Boyfriend 217

Partner in Crime.. 229

I'm So Proud of You 233

Let's Build a Park 245

Things They Don't Tell You About the Biz 271

Time Travel 279

Obligatory Drug Stories, or Lessons I Learned
on Mushrooms 287

My Boys 299

The Robots Will Kill Us All: A Conclusion 313

Acknowledgments 331

vii

MEADOWBROOK SCHOOL
BURLINGTON, MA

NAME _Amy Poehler_   TEACHER _Cynthia Systrom_

GRADE _Kdg._   DATE _June, 1977_

ACADEMIC READINESS:	ALWAYS		USUALLY		SELDOM	
Completes work			✓			
Knows letters	✓					
Knows beginning sounds	✓					
Knows numbers	✓					
Counts by rote	✓					
Listens carefully	✓					
Retains information	✓					
Contributes to group	✓					

COMMENTS: _Amy is an excellent student._

SOCIAL DEVELOPMENT:	ALWAYS		USUALLY		SELDOM	
Relates well to children	✓					
Relates well to adults	✓					
Shares willingly	✓					
Enjoys large group activities	✓					
Enjoys small group activities	✓					
Participates enthusiastically	✓					

COMMENTS:

writing is hard:

a preface

I LIKE HARD WORK AND I DON'T LIKE PRETENDING THINGS ARE PERFECT. I have learned that about myself. And I don't have any fear of writing. I have been writing my whole life: stories and plays and sketches and scripts and poems and jokes. Most feel alive. And fluid. Breathing organisms made better by the people who come into contact with them. But this book has nearly killed me. Because, you see, a book? A book has a cover. They call it a jacket and that jacket keeps the inside warm so that the words stay permanent and everyone can read your genius thoughts over and over again for years to come. Once a book is published it can't be changed, which is a stressful proposition for this improviser who relies on her charm. I've been told that I am "better in the room" and "prettier in person." Both these things are not helpful when writing a book. I am looking forward to a lively book-on-tape session with the hope that Kathleen Turner agrees to play me when I talk about some of my darker periods. One can dream.

———

It's clear to me now that I had no business agreeing to write this book. I have a job that keeps me shooting twelve hours a day, plus two children under six. I am going through a divorce and producing many projects and falling in love and trying to make appointments for cranial massage. All of these things are equally wonderful and horrible and keep me just off balance and busy enough to make spending hours alone writing seem like a terrible idea. Plus, I am forty-two, which is smack-dab in the middle. I haven't lived a full enough life to look back on, but I am too old to get by on being pithy and cute. I know enough now to know I know nothing. I am slugging away every day, just like you. But nonetheless, here we are. I've written a book. You have it.

Everyone lies about writing. They lie about how easy it is or how hard it was. They perpetuate a romantic idea that writing is some beautiful experience that takes place in an architectural room filled with leather novels and chai tea. They talk about their "morning ritual" and how they "dress for writing" and the cabin in Big Sur where they go to "be alone"—blah blah blah. No one tells the truth about writing a book. Authors pretend their stories were always shiny and perfect and just waiting to be written. The truth is, writing is this: hard and boring and occasionally great but usually not. Even I have lied about writing. I have told people that writing this book has been like brushing away dirt from a fossil. What a load of shit. It has been like hacking away at a freezer with a screwdriver.

I wrote this book after my kids went to sleep. I wrote this book on subways and on airplanes and in between setups while I shot a television show. I wrote this book from scribbled thoughts I kept in the Notes app on my iPhone and conversations I had with myself in my own head before I went to sleep. I wrote it ugly and in pieces.

———

I tried hard not be overly dramatic, like when I wrote this poem in Social Studies class at age thirteen:

Amy Poehler

May 21, 1985
Social Studies
1:10

When life attacks you from everyside.
It hurts —
too much
And the most
painless
easiest way out is —
death
        to survive.

———

———

At this very moment I am attempting to write this preface in the dark while my oldest boy, Archie, sleeps next to me. He is dreaming and talking, and I am turning down the light on the screen as I write about how hard it is to write. Writing a book is awful. It's lonely, even with Archie beside me and my editors nagging me. During this process I have written my editors e-mails with subject headings such as "How Dare You" and "This Is Never Going to Work" and "Why Are You Trying to Kill Me?" Most authors liken the struggle of writing to something mighty and macho, like wrestling a bear. Writing a book is nothing like that. It is a small, slow crawl to the finish line.

Honestly, I have moments when I don't even care if anyone reads this book. I just want to finish it.

If you are reading this, it means I have "finished." More likely, it means my editors have told me I can't keep tinkering anymore. I will take this time now to thank you for buying this and reading it and eventually turning it into a feature film with Kate Winslet/Katy Perry/Katie Couric as the star.

Let me offer this apology. Please excuse this self-indulgent preface. I know what I am doing. I am presenting a series of reasons as to why you should lower your expectations, so that you can be blown away by my sneaky insights about life and work. I am a grown woman. I know my own tricks! I know how good I am at bemoaning my process and pretending I don't care so that my final product will seem totally natural and part of my essence and not something I sweated for months and years. One of the things I have learned about me while writing about me is that I am really onto myself. I have got Amy Poehler's number, I'll tell you. I also learned that writing topless tends to relax me. Go figure. Life is a mystery.

———

While writing this book I made many mistakes. I kept a copy of Nora Ephron's *Heartburn* next to me as a reminder of how to be funny and truthful, and all I ended up doing was ignoring my writing and rereading *Heartburn*. I also kept a copy of Patti Smith's *Just Kids* nearby, which was awful because her writing is beautiful and poetic and how dare she. I also read and reread wonderful books by wonderful women: Rachel Dratch's *Girl Walks into a Bar . . .*, Sarah Silverman's *The Bedwetter*, Mindy Kaling's *Is Everyone Hanging Out Without Me?*, Lena Dunham's *Not That Kind of Girl*, Caitlin Moran's *How to Be a Woman*, and Tina Fey's *Bossypants*. All are superb and infuriating. My dear friend and *Parks and Recreation* cast-mate Nick Offerman had the nerve to start and publish his book *Paddle Your Own Canoe* in less time than it took me to write this preface. I congratulated him when he presented it to me and then immediately threw it in the garbage.

I made other terrible mistakes while I tried to write this book. I asked people who have already finished books for advice, which is akin to asking a mother with a four-year-old what childbirth is like. All the edges have been rounded and they have forgotten the pain. Their books are finished and in their libraries, so all they end up talking about is how you need to "stick to your guns" and "not let the editors push you around" and that "your title is important." Stick to my guns? I am hiding from my editors because I feel so guilty that I haven't worked hard enough and given them something genius or interesting or new. My title is important? Well, I am screwed, because right now I am vacillating between *The Secret 2* and *Mosquitos Love Me: A Woman's Guide to Getting Her Funk On*. The only people I can stand to read right now are Pema Chödrön, who reminds me that life is messy and everything is a dream, and Stephen King and Anne Lamott, who are two of my favorite writers on writing. But now that I think of it, both of them are funnier than me, so they can tie their sixty-eight books to their ankles and go jump in a lake.

Many people suggested ways I could carve out more time for my writing, but none of their suggestions involved the care and consideration of the small children who live in my house. Every book written by men and women with children under the age of six should have a "sleep deprived" sticker. I could find lots of discussion online about "waiting for the muse" but not enough about having to write in between T-ball games. I want more honesty from people who write books while they have small children. I want to hear from people who feel like they have no time. I remember once reading about J. K. Rowling, and how she wrote *Harry Potter* while she was a single mom struggling to make ends meet. We need to hear more stories like that. However, I do need to point out that J. K. never had to write a personal memoir AND make it funny AND do it while she had to be on camera with makeup on, AND she had ONLY ONE KID AT THE TIME IF I REMEMBER CORRECTLY. (This could be wrong; editors, please fact-check. Also let marketing know I am very interested in *Yes Please* becoming the next *Harry Potter*.)

In my desperation, I searched out other writers who were struggling and asked them if they wanted to take a break from their own misery and contribute to my book so I would have fewer pages to fill. I thought about asking Hillary Clinton but realized she was too busy writing, finishing, and publishing her own book. If I had timed it better, I could have contributed to her book and she could have contributed to mine. But I blew it. I guess my essay "Judge Judy, American Hero" will have to be read in *Harper's* at a later date.

Writing this book has been so hard I wrote a *Parks and Recreation* script in three days. It was a joy, writing in a voice that wasn't my own. I have also written two screenplays in the time it has taken me to crank this sucker out. (This isn't true but whatever. I can write a screenplay in my sleep. Shiiiiiit.)

So what do I do? What do we do? How do we move forward when we are tired and afraid? What do we do when the voice in our head is yelling that WE ARE NEVER GONNA MAKE IT? How do we drag ourselves through the muck when our brain is telling us youaredumbandyouwillneverfinishandnoonecaresanditistimeyoustop?

Well, the first thing we do is take our brain out and put it in a drawer. Stick it somewhere and let it tantrum until it wears itself out. You may still hear the brain and all the shitty things it is saying to you, but it will be muffled, and just the fact that it is not in your head anymore will make things seem clearer. And then you just do it. You just dig in and write it. You use your body. You lean over the computer and stretch and pace. You write and then cook something and write some more. You put your hand on your heart and feel it beating and decide if what you wrote feels true. You do it because the doing of it is the thing. The doing is the thing. The talking and worrying and thinking is not the thing. That is what I know. Writing the book is about writing the book.

So here we go, you and me. Because what else are we going to do? Say no? Say no to an opportunity that may be slightly out of our comfort zone? Quiet our voice because we are worried it is not perfect? I believe great people do things before they are ready. This is America and I am allowed to have healthy self-esteem. This book comes straight from my feisty and freckled fingers. Know it was a battle. Blood was shed. A war raged between my jokey and protective brain and my squishy and tender heart. I have realized that mystery is what keeps people away, and I've grown tired of smoke and mirrors. I yearn for the clean, well-lighted place. So let's peek behind the curtain and hail the others like us. The open-faced

———

sandwiches who take risks and live big and smile with all of their teeth. These are the people I want to be around. This is the honest way I want to live and love and write.

Except when it comes to celebrities without makeup. I want my celebrities to look beautiful. I don't need to see them pumping gas.

I tried to tell the truth and be funny. What else do you want from me, you filthy animals?

I love you,

Amy

———

instructions for
how to use this book

THIS BOOK IS A MISSIVE FROM THE MIDDLE. It's a street-level view of my life so far. It's an attempt to speak to that feeling of being young and old at the same time. I cannot change the fact that I am an American White Woman who grew up Lower-Middle-Class and had Children after spending most of her life Acting and Doing Comedy, so if you hate any of those buzzwords you may want to bail now. Sometimes this book stays in the present, other times I try to cut myself in half and count the rings. Occasionally I think about the future, but I try to do that sparingly because it usually makes me anxious. *Yes Please* is an attempt to present an open scrapbook that includes a sense of what I am thinking and feeling right now. But mostly, let's call this book what it really is: an obvious money grab to support my notorious online shopping addiction. I have already spent the advance on fancy washcloths from Amazon, so I need this book to really sell a lot of copies or else I am in trouble. Chop-chop, people.

———

In this book there is a little bit of talk about the past. There is some light emotional sharing. I guess that is the "memoir" part. There is also some "advice," which varies in its levels of seriousness. Lastly, there are just "essays," which are stories that usually have a beginning and an end, but nothing is guaranteed. Sometimes these three things are mixed together, like a thick stew. I hope it is full of flavor and fills you up, but don't ask me to list all the ingredients.

I struggled with choosing a quote that would set the table for you and establish an important tone once you started reading.

I thought about Eleanor Roosevelt's "A woman is like a tea bag; you never know how strong it is until it's in hot water."

I dabbled with "A woman who doesn't wear perfume has no future" from the seemingly hilarious and real "girl's girl" Coco Chanel.

I was tempted by "I always play women I would date" from Angelina Jolie.

But Wordsworth stuck with me when he said, "Poetry is the spontaneous overflow of powerful feelings: it takes its origin from emotion recollected in tranquillity." This book is a spontaneous overflow in the middle of chaos, not tranquillity. So it's not a poem to you. It's a half poem. It's a "po." It's a Poehler po. Wordsworth also said that the best part of a person's life is "his little, nameless, unremembered, acts of kindness and of love." I look forward to reading a book one day in which someone lists mine. I feel like I may have failed to do so. Either way, it's obvious I am currently on a Wordsworth kick and this should give you literary confidence as you read *Yes Please*.

The title *Yes Please* comes from a few different places. I like to say "Yes please" as an answer to a lot of things in my personal and professional life. The "yes" comes from my improvisational days and the opportunity that comes with youth, and the "please" comes

———

from the wisdom of knowing that agreeing to do something usually means you aren't doing it alone.

It's called *Yes Please* because it is the constant struggle and often the right answer. Can we figure out what we want, ask for it, and stop talking? Yes please. Is being vulnerable a power position? Yes please. Am I allowed to take up space? Yes please. Would you like to be left alone? Yes please.

I love saying "yes" and I love saying "please." Saying "yes" doesn't mean I don't know how to say no, and saying "please" doesn't mean I am waiting for permission. "Yes please" sounds powerful and concise. It's a response and a request. It is not about being a good girl; it is about being a real woman. It's also a title I can tell my kids. I like when they say "Yes please" because most people are rude and nice manners are the secret keys to the universe.

And attention, men! Don't despair! There is plenty of stuff in here for you too. Since I have spent the majority of my life in rooms filled with men I feel like I know you well. I love you. I love the shit out of you. I think this book will speak to men in a bunch of different ways. I should also point out that there is a secret code in each chapter and if you figure it out it unlocks the next level and you get better weapons to fight the zombie quarterbacks on the Pegasus Bridge. So get cracking, you task-oriented monkey brains.

I still wish this book was just a compendium of searing photographs I took in Afghanistan during my years as a sexy war correspondent, but hey, there is still time.

Shall we?

SAY

WHATEVER YOU WANT

...KING OF THE FOREST..." - Steve ... (right) delivers his lines as the ...rdly Lion, while Dorothy (Amy Poehler), ...n Man (Monica Stamm) and the Scarecrow... (Brian Doherty) look on during the ... Wildwood School presentation of "The W... Oz."

(Rick Karw...

how i fell in love with improv:

boston

I WAS IN FOURTH GRADE AND IN TROUBLE. The students of Wildwood Elementary School in Burlington, Massachusetts, shifted in their uncomfortable metal seats as they waited for me to say my next line. A dog rested in my arms and an entire musical rested on my shoulders. I was playing Dorothy in *The Wizard of Oz,* and it was my turn to speak. Dorothy is *Hamlet* for girls. Next to Annie in *Annie* and Sandy in *Grease,* it is the dream role of every ten-year-old. Annie taught me that orphanages were a blast and being rich is the only thing that matters. *Grease* taught me being in a gang is nonstop fun and you need to dress sexier to have any chance of keeping a guy interested. But *The Wizard of Oz* was the ultimate. It dealt with friendship and fear and death and rainbows and sparkly red shoes.

Up to this moment, I had only been onstage twice. The first was for a winter pageant in second grade. I was dressed as a snowflake and had to recite a poem. The microphone was tilted too high,

3

and so I stood on my tiptoes and fixed it. A year later I was in a school play in the role of a singing lion. My "lion's mane" (a dyed string mop worn on my head) kept slipping, and I surreptitiously adjusted it midsong.

My parents would later point to these two small moments and tell me that was when they knew I would be a performer. Honestly, I don't think I had a burning desire to act at that young age. Back then, I didn't know acting was a job, really. All I knew was I liked roller-skating in my driveway and making people sit and watch. I liked setting up dance contests in my basement and being the only judge. I liked attention. Attention and control. Attention, control, and, it turns out, laughs.

In *The Wizard of Oz,* the part of Dorothy isn't exactly the comedic lead. She spends a lot of time listening to other people explain themselves. She is the straight man among a bunch of much juicier character parts. The Wicked Witch of the West is more dynamic. The Scarecrow has a bigger arc. Even the Lollipop Guild has a killer song. Dorothy just asks a lot of questions and is always the last to know. I didn't care. At the time, I was in fourth grade, which, for me, was a heavenly time to be a girl. It was all elbows and angles and possibility. I hadn't gotten my period or kissed a boy. My beloved grandfather hadn't yet died of a heart attack on my front porch on the Fourth of July. I wanted to be an astronaut or a scientist or a veterinarian and all signs pointed to my making any or all of that happen. The worst things I had encountered to this point were lice (which I'd had), scoliosis (which I didn't), and the threat of nuclear war (a shadow that loomed over everything). My generation was obsessed with scoliosis. Judy Blume dedicated an entire novel to it. At least once a month we would line up in the gym, lift our shirts, and bend over, while some creepy old doctor ran his finger up and down our spines. Nuclear war was a high-concept threat, two words that often rang out in political speeches or on the six o'clock news. Our spines. Lice. Nuclear war. The Big Three.

AIDS was just around the corner, but we didn't know it yet. The only AIDS I knew were Ayds, an unfortunately named caramel diet candy my mom had in our kitchen cabinet. The anxiety-filled eighties would dovetail nicely with my hormonal teenage years, but in fourth grade, in 1980, I felt like I would live forever.

I stood onstage in my blue-checked dress, Toto in my arms, and looked at the audience of parents, teachers, and students. I breathed in and had a huge realization. I could decide right then and there what the next moment would be. I could try something new. I could go off script and give something a shot. I could say *whatever* I wanted.

5

It was because of this Dorothy Moment that I had the nerve, years later, to try out for the high school musical. It was my senior year and Burlington High School had been a great place for a floater like me. I weaved in and out of activities and groups, and hid on occasion. My school was big and sprawling, with four hundred students in my graduating class. I played basketball and soccer for a while and I thought I might be some kind of athlete. My dad was a semipro basketball player in college and I inherited his hand-eye coordination. I was a decent point guard and middling fullback. Softball was the most fun because of the opportunity to shit-talk. But my enthusiasm for team sports fell away once I realized I would never be great. (Once they move you from shortstop to second base, you might want to start making other plans.) I was a cheerleader for a while. I did student council. I started to hang with the popular crowd but was never considered the prettiest or most interesting. I tended to blend. In my high school yearbook I was voted third runner-up for "Most Casual." I never figured out if that meant most casual in dress or in overall manner. In any case, I didn't come in first. I guess the two ahead of me wanted it less.

Every year our school put on one musical, and in my senior year I auditioned for *Once Upon a Mattress*. I didn't know any of the "theater kids" by name. My experience with musicals was limited, at best. In our sophomore year, my class had taken a trip to New York City and gone to a few Broadway shows. We saw a production of *The Fantasticks,* which I liked, and *A Chorus Line,* which I loved. The part of Diana Morales spoke to me. I loved that she was short and blue-collar. I loved how she stood up to her grumpy and withholding acting teacher, Mr. Karp. I loved how she cried when that bastard died. Because she FELT NOTHING. So badass!

On the same trip, we visited the Empire State Building and the World Trade Center, as well as swinging by 30 Rockefeller Center

6

and taking the *SNL* studio tour. We pressed our noses against the glass and watched the *SNL* cast rehearse. It was 1985, and Anthony Michael Hall and Robert Downey Jr. were on the main stage. I would meet both of them twenty years later—I directed Anthony Michael Hall in a reenactment of *Sixteen Candles* for a VH1 program, and I met Robert Downey Jr. in a Hollywood coffee shop, where I pitched him my idea for a little indie film called *Iron Man*.

In *Once Upon a Mattress,* I was cast as Princess Winnifred, a part that had physical set pieces and lots of loud singing. It would be the beginning of me playing a long line of crazy big-mouths.

Carol Burnett had originated this role on Broadway and I loooooved *The Carol Burnett Show*. I loved Carol Burnett. She was funny and versatile and up for anything, but most importantly, I could tell that the ensemble around her loved her. I could tell that she was a benevolent captain of that team and was having a hell of a time. Watching that show proved that good comedy can be fun and you don't have to treat people badly to be on top. I felt the same when I watched Gilda Radner, Andrea Martin, and Catherine O'Hara. You could tell that the cast adored them. You could see Bill Murray look at Gilda in a way that told you he loved her, for real.

I was lucky enough to meet and do an interview with Carol Burnett once, for *TV Guide*. I told her that I loved everything about that show: how it represented time spent with my mother, how it reminded me of myself as a young woman learning to love comedy, how when she took off her makeup and answered questions at the end of the show it was such a generous act because she seemed like one of us. She said, and I quote, "Oh, Amy, you are my new best friend!" It's in print, I swear.

A lot of people ask me if I always knew I was going to be on *Saturday Night Live*. I think the simple answer is: yes. I don't mean to sound cocky. I didn't know if I had the talent or drive, I just had a tiny little voice whispering inside of me. That same voice would tell me I would meet Carol Burnett someday, I would find love, I would be okay. We all have a tiny whispery voice inside of us, but the bad ones are usually at a lower register and come through a little clearer. I don't know where the good voice came from. It was a mix of loving parents, luck, and me. But ever since I was a small child, I would look at places where I wanted to be and believe I would eventually be on the other side of the glass. I believed that someday in the future, I would be rehearsing onstage at *Saturday Night Live* while a gaggle of sophomore girls would be waving to me. All of them wearing cooler outfits than my classmates and I wore that day.

My high school musical did not offer a shirtless Zac Efron, but it did provide me with many lessons. I learned that I loved being in a theater, attending rehearsals, and building sets. I loved listening to the director and groaning about rehearsing choreography. When I would leave the bright sunlight of outside and enter into the dark and empty theater, I would feel like a real artist with a true sense of purpose. Time passed and the world spun, but all that mattered was the thing in the room you were making together. I started to go to theater parties and tried cigarettes. I had floated into the right pool, finally.

The play itself went well, from what I remember. It was a blur of adrenaline and costume changes. I reveled in this new feeling of being incredibly stressed and pulling things off last-minute. (A talent that I hope will help me finish this goddamn book—dear lord, when will I finish this book?) My parents rushed to congratulate me after the show. "You were so great, Ames!" my mom said. "You don't have to go to college if you don't want to!" my dad exclaimed. My mother hit him in the arm and told him he was crazy. This one-two punch of support and realism would help me deal with the many years of rejection I didn't know were ahead of me. I then thought about the idea of being an actress and tried it on for size.

Back to fourth grade, *The Wizard of Oz* and Dorothy. I stood onstage in soft Dearfoams slippers. My mother had bought two pairs at Bradlee's, and we spray-painted them silver and sparkly red. My hair was braided and I was wearing my own denim overall dress and blue-checked blouse. It was my time to speak during the tornado scene. All of the other actors were supposed to be running around and reacting to heavy winds. A teacher made a whistling-wind sound effect on a handheld microphone and construction-paper tumbleweeds were rolled across the stage. In my arms was Toto, played by a real dog. Some sucker had allowed us to cast their tiny poodle as Toto, which in hindsight begs the question: What kind of maniac hands over their tiny dog to a bunch of ten-year-olds for an elementary school play?

———

We were in the second night of a blistering two-night run. The previous evening I had delivered my line "Toto, Toto! Where are you?" during the tornado scene. The problem was the damn dog was in my arms at the time. The audience laughed. Lightning struck—and I discovered three important things. I liked getting a laugh. I wanted to get one again. But I wanted to get it in a different way and be in charge of how I got it. So, I stood onstage that second night and tried something new.

Trying something new was all I wanted to do when I graduated high school. I was so excited to go to Boston College that I distinctly remember wiggling in my seat as I wore my cap and gown. I wanted to go, go, go. Arriving at Boston College was like moving to a new country. I was unprepared for the fact that most of the kids were a lot wealthier than me. I met prep school kids who knew how to decorate their rooms with tapestries. I became friends with private school athletes who were familiar with living away from home. I studied with foreign students who had their own credit cards. When I got the name of my new freshman roommate sent to me in the mail, I noticed she was from Illinois and so I immediately assumed she lived on a farm. I was wrong. We spoke on the phone and I asked her if classical music was playing in the background and she informed me that was the sound of her doorbell. Her name was Erin and she ended up being very nice and fun. We would sing the soundtrack to *Les Misérables* by the light of a neon beer sign her dad sent us to put in our dorm room window.

I looked at my high hair and heard my New England accent and realized I was certainly bringing a lot of Boston to my Boston College experience. I decided I might want to tone both my hair and the lazy r's down a little. The accent is a really hard thing for me. It reminds me of my family and my childhood, but it's one of the

———

worst-sounding accents out there. I love Boston, but we sound like idiots. Our mouths never close and we talk like big, lazy babies. I might get shit for this but as a true Bostonian all I will say to that is FUCK YOU, AHHSOLE, IF YOU GOT A PRAWBLEM WIT ME THEN LET'S MEET BY THE RIVAH!

During my first week of freshman orientation I went to a performance at the Eagles Nest, the BC cafeteria and general social center. I was struck by how much fun it looked. It was ensemble comedy. It was improvisation. It was quick jokes and group mind dynamics. Everyone was getting to act and be funny and write and direct and edit all at the same time. The group was called My Mother's Fleabag and it was the oldest running improvisational group on campus. I wanted in. I met Kara McNamara, one of the performers. She was a Boston girl and would eventually be my roommate, and she pushed me to audition, though I have no memory of actually doing it. I think it was mostly short-form improvisational games. I do remember that it was thrilling. I went back to my room and waited.

We were told that we made the group by being woken up in the middle of the night and taken to a secret location to drink. It was like being hazed for one day, which is the exact amount of hazing I am able to withstand. We rehearsed constantly. We would spend hours arguing over one joke. Relationships were formed and trust was built. My Mother's Fleabag performed shows a couple of times a year. A cover band played "Pulling Mussels (from the Shell)" by Squeeze, and we would run out in baseball shirts. We did short-form improv games, sketches, and songs based on specific Boston College humor. It was fun but not too cool, and it got me in front of an audience. I had a theater I went to every day and a group that needed me all the time. It was heaven.

Kara and I moved in with a bunch of men and women off campus and my college life sort of exploded in happiness. We used to host big and boozy parties. We had a "Good-bye to the Eighties" party and everyone dressed in costume. At least twenty different women arrived in sexy Robert Palmer–girl outfits. I dressed as Baby Jessica, the little girl who fell down the well. (And was successfully rescued! Important fact!) I wore pajamas and pigtails and made my face a little dirty. Sexy stuff. We lived on a street called Strathmore and our motto was "Live More, Love More, Strath More." I learned about Charles Busch and Kate Bush. I sat with the cool Jesuit priests and talked about Edna St. Vincent Millay. I took classes like "The Medium Is the Message" and "The Male Lens." I carved out a pretty groovy off-campus curriculum in what was a very competitive academic program. I spent my days directing scenes from *True West* and my nights writing sketches about bad cafeteria food. I studied Shakespeare and learned to control my voice, and at night I huddled with a bunch of misfits and practiced being stupid on purpose.

I didn't really know what kind of actor I wanted to be back then. I didn't have a real plan or even a mentor to follow. I just knew the things I didn't want. I didn't want to be tied down and stuck. I didn't want to decide who I was going to marry or where I was going to live. I took a public speaking class in college with Craig Finn, a friend of my cousin Lynn (Sheehan) Gosselin. Craig is a great musician who is now the lead singer of the band Hold Steady. I remember feeling like we both knew a secret: we were going to keep performing no matter what, and we both were going to have no money, stability, or children for the next ten years. I think we should stop asking people in their twenties what they "want to do" and start asking them what they don't want to do.

Instead of asking students to "declare their major" we should ask students to "list what they will do anything to avoid." It just makes a lot more sense.

I was in my off-campus Strathmore kitchen when Kara told me she was going to move to Chicago after she graduated. She was a year ahead of me and had heard about these classes at the comedy mecca Second City. Further investigation led us to research ImprovOlympic, and they also had classes. That settled it. Kara was going to Chicago and was going to get an apartment, and I would join her a year later. "I can be a waitress anywhere!" I said to my horrified parents, who had remortgaged their small house twice to pay for my brother and me to go to college.

I started to believe in myself. I realized I could say whatever I wanted.

In the second and final performance of *The Wizard of Oz,* I decided to take control during the tornado scene. I paused, put the blinking dog down on the stage, and walked a few feet away from it. "Toto, Toto! Where are you?" I said, pretending to look for my lost dog in the fearsome storm. The dog froze and played it perfectly. I got laughter and some light applause for my efforts. I had improvised and it had worked. One could argue that it worked because of the dog. A good straight dog can really help sell a joke. Whatever. I have been chasing that high ever since.

1989

2014

plain girl vs. the demon

I HATE HOW I LOOK. That is the mantra we repeat over and over again. Sometimes we whisper it quietly and other times we shout it out loud in front of a mirror. I hate how I look. I hate how my face looks my body looks I am too fat or too skinny or too tall or too wide or my legs are too stupid and my face is too smiley or my teeth are dumb and my nose is serious and my stomach is being so lame. Then we think, "I am so ungrateful. I have arms and legs and I can walk and I have strong nail beds and I am alive and I am so selfish and I have to read *Man's Search for Meaning* again and call my parents and volunteer more and reduce my carbon footprint and why am I such a self-obsessed ugly asshole no wonder I hate how I look! I hate how I *am!*"

There have been forty million books and billions of words written on this subject, so I will assume we are all caught up.

That voice that talks badly to you is a demon voice. This very patient and determined demon shows up in your bedroom one day and refuses to leave. You are six or twelve or fifteen and you look in the mirror and you hear a voice so awful and mean that it takes your breath away. It tells you that you are fat and ugly and you don't deserve love. And the scary part is the demon is your own voice. But it doesn't sound like you. It sounds like a strangled and seductive version of you. Think Darth Vader or an angry Lauren Bacall. The good news is there are ways to make it stop talking. The bad news is it never goes away. If you are lucky, you can live a life where the demon is generally forgotten, relegated to a back shelf in a closet next to your old field hockey equipment. You may even have days or years when you think the demon is gone. But it is not. It is sitting very quietly, waiting for you.

This motherfucker is patient.

It says, "Take your time."

It says, "Go fall in love and exercise and surround yourself with people who make you feel beautiful."

It says, "Don't worry, I'll wait."

And then one day, you go through a breakup or you can't lose your baby weight or you look at your reflection in a soup spoon and that slimy bugger is back. It moves its sour mouth up to your ear and reminds you that you are fat and ugly and don't deserve love.

This demon is some Stephen King from-the-sewer devil-level shit.

I had a lucky childhood. My demon didn't live in my room. My demon just walked around my neighborhood. I grew up with a naturally pretty but very earthy mother who never told me to put on makeup or change my outfit. I didn't have the kind of mother who flirted with my friends or wore tight jeans.

In middle school I was small and flat chested, which was also a lucky break. You can kind of slip around unnoticed that way, which is exactly what you want. I was made fun of for being short, but it was mostly by boys who were shorter than me. I rarely brushed my hair

16

and I was skinny. I bordered on being a tomboy, but not enough to be labeled one. It was a wonderful but short-lived time when I was in my body but not critical of it. If you ever want to see heaven, watch a bunch of young girls play. They are all sweat and skinned knees. Energy and open faces. My demon would receive my school picture and maybe gently suggest I "do something about those eyebrows," but for the most part it left me alone. I felt safe in the middle—a girl who had a perfectly fine face but not one that drew any attention.

Then I started caring about boys and the demon pulled into my driveway.

The eighties were a strange time for teenage fashion. We wore silk blouses and shoulder pads, neon earrings and jodhpur pants. Come to think of it, our pants were especially weird. We also wore stirrup pants, parachute pants, and velvet knickers. It was a real experimental pant time. We curled our hair and sprayed it until it was crunchy and high. We wore jewel tones and too much makeup. With the exception of a few naturally beautiful girls who knew how to balance all of these elements, we looked ridiculous.

———

Dating in middle school often meant walking around the mall together and spending hours on the phone picking "your song." There was light hand-holding and maybe a kiss on the cheek, but it was really all very innocent. I "dated" one boy and our song was "Faithfully" by Journey. Every time it played my body would turn electric, and I would stare out whatever window I was near and reminisce about experiences I hadn't had. Is there a word for when you are young and pretending to have lived and loved a thousand lives? Is there a German word for that? Seems like there should be. Let's say it is *Schaufenfrieglasploit*.

Dating in high school was very different. Boys suddenly went up your shirt. Girls were expected to give blow jobs and be sexy. You had to be hot but not a slut. You had to be into sex but never have it, except when your boyfriend wanted it. If you had sex you had to keep it a secret but also be very good at it, except not too good, because this better be your first time. Darling Nikki masturbated to a magazine, but Madonna was supposedly still a virgin. It was very confusing. Once high school started, I began to see the real difference between the plain and the pretty. Boys, who were going through their own battles started to point out things about me I hadn't yet noticed. One told me I looked like a frog. Some told me I smiled like a Muppet. A senior told me to stop looking at him with my "big, weird eyes." I looked in the mirror at my flat chest and my freckles and heard a sound. It was the demon, suitcase in hand. He moved in and demanded the top bunk.

Now, as I continue, please know a few things. I usually find any discussion about my own looks to be incredibly boring. I can only imagine what a yawn fest it is for you. But I cannot, in good faith, pretend I have fallen in love with how I look. The demon still visits me often. I wish I could tell you that being on television or having a

———

nice picture in a magazine suddenly washes all of those thoughts away, but it really doesn't. I wish I were taller or had leaner hands and a less crazy smile. I don't like my legs, especially. I used to have a terrific flat stomach but now it's kind of blown out after two giant babies used it as a short-term apartment. My nose is great. My tits are better than ever. I like my giant eyes, but they can get crazy. My ass is pretty sweet. My hair is too thin for my liking. My Irish and English heritage and my early sun exposure guarantee that I am on the fast track to wrinkle city.

Bored yet? Because I can't stop.

I went through high school and college and the years after dating all different types of people. I think if you lined them up in a row there would not be one single physical characteristic that they all shared. Most were white. Not all. Some were short and hairy, some were weird, some pretty, sweet, athletic. I would say that maybe most of the men I dated had a small current of anger fueling them, but that is the case for most funny people. I dated a lot of really funny people. And some medium funny. The best-looking ones were medium funny at best—it's tough to be both. In Chicago I dated a "male model" for a hot minute. It was the first time I had dated someone that "handsome" but the truth was he was in my improv class and not that funny, so I felt weirdly superior.

I made the mistake of snooping and reading the model's journal. We finished having medium-to-boring sex and I rifled through his things while he took a shower. I am pretty good at snooping around. It started in my own house, where I would go through every drawer and every pocket in my parents' room. Luckily, I didn't find much at home except for some well-worn copies of *Playboy* that seem positively charming compared to the up-close butt fisting that pops up on my computer these days when I am trying to order salad tongs from Target. I honed my snooping skills when I babysat. It was then that I saw my first diaphragm, laxatives, and stacks of cash in an underwear drawer. I have basically ransacked every house I have been allowed into. My snooping tendencies have now abated somewhat, but I still have to fight the urge to immediately go through people's shit. I am not proud of this and I realize that by admitting this I am limiting future opportunities to be a houseguest.

Anyway, the bad part about snooping is you can find stuff you don't want to find. Snooping in e-mails, texts, or journals is a disaster. No one says good things about people in diaries. You tell people the good things. Diaries are for the bad things! I found an entry from model man that basically said he was kind of proud of himself for dating someone like me. He thought I was "funny but not that pretty, which was kind of like cool, you know?" He, like, wasn't "into me but like was totally down for the journey." Like, cool, man. I remember thinking, "HA HA! I know that already, dummy. We just had boring sex and I win because I tricked you with my personality! I don't even like you!"

Then I went home and cried and took way too long to break up with him.

But I was eventually okay. And you will be okay too. Here's why. I had already made a decision early on that I would be a plain girl with tons of personality, and accepting it made everything a lot easier. If you are lucky, there is a moment in your life when you have some say as to what your currency is going to be. I decided early on it was not going to be my looks. I have spent a lifetime coming to terms with this idea and I would say I am about 15 to 20 percent there. Which I think is great progress. I am not underestimating the access I get as a BLOND, WHITE lady from AMERICA.

Believe me, blond hair can take you really far, especially with the older men. It can really distract from the face. I am convinced I could have had sex with both Tony Bennett and John McCain if we weren't each happily married at the time we all met.

Decide what your currency is early. Let go of what you will never have. People who do this are happier and sexier.

Being considered beautiful can be tough. I know this because I work in Hollywood, which is filled with the most conventionally beautiful people in the world. Beautiful people can get objectified and underestimated. They didn't do anything to earn their genes so they have to struggle to prove they are more than their hot bods. People assume they are happy and good in bed, and most times this is not true. Plus, some beautiful people get a little addicted to being told they are beautiful and have real trouble when they get older, get less attention, or have their spouse cheat on them with someone considered "plain."

Improvisation and sketch comedy helped me find my currency. My plain face was a perfect canvas to be other people. There is nothing I like more than picking out wardrobe for a character. An *SNL* hairstylist once told me I had a great face for wigs. A Great Face for Wigs! What a compliment. (And also the title of my second book.) Looking silly can be very powerful. People who are committing and taking risks become the king and queen of my prom. People are their most beautiful when they are laughing, crying, dancing, playing, telling the truth, and being chased in a fun way.

Improvisation and sketch comedy let me choose who I wanted to be. I didn't audition to play the sexy girl, I just played her. I got to cast myself. I cast myself as sexy girls, old men, rock stars, millionaire perverts, and rodeo clowns. I played werewolves and Italian prostitutes and bitchy cheerleaders. I was never too this or not enough that. Every week on *SNL* I had the opportunity to write whatever I wanted. And then I was allowed to read it! And people had to listen! And once in a blue moon it got on TV! And maybe five times it was something really good. Writing gave me an incredible amount of power, and my currency became what I wrote and said and did.

If you write a scene for yourself you can say in the stage directions, "THE MOST BEAUTIFUL WOMAN IN THE WORLD ENTERS THE BAR AND ALL THE MEN AND WOMEN TURN THEIR HEADS." Then you can write a scene where you say, "SERGIO, THE MOST GORGEOUS MAN WE HAVE EVER SEEN, STARTS TO KISS HER." If you are lucky enough to be directing this scene you can have casting sessions and bring in various attractive men and see if they are good at kissing you. You will arrive on set and the call sheet at the start of your day can read, "JASMINE HAS SEX WITH SERGIO IN A ROWBOAT," and then you can go have fake sex with someone and still not cheat on anybody. Men do this all the time. Acting isn't all bad.

Hopefully as you get older, you start to learn how to live with your demon. It's hard at first. Some people give their demon so much room that there is no space in their head or bed for love. They feed their demon and it gets really strong and then it makes them stay in abusive relationships or starve their beautiful bodies. But sometimes, you get a little older and get a little bored of the demon. Through good therapy and friends and self-love you can practice treating the demon like a hacky, annoying cousin. Maybe a day even comes when you are getting dressed for a fancy event and it whispers, "You aren't pretty," and you go, "I know, I know, now let me find my earrings." Sometimes you say, "Demon, I promise you I will let you remind me of my ugliness, but right now I am having hot sex so I will check in later."

———

Other times I take a more direct approach. When the demon starts to slither my way and say bad shit about me I turn around and say, "Hey. Cool it. Amy is my friend. Don't talk about her like that." Sticking up for ourselves in the same way we would one of our friends is a hard but satisfying thing to do. Sometimes it works.

Even demons gotta sleep.

———

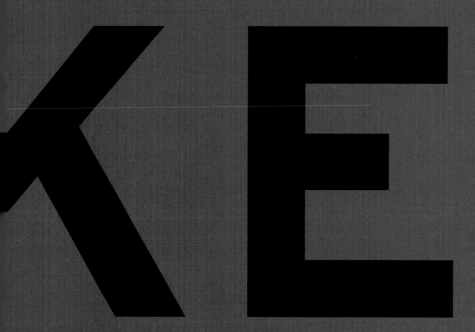

KE

WHO LIKES YOU.

PLASTIC SURGERY HAIKU

If you plump your lips
The words that come out of them
Sound ridiculous

We know it's Botox
And not your vegan diet
Nice try, Margaret

A face-lift does not
Make daughters comfortable
When you chaperone

Fine, get your boobs done
But only make them smaller
Fake boobs are weird, y'all

Asymmetrical
Looks cool while cheek implants are
Less interesting

Plastic surgery
Requires a good amount
Of lying to friends

Can I be honest?
You look like a lady from
The Broadway show *Cats*

I have no idea
If you are angry or sad
Since you got fillers

Hey, shooting poison
In your face does not keep you
From turning fifty

laughing to crying to laughing

DOING SKETCH COMEDY ON LIVE TELEVISION WHILE PREGNANT IS LIKE WEARING A SOMBRERO. You can pretend to be a serious person, but the giant hat gives you away. I have spent an inordinate amount of time on camera being pregnant. Sometimes it was real and sometimes it was not. When I shot the film *Baby Mama* I wore a fake belly. It was shaped like a watermelon cut in half and it was strapped onto my body with flesh-colored Velcro. I would adjust it to where it felt comfortable and then giggle at the sight of it under my clothes. I would rip my belly off at lunch and the satisfying Velcro rip would announce that my pregnancy was over. Many times I patted my sweaty and firm stomach and thought about how cool it was going to be when I really was pregnant.

Real pregnancy is different.

I always wanted to have kids. I like them. They like me. I'm a mother now and I think I am pretty good at it. I think I am a decent person and very good listener and excellent at funny faces, all necessary when mothering a child. When I was twenty-six, a Japanese healer felt my abdomen and told me I had a joyful uterus and I would have three children. He worked in a dusty office that smelled like envelope glue. He gave me a bunch of herbs to help with my anxiety, which is why I was actually there, but when I boiled the herbs the smell was so horrible that I became instantly anxious at the thought of ingesting them and threw them in the garbage. In addition to my joyful uterus, I have what my nana referred to as her "Irish stomach." This means that when I get old I should limit myself to buttered saltine crackers and the occasional hot dog. I associate hot dogs with the very young and the very old. Once after a grueling rehearsal at *SNL* for a Mother's Day show (where I was six months pregnant with my second son) I asked the indefatigable Betty White what she was going to do when she got home. She told me she was going to fix herself a "vodka on the rocks and eat a cold hot dog." In one sentence, she proved my theory and made me excited for my future.

Most of my thirties were spent married and without children, which is a state of affairs that I would highly recommend most people try for a while. Married and without children means you can go on vacations with other childless couples. You can eat in any restaurant at any time and have conversations about interesting things. You can decide to learn how to surf or write a slim book on the best place to buy a fedora in Los Angeles, because your spouse will be supportive and no one has to go home to relieve the babysitter. I was in no rush to change this wonderful lifestyle. Then I woke up and realized I was thirty-seven and might need to get cracking.

———

Pregnancy is such a sensitive and subjective experience. Trying to get pregnant is the most vulnerable thing in the world. You have to openly decide you are ready and then you have to put sperm in your vagina and elevate your legs like you are an upside-down coffee table. It's all ridiculous and incredibly sci-fi. Everyone's journey is different and I have nothing to say about how and when someone decides to become a mother. The legacy of my generation will be that we have truly expanded the idea of what "family" means. It is no longer unusual for people who choose surrogacy, gay adoption, IVF, international and domestic adoption, fostering, and childlessness to live side by side and quietly judge each other. We can all live in peace thinking our way is the best way and everything else is cuckoo. I was lucky. I tried for a little while to get pregnant, and at thirty-seven I did.

I didn't tell anyone at first, as you are supposed to keep it secret. It's a really magical time, those first few weeks. It almost makes you wish you didn't have to tell anyone, ever. You could just watch your belly grow bigger and no one would be allowed to ask you about it and you would have your baby and a year later you would allow visitors to finally come and meet your little miracle. I was halfway through my seventh season at *SNL,* and no one really noticed my nausea or extreme tiredness. That was par for the course at a job that made you stay up all night long and eat cold mozzarella sticks you had to buy yourself.

My ob-gyn was a wonderfully old Italian man I will call Dr. G. Dr. G had delivered Sophia Loren's children. I know this because everyone from his receptionist to the other doctors in his practice liked to tell me this fact. I was happy to hear that Dr. G was comfortable with beautiful and famous vaginas. I don't consider myself beautiful or famous, but my vagina certainly is. Everyone knows this.

———

I have the Angelina Jolie of vaginas. And there is your pull quote, editors.

"I have the Angelina Jolie of vaginas."

But even with my glamorous vagina, I worried about delivery. I have many friends who have had natural childbirth. I applaud them. I have friends who have used doulas and birthing balls and pushed out babies in tubs and taxicabs. I have a friend who had two babies at home! In bed! Her name is Maya Rudolph! She is a goddamn baby champion and she pushed her cuties out *Little House on the Prairie* style!

Good for her! Not for me.

That is the motto women should constantly repeat over and over again. Good for her! Not for me. I knew early on that my big-headed babies were going to be tricky to get out of my five-foot-two-inch frame. I knew that I was worried about pain and wanted to have the right measures in place. I knew I was the kind of person who could barely go to the movies without being stoned, let alone a delivery room. I remember a very important day when I told my dentist I wanted nitrous oxide at the ready every time I came for an appointment. No matter the procedure. No questions asked. This is what adults do. They demand or deny drugs on their own terms. Luckily, Dr. G made me feel like I would be able to handle anything.

Dr. G was European and old-fashioned in all the right ways. He reassured me I didn't need an amniocentesis by reminding me that Italian women don't worry about that sort of thing. I imagined Sophia Loren laughing off the idea of a needle being driven into her pregnant belly as she sipped an espresso. Dr. G dressed in stylish suits and moved very gently, squirting cold gel on my tummy while whistling a slow tune. He didn't have a 3-D imaging machine. He had a utilitarian black-and-white deal that showed you a blurry picture of what looked like a big-headed frog. "Your baby is very smart," he would say to me and my husband, Will Arnett. "You are doing everything right. Please drink one or two glasses of red wine a night."

I was so lucky to have Dr. G as my doctor. I didn't feel neurotic or stressed. I felt like a success. I ate what I wanted and felt super sexy. I was lucid enough to realize that I was on a total hormonal high and that a crash was just around the corner, but I didn't care. I loved being pregnant. I loved being at work and still feeling vital and busy while this extraordinary thing was happening inside me. I never felt alone. I always had a companion. I reveled in all the new space I was taking up. When your stomach is big you knock things over and everyone stays out of your path. I was big in brand-new ways and I felt very powerful and womanly.

I couldn't have chosen a better doctor to deliver my first child. Unfortunately that never happened. Dr. G died the day before I went into labor.

Yup.

But before I get to that . . .

The last week of *SNL* before my son Archie arrived was incredibly exciting. The 2008 presidential race was almost a dead heat and the entire year leading up to the election had been a magical time to work on a live satirical sketch comedy show. Everything felt electric. The audience knew the ins and outs of every political story, and a lot of it had to do with what *Saturday Night Live* was doing. I think everyone was crushing it that season and the show had never been better.

We could barely keep up with the daily goodies and produced four prime-time *Weekend Update Thursday* specials during September and October. I was eight months pregnant and did fifteen live shows in thirteen weeks. Everyone came on. I met then presidential candidate Barack Obama while I was dressed as Dennis Kucinich. Maya was dressed as Barack Obama at the time, so the introduction might have been slightly more embarrassing for her. We were doing a sketch about how hot Kucinich's wife was. That's how much America was paying attention! Then Tina played Sarah Palin for the first time and blew the roof off the joint.

The anticipation of Tina playing Palin was so fun to witness, and she explains it well in her book *Fifty Shades of Grey*. She totally took on what was expected of her and it was awesome to stand next to her as she killed. The sketch that night dealt with Hillary Clinton coming to terms with the possibility of a Vice President Sarah Palin. It dealt with fierce competitiveness in politics. It dealt with power and entitlement. It dealt with the way society forces women to define themselves and compete against each other. It tackled old theories about Madonna vs. Whore and Slut vs. Shrew. But most importantly, it was really funny. That sketch was written by Seth Meyers. Tina and I added jokes. *SNL* and now *Late Show with Seth Meyers* producer Mike Shoemaker wrote the legendary line "I can see Russia from my house."

I remember standing onstage and it being one of the few times that something felt perfectly whole. Archie did flips in my stomach each time the audience clapped. It was the closest to what I imagine it feels like to write a hit song. Here is a picture of Shoemaker and Seth rehearsing that skit with us. Look how in love with us they are.

My stomach grew bigger and the election grew closer. With just a few weeks left, Governor Sarah Palin was asked to come on the show. I had never met her, but many years before I had met Senator John McCain when he hosted and liked him instantly. We did a scene in a shower together and he was totally appropriate while also being very pleased. He was vigorous and honest. He noticed me smoking and told me if he knew the world was going to end the first thing he would do is start smoking again. He invited me to his house in Arizona. We hit it off.

———

I knew Tina would do a great opening sketch with Sarah Palin, and Seth and I were trying to think of something to do with her at the "Update" desk. I think I made some kind of joke about getting her to do a hard-core rap or something. Then I laughed at the thought of my doing one near her, in the gigantic state I was in. Seth laughed too. It was certainly not some wildly original idea, but as usual at *SNL,* the time pressure let us do things without overthinking. When you are pregnant you can get away with a lot of shit. Women really are at their most dangerous during this time. Your hormones are telling you that you are strong and sexy, everyone is scared of you, and you have a built-in sidekick who might come out at any minute. There should be some kind of pregnancy superhero movie. Calling Hollywood now. What's that, Hollywood? It's a weird idea and also you don't do movies with female superheroes? Copy that.

I went into my dressing room and wrote the rap. Seth helped. Andy Samberg helped. I met Palin in her dressing room beforehand to go over things and I was honestly surprised that they didn't make us change more of it. She and her team only wanted to modify a small joke about Todd being a real ladies' man, I think. Her daughter Bristol was pregnant at the time, and we made small talk about babies. I did the rap and it was super fun. My stomach looked so big it almost seemed fake. It was ridiculous. I was so tired between dress and air that I remember lying in my dressing room like a bear and sleeping deeply in between sketches.

Which brings us to Friday, October 24, 2008. The day I went into labor. The day after my doctor died. The musical guest that week was Coldplay, and it was going to be Jon Hamm's first time hosting the show. I had been working the whole time and feeling pretty good. Exhausted, yes. But invigorated. And honestly, at the

———

———

end of a pregnancy any lady will tell you she is searching for anything to take her mind off the creature that is about to burst forth.

So I had done my rap the previous Saturday and slept all day Sunday feeling happy. Will and I had our suitcases packed and a name picked out. We were both so happy and so in love. Nothing brings a couple closer than a baby about to arrive. Each person needs the other so desperately and in such new and deep ways. Each day through the week, I was doing my check-in with the doctor. As we all know, a watched cervix never dilates, and I'd still been tight and sassy that Thursday morning. Dr. G assured me I would probably deliver a few days late like most new mothers. I told him that I was doing the show on Saturday, even though it was technically my due date, but any time after that would be fine. It was the first of many times I ridiculously thought I had any control over my schedule, this baby, or life and death in general.

I was in the middle of rehearsing a *Mad Men* parody Friday morning and called to confirm my three P.M. appointment. The receptionist answered the phone crying. She told me Dr. G had passed away from a heart attack in his sleep. I burst into tears so loudly and violently that I think water was squirting out of my eyes like in a *Cathy* cartoon. Nothing is more horrifying than a giant pregnant lady sobbing. Everyone got very quiet. I hung up the phone and told Jon and the hair and makeup people that my doctor had just DIED. And I was DUE TOMORROW. And that I knew it seemed like a weird punch line, but my beloved and dear Italian grandpa was not going to be able to help me. I felt so terrible about the fact that all I was thinking was "What about meeeeeee!" I cried and cried in my *Mad Men* dress. Jon Hamm held me by the shoulders and looked at me and said, "I know this is very sad, but this is a really important show for me, so I'm going to need you to get your shit together." This made me laugh so hard I think I

———

37

peed. Going from crying to laughing that fast and hard happens maybe five times in your life and that extreme right turn is the reason why we are alive, and I believe it extends our life by many years.

I told everyone at dress rehearsal. It freaked them out. At three P.M. I went to Dr. G's office and was met by his grieving colleagues who had worked with him for decades. One of them, the lovely Dr. B, examined me and told me I shouldn't worry. Nothing was happening and I would probably deliver a few days late. He had already treated and met with Dr. G's other patients and would spend the next twenty-four hours delivering five babies. He was kind and professional, but it was extremely weird. He was a stranger. I went back to *SNL,* where I stayed until two A.M. Maya and Fred Armisen were doing bits on the main stage pretending to be robot versions of themselves, and I laughed and laughed and for the millionth time thought about how lucky I was. Eddie the security guard walked me to the car and asked me how I was doing. "I'm tired," I said. I went home and got in bed. It was three thirty in the morning and I put on my favorite TV show, *Law & Order,* to go to sleep. I heard the "bam bam" sound effect in the opening credits and my water broke.

Did you know that when your water breaks the best thing to do is stand up? Your baby acts like a plug. Isn't that insane? Strange thoughts like this and others filled my head as Will and I tenderly got ready to go to the hospital. I had that nervy feeling you get when you know your whole life is going to change and you realize you're made of tissue paper. Will raced around and I weirdly brushed my teeth. As we got our car from the garage our doorman predicted we were going to have a girl. I sat down in Will's car and gushed all over it. I was worried that he would be upset, but he laughed as he helped me in. I looked at him and thought, "I've turned into an animal now and I have a feeling this will be the nicest thing you see all night."

I took drugs and pushed. It was hard and long. I texted Shoemaker and Seth and told them I wouldn't be coming to work. While I tried to get my little bugger out, *SNL* scrambled to replace my parts. The real Elisabeth Moss came in to play herself, and she met Fred Armisen, who one year later to the day would become her husband. I would go to their wedding on my one-year-old boy Archie's birthday. Seth Meyers prepared to do "Update" alone for the first time. He would go on to do it alone successfully for years, although I like to think it was a tiny bit less fun. My big-headed wonder couldn't get out, and I started to think crazy thoughts. What if this was the one baby they couldn't get out? What if they just handed me back my clothes and sent me home and said, "We are so sorry, we did what we could but we just couldn't get him out. We wish you the best." I felt like the bouncer of my own uterus. I was ready to turn on all the lights and kick that baby out. "Time to wrap it up. I don't care where you go but you can't stay here."

I finally had a C-section. As I was wheeled into the operating room one of the nurses said, "Hey, it's Hillary Clinton!" and I answered by barfing all over her. Full circle.

Archie was born Saturday, October 25, at 6:09 P.M., just about when we would have been getting ready to do our first run-through for "Weekend Update." He was, and remains, perfect. My whole world cracked open and has thankfully never been the same since. I watched *Saturday Night Live* that night, drugged to the gills. I watched scenes that I had rehearsed hours before. I watched Maya and Kenan sing a song to me, and Seth tap my spot at the "Update" desk and tell me they loved me. I cried and cried and then laughed and laughed. I added a few more years to my life. I kissed Archie's giant head, which was shaped like a beautiful balloon. Today we wear the same size sombrero. He is six.

HELLO, EVERYONE. MY NAME IS SETH MEYERS and I will be writing this next chapter so that Amy can take a break. It is very hard to write a book. I haven't written one myself but I know it's very hard because every time I have seen Amy in the past year she has greeted me by saying, "Hello," quickly followed by, "It is very hard to write a book." At one of these meet-ups I offered to write a chapter for her so she could rest. She said, "Yes please." After I complete this favor for Amy I will only owe her one thousand more favors. I am not unique in my great debt to her. Most of Amy's friends owe her around one thousand favors. She never holds it over you though. She's not that kind of person.

I'm going to write about the night that Amy gave birth to her first son, Archie.

Before I get there, a bit of background. I first saw Amy Poehler perform in Chicago at a theater called ImprovOlympic in the midnineties. That theater is now called "iO" because the Olympics threatened to sue. The International Olympic Committee was worried people would walk into a one-hundred-seat theater on the corner of Clark and Addison and wonder why no one was jumping over hurdles.

The night I first saw Amy, she and the other performers were playing an improv game called "The Dream." She asked for a volunteer to come onstage and tell her about their day. I raised my hand and she picked me. My first conversation with Amy was in front of an audience: me in a chair, her standing beside me. She was charming, funny, sweet, and sharp, and I left thinking, "I would like to be her friend."

The next time I saw Amy perform was with Tina Fey in the same theater. They were workshopping a show called *Women of*

Color. I would learn later that it was the only performance of that show. Amy would move to New York soon after and Tina would quickly follow. There weren't a lot of people in the audience that night and for a while I thought seeing Amy and Tina perform in Chicago right before they left and got famous would be the most interesting thing that ever happened to me. In my mind it was like seeing the Beatles in Hamburg. And much, I'm sure, like someone who saw the Beatles in Hamburg, I talked about it so much that my friends eventually said, *"Genug."*

At this point, my relationship to Amy was the same as everyone else's. I was a fan.

I auditioned for *SNL* in 2001. My manager called me to tell me I had been hired. He then listed the other new cast members, one of whom was Amy. My first thought after hanging up the phone wasn't "Oh my god, I'm going to be on *SNL*," it was "Oh my god, I might get to be friends with Amy Poehler."

I am happy to say we were friends right away.

I won't bore you with the details of our many years of friendship and collaboration on the show for no other reason than it is likely Amy has dedicated dozens of pages to that topic in this very book. I wouldn't be surprised if a photo of me graces the cover of this book. To take up any more time talking about it would be redundant.

Instead I will pick up the action years later on the Saturday before the Saturday Amy became a mother. Josh Brolin was hosting the show that week, but this fact would soon be rendered a footnote when Sarah Palin agreed to do a cameo.

In 2008, under intense pressure from the comedians' lobby, Senator John McCain selected Alaska governor Sarah Palin as his running mate. This brought much good fortune to *SNL* in the form of Tina Fey's mimicry. However, the fact that Governor Palin would actually be appearing on the show was not immediately greeted with cheers.

It wasn't that we weren't excited to have her on; we just didn't know what to do with her once she got there. When you perform a sketch about a person when they're not in the room you have a great deal more freedom than when they are in the room. It was understood that we'd have to write a sketch with Tina and the governor, and we did. It was a soup of moving parts; Alec Baldwin, Lorne, and Mark Wahlberg made cameos, there were some jokes, and it went well.

Sensing that the audience might want more, on Friday night Lorne suggested using Governor Palin a second time, on "Weekend Update." We sat in our weekly joke read kicking around ideas that failed to inspire any enthusiasm. For a laugh, someone said the governor could do a rap, perhaps starting with the line "I'm Sarah Palin and I'm here to say . . ." Someone else suggested that the governor could get cold feet and Amy could do the rap instead. I don't remember if either of these ideas was meant to be real but I do remember that Amy's eyes went wide with glee and she left the room with a notebook in hand. The next time I saw her she was on the phone with the wardrobe department barking orders like mission control trying to get a shuttle back. "I need Eskimo suits for Fred and Andy, a snowmobile suit for Jason, and a moose suit for Bobby."

Take a second here. Go back and watch the Palin Rap one more time. Maybe you forgot how convincing and believable Sarah Palin was when she said she wasn't going to do the piece; maybe you forgot exactly how pregnant Amy was when she stood up from behind the desk; you probably remember that Amy was good but you likely forgot exactly *how* good. It is a performance without artifice. She's not play-rapping. She's rapping. I still get goose bumps when I think of Amy screaming, "I'm an animal and I'm bigger than you!" And the whole time she was doing it, for every single second of it, there was a little person sloshing (that's the correct medical term, yes? Sloshing?) around in her belly.

That person, Archie, is getting older every day, and soon he will be aware enough to watch and appreciate what his mother was doing on national television the week before he was born. When I want to smile, I think of that.

A week later, on the Friday before the Saturday that Amy became a mother, the entire cast stayed late to block a sketch called "The Barack Obama Variety Half Hour." On a normal week, the last piece rehearsed was usually a smaller piece with a handful of cast members cursing their luck that they had to stay at the studio until eleven P.M. the night before a show. This time, having everyone there together was a luxury and a delight.

While we waited for the cameras to set up, Maya and Fred started a bit pretending they were onstage for the seventy-fifth anniversary of *SNL*. Moving slowly and speaking softly, they delighted us with wooden award-show banter wherein they tried to remember the lines to their old sketches. Bill Hader took the stage pretending to be his own son and gave a speech about how much his "pops" had talked about working on the show before he died.

We were all enjoying ourselves that night, but no one more than Amy. She was laughing the hardest but that wasn't surprising. In my time at *SNL* no one was quicker or more gracious with a laugh than Amy—never more so than at the weekly table read, when it was needed most. When a new cast member or writer had a piece bombing to such silence that you could almost hear their pores expelling sweat, you could always count on Amy to give them a laugh. Though to be fair, it was less a laugh and more of a cackle. The writer Alex Baze described it as the sound one hears when running over a raven's foot with a shopping cart. It is, without exaggeration, one of my favorite sounds on earth.

We all headed home around midnight, in a great mood.

A quick but necessary tangent: For years Amy has called me "Coco" and I have called her "Moses." These nicknames sprung from a "Weekend Update" joke about a six-foot-tall camel named Moses and his tiny pony sidekick, Coco, who had escaped from a zoo in Texas. I don't remember the joke but I do remember that we laughed every time we said "a six-foot-tall camel named Moses and his tiny pony sidekick, Coco."

At three A.M. or so on Saturday morning Amy texted me. "Water broke, Coco! You're gonna do great!"

And that text is pretty much all you need to know about Amy. Instead of focusing on any of her fear, her excitement, or the anticipation that comes with giving birth for the first time, she sent *me* words of encouragement. And when I went out to do "Update" without her I was glad she had. I was nervous and lonely but I remembered that "You're gonna do great!" and felt better. Amy is rarely wrong.

Doing comedy for a living is, in a lot of ways, like a pony and a camel trying to escape from the zoo. It's a ridiculous endeavor and has a low probability of success, but most importantly, it is way easier if you're with a friend.

So that's my chapter. I am going to shake Amy awake now so she can continue with the hard work of writing a book for all of us. I hope she got some rest!

October 25, 2008

Archie Arnett

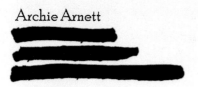

Dear Archie,

Happy Birthday! I know that your arrival brings great joy to your parents and entire family and I am pleased to join with them in welcoming you to New York and our nation. Best wishes for a lifetime that includes lasting friendships, boundless curiosity, a love of learning and a future that is shining and bright.

Sincerely yours,

Hillary Rodham Clinton*

Hillary Rodham Clinton

* otherwise known as your mother's double!

FIGURE OUT WHAT YOU WANT

SAY IT LOUD. THEN

SHU

T UP.

BIRTHING PLAN

To all Caregivers, Doctors,
Obstetrical Fellows, TMZ Interns,
and Hospital Staff:

We are looking forward to the birth of our child and ask that
the following wishes be respected during our birth process.

We have chosen to give birth in a hospital because of the
outstanding facilities it makes available to us. We would also
like to deliver our baby in a hospital since we spent most of
our twenties getting stoned and watching episodes of *ER*, and
so we know that delivering a baby is the best way to cheer up
an attractive but beleaguered doctor. Please make sure our
doctor is handsome and "cares too much." We considered
a home birth, but we just got our hardwood floors redone.
We also considered a birthing tub, but the mother is concerned
the water won't be warm enough. Is it too late to flood the
hospital room? Or turn it into a really fun foam party? We are
sorry for asking. The mother is very pregnant and would like
to remind everyone her brain has turned into spaghetti.

Those we plan to have present at our birth include: Baby, Mother,
Father, Grandparents, Lawyers, Agents, Lottery Winners,
Lookie-Loos, Midwife, First Wife, Life Coach, Finnoula the
Doula, Unexpected Ghosts, Bossy Astrologist, and the entire
cast of *Cheers*. All other visitors and unnecessary staff may
be turned away, unless they are wearing something cute.
Or bring hot wings for the father.

The birth environment is very important to us. For that reason we ask that the lights be kept dim, noise be avoided, and the door be closed for privacy. We would also like people to stay "chill" and not "bring their own shit" into the room with them. It's really important we feel "cool." Please decorate the room with Nan Goldin prints and leather beanbag chairs. We would love it if you could bring in a silk Persian rug for us to destroy. Think Chateau Marmont if it was closed for repairs. Or the set of *MTV Unplugged.*

Speaking of music, we will arrive with our own. We plan on delivering our baby to the soundtrack of Pink Floyd's *The Wall* while simultaneously watching *The Wizard of Oz.* If this kid works with us, we guarantee your minds will be blown!

The mother will wear her own clothes to the birth. If the delivery is on "Casual Friday," the mother will be wearing a tube top and bike shorts. Regardless of the day, the father will be in a fun tuxedo with jokey suspenders. Both the parents are in entertainment and have no business wear to speak of. Everyone else should be wearing open hospital gowns with nothing underneath. It only seems fair.

We plan on handling pain in a variety of natural ways. Please have a birthing ball and back massager available upon request. An annoying nurse with an unfunny and teasing manner on whom we can focus our anger would be a welcome addition. The mother would also like a punching bag, a screaming pillow, a mirror to smash, and a small handgun. The father would like a George Foreman grill, just to have.

We ask for vaginal exams only upon request. The mother requires at least a minute or two of chitchat before cold fingers are introduced. The mother would like to remind the staff that her vagina is the absolute last thing that she wants to have touched right now. The mother can think of a thousand things that she would rather have presently poked at than her vagina. Honestly, the mother doesn't know how the hell that baby is going to get out of there. The mother also would like to request that the handsome doctor maintain eye contact at all times during said poking.

If induction becomes necessary, we are aware of the nonchemical methods and would like to try them in this order: breast stimulation, sexual intercourse, and cervical cream. That's right, you heard us. If this baby isn't coming out, we are going to start doing it and make you all watch. So, let's get cracking.

We will use the squatting or semi-squatting position for pushing. Preferably the mother would like to "drop it like it's hot." The mother would like to push at her own pace. The father would like to add that he hopes it doesn't "take all day." We would like to feel our son's head as he descends with the option to stick him back up in there if we don't feel ready. The mother should be given the freedom to walk around during labor. Light choreography is expected.

If drugs become necessary, we would like to go all in. We are talking epidural, helium, and roofies. The mother would like to ask one last time why no one is taking seriously her request for nitrous oxide. The mother heard about women in England and Sweden and Canada being offered this at birth and apparently it works wonderfully to calm nerves and help with delivery. The mother still resents the judgment she received from doctors and friends when she brought up this idea. Either way, if drugs have to be administered, both mother and father know a guy.

If delivery assistance is needed, we prefer "suction" over "forceps." If episiotomy is needed, we prefer "buttonhole" over "backstitch." If cesarean is needed, please inform us early so we don't have to go through the above first.

In the event of a cesarean, the mother would like to be conscious. The mother would also not mind if you tweaked her abs while you're down there. The father would like to be present and totally freaked out when he accidentally looks past the curtain and sees his wife's organs stacked next to her like laundry.

The father would like to be involved in the "catching" of the baby and the "cutting" of the cord. At least that's what he is saying right now. We'll see. Please don't cut the cord until it stops pulsing. Please immediately let the cord blood guy in with his titanium suitcase so he can put the cord blood in a vault and keep it fresh. It will help us during the robot apocalypse.

After birth we wish to nurse immediately. Please do not introduce formula or bottles or pacifiers or water, unless those things stop this baby from crying. Why won't he stop crying? Wait, where is everybody going?

We prefer our stay in the hospital to be extended to the longest period our insurance will allow. We need time for our heads to catch up with our bodies. We also need to catch up on some *Judge Judy*. Please know we are grateful and sore and happy and scared. We will hear our baby down the hall and recognize his cry and we will realize this truly is a sci-fi miracle sent to us from G-O-D.

That being said, if people buy gifts that aren't on the registry the mother will lose her shit.

The mother would like to take this moment to admit a few things. She thinks natural childbirth is amazing but she also likes drugs. She didn't put baby oil on her perineum and try to stretch it because she just never felt like it. She lied when she said she completely stayed away from lunch meat. She also skipped Lamaze because sometimes she can't stand being around other people. That's all. We good?

Thank you in advance for your support of our choices. We look forward to a wonderful birth. We are excited but mostly scared. Have you SEEN the mother? She is TINY! How is this going to WORK exactly? Please advise.

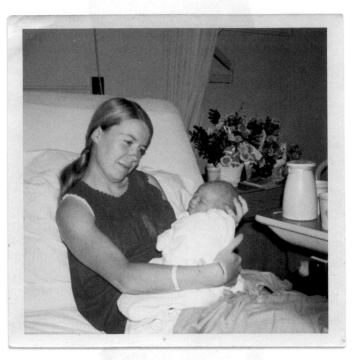

the day i was born

I REMEMBER MANY DETAILS ABOUT THE DAYS MY SONS CAME INTO THE WORLD BUT VERY LITTLE ABOUT MY OWN BIRTHDAY. Partly because I was a newborn baby, and partly because my mother was always a little coy about how the birth went down. When people celebrate birthdays I like to have them describe the day they were born. Sometimes it's fun to see if the birth matches the personality. Does a big baby turn into a big adult? Does a baby born at home turn into a homebody? Does a baby born on New Year's Eve end up being a real party monster?

I was born September 16, 1971, in Newton, Massachusetts. The most popular song at the time was "Joy to the World" by Three Dog Night. *All in the Family* had been on for less than a year, Evel Knievel had just set a world record jumping over nineteen cars, and Disney World would open a month later. My mother was twenty-four years old and my father was about to turn twenty-five, and they had been married for a short eleven months. Mom wore yarn in her hair and claims she doesn't remember a thing about labor. Back then there was this wonderful thing called "twilight sleep" where women were given anesthesia at the onset of labor and woke up with a baby. Today "twilight sleep" is when you pass out on your bed while looking at paparazzi photos of Robert Pattinson eating an omelet. I always pictured my mom in a deep sleep, her beautiful thick hair (that I didn't inherit) spread out like a fan on the pillow. *The Best of Bread* played on the radio while some doctor pulled me out using groovy seventies fondue forks. I figure now would be a good time to ask her how that day went down.

I T WAS 1971, THE AGE OF ALMOST "UNNATURAL CHILDBIRTH." I had no childbirth education classes, no prenatal diagnostic tests, no ultrasound. I started labor and Dad took me to the hospital. He went home to await the birth at Nana and Gunka's house. There was no push to include fathers in the delivery room at the time, so that didn't feel strange.

I didn't feel afraid. My contractions stalled, so they had to break my water. Things moved pretty fast from then on. I remember the pain, being administered a "saddle block" anesthetic, and then helpful nurses and my doctor encouraging me at the moment of birth. You were slight in weight but unusually long, making for an easy delivery.

I was thrilled to have a daughter. My mother had modeled so successfully how to bring up daughters. I can still remember that first rush of motherly pride, that assurance that my child was perfect, and then that first twinge of self-doubt. Was I ready for this job? I look like a kid in the pictures, with a long ponytail, smiling and probably overly confident. Right after you were born, you were happily bottle-fed and then returned to the nursery and I was given four days in the hospital to recuperate. It all seems so separate and sterile now, so different from today's emphasis on instant mother-child bonding. Yet I felt great and it had all gone so smoothly.

Pregnancy had been a different story. I was sick almost every day up to your birth, sometimes on the way to work. I was teaching third grade in a nearby elementary school in 1971 and the policy was that I was supposed to resign my job upon finding out I was pregnant. An understanding principal looked the other way and I made it through the school year. Over the summer, I gave up my job in preparation for stay-at-home motherhood. There were virtually no other options available. My parents were still young and working full-time. There was no day-care facility nearby. For me, it just wasn't socially acceptable to go back to work full-time and I had always followed the rules. I was the oldest daughter in my family, the one who was working her nine-to-five shift at the bra department in our local store while her sister was at Woodstock. I studied, graduated, got a job, fell in love, got married, and had a baby. I left my job to take care of my daughter. That's the way things were done. That's the way all of my friends were doing it.

We moved away to a not-so-neighboring town. Dad went to work every day with the car and you and I were alone all day, in unknown territory. No one knew about postpartum depression then, or dared to speak its name ("Snap out of it!" was the more common reply), but knowing what I know now, I am quite sure that the signs were there for me. I was often overcome with

59

———

loneliness, unsure about my choices, missing my friends. Motherhood was a twenty-four-hour-a-day, all-encompassing job. It was the hardest job I had ever had. Everything that happened to you happened to me. I had once heard children described in a novel as "hostages to fortune" and certainly my happiness depended on yours. You were not a sleeping baby. You stared at me with those blue eyes at all hours of the day and night.

I would walk the length and breadth of our town, singing Helen Reddy's "You and Me Against the World." It was the time of the burgeoning women's movement and the National Organization for Women had just been launched, and I was curious and bewildered at the same time. Where did I belong in this new world?

Moving to a new suburban town when you were five made all the difference. Here lived some college friends and a host of other educated women. Most of them were also at home providing full-time child care. These women and I "volunteered" and you came with me. We made paths for a town walking trail, read to kindergartners, delivered meals to shut-ins, and constructed floats for the Fourth of July parade on which you and your brother sat proudly and waved. We were busy and productive, involved in town politics and issues. It was the beginning of networking for me, a time of making connections and defining goals and career plans. You were always part of all this, watching me become my own person, motivated and ready for change.

—EILEEN POEHLER

———

I WAS THRILLED TO HAVE A DAUGHTER AND SPECIFICALLY asked the florist to put a card on the arrangement that read, "Glad it's a girl!" I have never forgotten holding you as a newborn, with your whole fanny fitting in the palm of my hand. I figured I would wait for the appropriate time to describe this to you, and now seems like a nice, private moment!

—BILL POEHLER,

also chiming in

That's my birth story. I was small and fussy, and remain so as an adult. Three years later my younger brother and only sibling, Greg, was born. I remember my father dressing me to go to the hospital and my mother commenting on how he put the wrong pants on me. I remember loving my brother instantly. He was my first friend.

If your parents are still alive, call them today and ask them to describe the day you were born. Write the details down here, on the following pages. Tell the story every year on your birthday until you know it by heart.

The Day I Was Born

sorry, sorry, sorry

I SAY "SORRY" A LOT. When I am running late. When I am navigating the streets of New York. When I interrupt someone. I say, "Sorry, sorry, sorry," in one long stream. The sentence becomes "Sorrysorrysorry" and it's said really fast, as if even the act of apologizing is something to apologize for. But this doesn't mean I am a pushover. It doesn't mean I am afraid of conflict or don't know how to stand up for myself. I am getting to a place right in the middle where I feel good about exactly how much I apologize. It takes years as a woman to unlearn what you have been taught to be sorry for. It takes years to find your voice and seize your real estate.

I am still learning the right balance. Sometimes I go too far the other way. I have a quick temper and I'm not afraid to argue. Once, I was flying from New York to Toronto with Tina Fey and Ana Gasteyer on our way to shoot *Mean Girls*. We were flying in first class and spent the hour-long, ten A.M. flight chatting about life and

---

65

work. The man sitting next to me was in an expensive suit on his way to a meeting, and I got the sense that he hated us and our friendly back-and-forth. A few times during the flight he sighed loudly, which I took as a sign that we were bothering him. I ignored it. Maybe that was a mistake, but sighing doesn't really work on me. As we got off the airplane and headed toward the moving walkway, the man pushed past me and jostled me a bit.

"Excuse me," I said.

"Excuse me? Excuse you!" he said.

I looked up at his boring, rich-guy face. He was turning red. I realized he was preparing to scold me. He had bumped into me on purpose to teach me a lesson.

"You girls were talking the entire flight," he said. "You should not be in first class!"

All of my lower-middle-class Boston issues rose to the surface. I don't like it when bratty, privileged old white guys speak to me like I am their mouthy niece. I got that amazing feeling you get when you know you are going to lose it in the best, most self-righteous way. I just leaned back and yelled, "FUUUUUUUUUUUCK YOU." Then I chased him as he tried to get away from me.

"You rich motherfucker! Who do you think you are? You're not better than me. Fuck you and your fucking opinions, you piece of shit."

And on and on. Tina was laughing. Or horrified. I don't remember; I was in a rage haze. Also I was showing off, which can be at the very least embarrassingly transparent and at the very worst careless and dangerous. But who doesn't love self-righteous anger? It's great. When I yell at the dads drinking coffee and looking at their phones at the playground while their seven-year-olds play on the preschool monkey bars, I feel like I am fully alive.

But for the most part I try not to yell "fuck you." I try to say "yes please." And "thank you." "Yes please" and "thank you" and "sorry, sorry, sorry."

But there was one "sorry" that I took too long to say, and it haunted me for years.

Saturdays at *SNL* were a tornado of activity. I would typically be in eight or nine sketches a night, which meant fast costume changes and lots to prepare. Costume changes at *Saturday Night Live* are a dance all to themselves. Each week I would confab with my human pit crew and figure out how much time I had to change between sketches. I would change under bleachers and tucked away in corners. Hearing the sound of the audience while I was in my underwear was thrilling and terrifying. My job was to stay still and obey directions as they were shouted: "Lift your foot!" "Snap this shut!" "Close your eyes!" Bruce would pull off my pre-Velcroed shirt as Robert glued on my fake mustache. I would hold up my two index fingers next to my head while Jeffrey put on my old-man wig, and Spivey would stand next to me telling me that my new cue to enter was "Thanksgiving is ruined!" Everyone was equal during those moments, all of us actors in a play trying to get changed in time. I watched Robert De Niro wiggle into spandex pants as Siegfried. Or Roy. I witnessed Donald Trump stepping into a chicken suit. I engaged in small talk with Derek Jeter as he was buttoned into a dress. "How are you doing?" I asked. "Are you nervous?" He just laughed and said, "No," thus settling the long-standing debate about what is more nerve-racking: live comedy or the World Series.

"*SNL* time" is completely different from real-world time. Gena, our stage manager, would peek in and reassure us that we still had "a minute twenty." Our shoulders would relax and we would joke around like emergency room doctors. We would chat about someone's

———

boyfriend as we hustled to the stage floor, and more than once a prop was thrown to me with seconds to go. I would catch it, the crowd would clap, and the scene would start. It was chaos. It was so exciting.

The problem with busy shows is that details get lost. Attention is not equally paid and things slip through the cracks. It was in one of those cracks that I did the only sketch I regret from *SNL*. The crack is not an excuse. Or maybe it is. This essay is about apologies, and I have learned an important part of apologizing is not making excuses. But that night was particularly busy.

It was March 2008 and I was newly and secretly pregnant. I remember feeling tired and worn out. Hillary Clinton was in the cold open and I stood beside her wearing a matching outfit. It's always extremely weird to play someone as they stand next to you. Coming down from that much adrenaline can drain you. Later that night, I played Dakota Fanning, hosting *The Dakota Fanning Talk Show*. I don't do an impression of Dakota Fanning, or look anything like her, so the sketch depended on my creepy ability to play a ten-year-old girl with relative ease. It was written by two *SNL* writers who liked the idea of a highly intellectual Dakota Fanning discussing things that were far too mature for her young age. Her references were often lost on her beleaguered bandleader, Reggie, played by the always-brilliant Kenan Thompson. Dakota would confess that she was a big fan of Vonnegut but "not familiar" with Harry Potter. She loved Tom Waits and enjoyed discussing Japanese poetry. She treated her mom like her manager and claimed she never watched TV. Her upcoming projects were always serious and much too adult. You get the idea.

On this particular night, the awesome Ellen Page was the host. Ellen was playing a young and innocent Miley Cyrus. This was in the *Hannah Montana* days, and Miley/Ellen was showing Dakota her new doll. The script read like this:

———

ELLEN/MILEY

Hey Dakota, check this out! It's my new Hannah
Montana doll! Pretty awesome, right?

(ELLEN TAKES OUT A CUTE DOLL AND MAKES IT DANCE)

AMY/DAKOTA

I've also got a new doll. It's from my upcoming film
Hurricane Mary, where my sister and I play severely
disabled twins.

(AMY/DAKOTA TAKES OUT A CREEPY DOLL)

ELLEN/MILEY

(AS HER DOLL)

Hey Dakota, want to play?

AMY/DAKOTA

(AS HER DOLL)

I wish I could but I am severely disabled.

I rehearsed the sketch and went over the blocking. The entire time I assumed that *Hurricane Mary* was something the writers had made up. We did a run-through and I was told the doll was being made and would be ready by air. The night of the show came, and the doll arrived. As it was put into my hands, I remember feeling my stomach tighten. It had been manipulated to look like a strange and twisted girl. But there was no time. Jeffrey adjusted my wig. Gena told me I had five seconds. The scene played fine. I ran to the next quick change. Robert glued on a beard. I forgot about my weird feeling, finished the show, and went to the after-party.

Months later I received a letter from Marianne Leone and Chris Cooper. It was simple and painful. It said something like "Shame on you for making fun of a real girl. Her name is Anastasia and she is amazing. You should know her story." I knew Chris Cooper from his work in films like *American Beauty* and *Adaptation*. I had always heard he was a wonderful person and a delight to work with. I didn't know his wife, Marianne, but a quick Google search told me a few important things: Marianne was an actor and had written the television movie *Hurricane Mary* mentioned in our skit. *Hurricane Mary* was based on the real story of Alba and Anastasia Somoza, twin sisters with cerebral palsy, and their mother's battle to ensure their right to an equal-opportunity education, as well as their full integration into society. Marianne and Chris had come to know Anastasia's story through their advocacy for disabled children. The cause was personal for them: their beloved son, Jesse, had been born with special needs. Sadly, he had passed away in 2005.

I'd like to tell you that I responded to the note. Or that I turned around and faced that letter head-on. I'd even like to tell you that I checked my body and heart and realized I was fine with the sketch and felt no need to apologize. Nope. Instead, I got angry. Anger and embarrassment are often neighbors. Sometimes we get defensive about what we feel guilty about. I was angry about the fact that I was being accused of something I didn't do. I didn't make fun of a real girl on purpose! I would never do that! That's not me! That's not me at all! I reread the note over and over again. I shared it with other people in the hopes they would agree that Marianne and Chris were overreacting and I was right to believe I was a good person. I told everyone about it and asked everyone to say it wasn't my fault. I threw the note in the trash like it was evidence of a crime. I stomped around for a bit and then pretended it went away. I was a shitty version of myself. The shadow side. I made a lot of noise because I felt bad about hurting someone's feelings and I didn't want to get quiet and really figure out how I felt. I was afraid to lie down and put my hand on my heart and hear the tiny voice whispering inside me saying that I had screwed up.

Your brain is not your friend when you need to apologize. Your brain and your ego and your intellect all remind you of the "facts." I kept telling myself that the only thing I was guilty of was not paying attention. Sure, I was being self-absorbed and insensitive, but who isn't? Sure, I should have been more on top of what I was saying, but wasn't that somebody else's job? Didn't everyone know how busy I was? Didn't Marianne and Chris take into consideration what a NICE PERSON I was? My brain shouted these things loud and clear. My heart quietly told a different story.

Shame is difficult. It's a weapon and a signal. It can paralyze or motivate. My friend Louis CK likes to say that "guilt is an intersection." Getting out of it means making a choice and moving forward. I felt guilty and I felt shame, but I didn't really move. For years. I parked my car in the intersection and let it sit there until the battery ran out. Then Spike Jonze helped me.

I bet you didn't expect so many A-list names in my apology story!

A word about apologizing: It's hard to do it without digging yourself in deeper. It's also scary and that's why we avoid the pain. We want so badly to plead our case and tell our story. The bad news is that everybody has a story. Everyone has a version of how things went down and how they participated. It's hard to untangle facts and feelings. For me, as a person in comedy, I am constantly weighing what I feel comfortable saying. There are big differences between what you say on live television and what you say at dinner, but you realize you have to be responsible for all of it. Each performer has to figure out what feels right. I am a strong believer in free speech and have spent most of my adult life in writers' rooms. I have a high tolerance for touchy subject matter. There isn't a taboo topic I can think of that I haven't joked about or laughed at. But I have an inner barometer that has helped me get better at pinpointing what works for me and what feels too mean or too lazy. I like picking fair targets. I don't like calling babies on websites ugly or comedy that relies on humiliation. I love ensembles and hate when someone bails or sells their partner out. I love watching a good roast but don't think I would be particularly good at roasting someone. Maybe it all comes down to what you feel you are good at. I have a dirty mouth but know that I don't always score when I work really blue. I have a sense of what kind of jokes I can get away with and still feel like my side of the street is clean. I like to lean my shoulder against limits and not depend on stuff that is shocking.

That being said, I still made a joke about someone being disabled. I didn't know it was a real person, but why does that matter? All of this left me stuck in that guilt intersection. I knew I was wrong but couldn't move. I lived in fear of running into Chris and Marianne, which was strange, because there really wasn't anyone else in the world I was afraid to be in a room with. This made famous-person stuff stressful, because Chris was famous and an actor and there was a high chance I would run into him at an award show.

I don't want to back-door brag as I make my way to the end of this apology tale, so let me just front-door brag and talk about the cool people I get to be friends with. I am friends with Kathleen Hanna and Adam Horovitz, aka Ad-Rock from the Beastie Boys. I can't believe I am friends with them. I love Kathleen's music and I am in awe of her social activism and general awesomeness. I asked her to interview me for *Interview* magazine when I was just a sketch performer whom nobody knew. She said yes because she supports young women. This is the artist who pulled women to the front at her rock shows. She shows up and does the work and is the real deal. Now she is my friend. Her husband, Adam, is also my friend. I used to listen to the Beastie Boys on my Walkman and dream about meeting them. Now I have Adam's e-mail. I'm blowing my cool cover but I am so psyched we are friends. I am also friends with Spike Jonze. Guess who else I am friends with? Kim Gordon! Norman Lear! Martin Short! It's awesome! I can't lie, it's so awesome!

See how I am trying to distract you from the shitty thing I did?

Anyway I was at dinner with some of these people and Spike mentioned working with Chris. I told him my story, and how five years had passed and I was still sitting on this feeling that I had blown it. Spike gently reminded me that it's never too late to reach out and apologize.

Spike told me he was looking at some similar themes in his new movie *Her*. What I didn't know then was how a year later I would watch that beautiful movie about loss and love with my wonderful new boyfriend, Nick Kroll. I would watch the scene where Joaquin Phoenix reads an apology letter he writes to his ex-wife, and I would cry for all the things behind me and all the things yet ahead. Spike offered to connect me to Marianne, and I gratefully agreed.

Then he sent me this:

———

From: Spike Jonze
Date: March 11, 2013
To: Amy Poehler
Subject: Fwd: Hey from Marianne & Chris

I didn't realize the whole situation.
I'll leave it in your hands.
I'm sorry, Amy.
Being a grown-up is hard.
Marianne is an awesome woman. I'm sure you guys would get along great if you met in a different situation.
big hugs
x

On March 11, 2013, Leone, Marianne wrote:

From: Marianne Leone
Date: March 11, 2013
To: Spike Jonze
Subject: Re: Hey from Marianne & Chris

Yeah, I was furious at the skit she did on *SNL* and wrote her a letter to tell her. The skit was a gratuitously cruel slap at disability which wasn't funny in the least. What made it so, so horrible was that she was talking about the Somoza twins and the script I wrote about their lives. It was also the same night Hillary Clinton was on and I knew that Anastasia was watching it with friends, since she was in Texas stumping for Hillary, so I knew she saw herself being parodied in a horrible, unfunny, cruel way. I was doubly insulted for the twins that Poehler never had the class to answer the letter, so, quite frankly, I am glad that it bothered her. (We had our return address on the letter, and, face it, we're not that hard to find.)

So, Spike, what I feel now is that I, we don't need an apology from her, but if she wants to make it up to ANASTASIA, she can

———

contribute to her staying at London School of Economics for another year to get her Master's in Human Rights. Nothing will stop Anastasia. She will effect change in the world.

Love always,
Marianne

I read Marianne's e-mail and was devastated. I pictured Anastasia watching the show and seeing me make fun of her. I waited almost a month and sent this.

From: Amy Poehler
Date: April 1, 2013
To: Marianne Leone
Subject: Truly sorry

Dear Marianne and Chris,

I am writing to apologize. This is most likely an example of "too little too late" but I am writing to you to apologize for a Dakota Fanning sketch I did on *SNL* many years ago. It was a sketch that upset you and Anastasia, and one that moved you to write to me.

It has always bothered me that I never contacted you both. I regret that. I spoke of this to Spike and he very nicely connected us. I am grateful to him for giving me this opportunity, and appreciate you taking the time to read this.

I am very sorry for any pain I caused. I apologize for an insensitive portrayal of what was a loving and important project. I am truly sorry for hurting Anastasia in any way.

I do not think it's funny to make light of disabilities. This is not the kind of person I am or have ever been. The sketch was not written by me. The mean prop used was not seen by me until live on air. In fact, I had no idea that we were referencing a real film. I assumed it was yet another "adult" project that we would joke about Dakota Fanning working on. These are not excuses. I take responsibility for my negligence in understanding the context of what I was saying, but it's important for me to tell you these details.

Anastasia deserves an apology from me. Feel free to pass this along if you feel that is helpful or send me her email if you deem it appropriate. I visited her Indiegogo page. She is an awesome young woman and I have no doubt she will continue to live an amazing life.

Again, I am sorry. I send my best wishes to you and your family, and my deepest condolences regarding the loss of your son.

Thank you for reading this.
Amy

Rereading it now I notice a few things. I got a little caught up in the facts. I was hoping to defend myself. But it felt really good to try. Apologies have nothing to do with you. They are balloons in the sky. They may never land. They may even choke a bird.

Then I got this.

From: Anastasia Somoza
Date: April 7, 2013
To: Amy Poehler
Subject: Re: Fw: Truly sorry

Dear Amy,

Wow!!!! Oh my goodness, what a lovely surprise!! Thank you so very much for your donation to my campaign launched to raise funds that will hopefully cover the cost of my caretakers in my 2nd year at LSE, and for the kind message you wrote to Marianne and Chris, which they graciously forwarded along to me.

They are two of the most amazingly wonderful, loving people I know and have been incredible supporters of me and my family!! I adore and admire them just as much as I do my own parents, for countless reasons, but most importantly for being a spectacular Mom and Dad duo to gorgeous Jesse!! It is thanks to them, Spike, many more of their closest friends and other fabulous people that I am at LSE today stressing out (like a typical grad student) over first year final papers and comprehensive exams that are fast approaching!

I always knew you never meant to hurt us in doing the skit. After all, you didn't even know we actually existed so I realized it wasn't personal. It also certainly helps to know that you weren't aware of the back story or real life references portrayed. That being said, Chris, Marianne, my family and I have worked tirelessly to make equal opportunity, the inclusion and positive portrayal of people with disabilities in society the norm rather than the exception. As such, I was upset more generally speaking, about the skit contributing to a severe lack of knowledge, awareness, understanding and empathy around disability. Too

77

———

many people already fear, and are often disgusted or put off in other ways by disability and it saddened me to think of the impact the skit may have had in adding fuel to that fire.

Just as you felt relieved I'm sure, to have the opportunity to apologize and express certain details to Marianne, it is important to me that you now know more about why the skit mattered. I hope you understand that Marianne wrote to you out of a deep love for her son, and my family for sure, but also precisely because the struggle to change the perception of disability goes far beyond us and the more people exposed to this reality the better.

I've seen several episodes of your web series *Smart Girls at the Party* and I truly believe that the show's goal in celebrating "extraordinary individuals who are changing the world by being themselves," represents who you are and what you believe in, far more than the skit. It takes strength and character to admit responsibility by acknowledging, to Marianne and Chris, that you could and indeed should have done more to inform yourself about what you were being asked to act in the skit. I agree and greatly appreciate, admire and thank you for your honesty and willingness to recognize that.

The sincerity of your apology and your generosity mean more to me than you will ever know and it made my younger sister Gabriella giddy with excitement!!! I hope you're enjoying a sunny Sunday and thanks again from the bottom of my heart!!

Warmly,
Anastasia

———

Look at this woman. This beauty. What an act of grace. What a gift she gave me.

Shame makes people abandon their children and drink themselves to death. It also keeps us from true happiness. An apology is a glorious release. Anastasia gave me a huge gift. That e-mail changed me. It rearranged my molecules. She has lived a life of struggle and decided not to pick up the armor. She teaches me about compassion. She makes her journey about open hearts. She is not ashamed.

Thankyouthankyouthankyou.

apology letter from
the brain

Hey there,

I'm sorry, okay? But can I say something?

Look, I admit I wasn't perfect. No one is perfect.
That's a fact. Speaking of facts, don't you think we
all need to take a minute and decide who is right
and who is wrong? Every side is different; it's just
that my side seems more right. I am not just saying
that because it's my side. I think a lot of other
people would agree with me if given the chance.

If I upset you in some way, please know that wasn't
my intention. I didn't know how sensitive you were.
It's obvious I can set you off very easily. That's
not an insult, it's just an observation.

I think it would help if we talked about this more
and argued about who is telling the truth. I would
like to see you in person to tell you how this
situation has affected me. I may use this opportunity
to bring up other times you have hurt me in the past.
If possible, I would like to hurt you back. Either way,
I want to be in control.

Until then, take care and please remember I reached
out first.

I Remain,
THE BRAIN

apology letter from
the heart

Hey there,

I'm sorry.

I've found it hard to tell you this and I realize
my apology may be too little or come too late.

It is important for me to let you know that I am
sorry for what I did or said or didn't do or say.
I was wrong. I make mistakes. I hate that I made
one with you.

I am reaching out because life goes by fast. I
don't want my one life to go by without expressing
this to you. I want to do and be better.

This apology is yours. Feel free to do whatever
you want with it. My hope is that it gives you
comfort, but my goal is that it doesn't cause you
any pain.

Again, I am truly sorry. Thank you for taking the
time to read this.

Love,

The Heart

P.S. I'm sorry.

FOR

GET

THE FACTS
AND REMEMBER
THE FEELINGS.

my books on divorce

I UNDERSTAND WHY PEOPLE READ SO MANY BOOKS ON DIVORCE. When you are a person going through a divorce you feel incredibly alone, yet you are constantly reminded by society of how frequently divorce happens and how common it has become. You aren't allowed to feel special, but no one understands the specific ways you are in pain. Imagine spreading everything you care about on a blanket and then tossing the whole thing up in the air. The process of divorce is about loading up that blanket, throwing it up, watching it all spin, and worrying what stuff will break when it lands. It's no wonder we want to find answers and comfort.

I don't want to talk about my divorce because it is too sad and too personal. I also don't like people knowing my shit. I will say a few things. I am proud of how my ex-husband, Will, and I have been taking care of our children; I am beyond grateful he is their father; and I don't think a ten-year marriage constitutes failure. That being said, getting a divorce really sucks. But as my dear friend and relationship sponsor Louis CK has noted, "divorce is always good news because no good marriage has ever ended in divorce."

Any painful experience makes you see things differently. It also reminds you of the simple truths that we purposely forget every day or else we would never get out of bed. Things like, nothing lasts forever and relationships can end. The best that can happen is you learn a little more about what you can handle and you stay soft through the pain. Perhaps you feel a little wiser. Maybe your experience can be of help to others. With that in mind, here are some titles for a series of divorce books I would like to pitch to you and my editors for future discussion. After review, I realize that all of my books have exclamation points at the end of their titles, but I think people want exclamation points in the titles of their books and I don't think I am wrong!!!!

1.

I WANT A DIVORCE!
SEE YOU TOMORROW!

If you have small children you will understand this book. This book deals with the fact that most people who divorce with small children still need to see each other every day. Any good parent will try to put their children's needs first, and so this book will help teach you how to have a knock-down, drag-out fight and still attend a kid's birthday party together on the same day. Are you in your early twenties and recently broke up with someone over Skype? This book is not for you. Have you successfully avoided your ex for over six months except for a close call at your friends' art opening? This book is not for you. Have you heard secondhand that your ex is building houses for Habitat for Humanity and you rolled your eyes at how fucking phony the whole thing sounded and then sighed because you don't miss him but you liked playing with his dog? This book is not for you. This book is for the people who have to work together or live together or co-parent together while going through a divorce.

Chapters include:
- FAKE SMILING
- HOW IMPORTANT IS THE LAST WORD?
- PHONE CALLS ON THE WAY HOME FROM THERAPY
- EVERYONE NEEDS TO STOP BUYING TOYS

2.

GET OVER IT! (BUT NOT TOO FAST!)

When you are going through the trauma and drama of divorce, you learn who your real friends are. They guide you and take care of you and save you from your darkest days. The problem is, you also have to talk to other people about this bullshit, and it's often people you don't care about or like. Usually these people are very interested at first and then have to go back to their own lives and want you to do the same. This book is here to remind you that even though you are in pain and still in transition, everyone else has moved on and is a little tired of your situation. This book will remind you that unless you and your ex-spouse got into a juicy fight or there are some new boyfriends and girlfriends in the mix, most people don't want to talk about it anymore. This book will also teach you how you need to move on, but not too fast. It will remind you that you are allowed to be upset, but for god's sake please keep it together. You need to seem sad at just the right times or else other people will think you're weird. You also need to be able to act normal at the parties they invite you to.

Chapters include:
- SHE DOESN'T CRY ENOUGH
- HE SEEMS GAY TO ME
- THIS WON'T GET YOU OUT OF A SPEEDING TICKET
- I'M SORRY TO INTERRUPT, BUT WHEN DO YOU THINK YOU WILL BE OVER IT?

3.

DIVORCE: TEN WAYS TO NOT CATCH IT!

Divorce is contagious! Haven't you heard? It's like cancer but worse because no one really feels that bad for you. This book will teach you how to discuss your divorce with your currently married friends. Some married couples get freaked out when you talk about your divorce and like to tell you how they aren't going to get one. Usually they point to their hard work through therapy, their fear of being alone, or their total acceptance of a dead marriage devoid of sex and love. This book will help you not strangle them when they both stand in front of you and talk about how great their relationship continues to be. This book will also help you deal with the divorce voyeur, the friend who wants to hear every detail and live vicariously through your experience. This book will point to ways you can talk about your divorce without feeling like it's a fancy fur coat that people like to try on but then throw back at you in disgust because they would never wear something so vile. This book contains illustrations of happy couples looking at you with pity, and some weird aphorisms that intimate it's somehow easier to get divorced than to stay in an unhappy marriage.

Chapters include:
- DIVORCE IS NOT AN OPTION FOR ME, BUT I AM HAPPY FOR YOU
- C'MON, WHO HASN'T CHEATED?
- I JUST COULDN'T DO THAT TO MY KIDS
- MAYBE YOU GUYS JUST NEED TO GO TO OJAI FOR A WEEKEND

4.

HEY, LADY, I DON'T WANT TO FUCK YOUR HUSBAND!

Newly divorced and attending a wedding for the first time alone? This book is for you! Inside you will find ways to deal with the strange stares and drunk accusations that come along with not having a date. You will find tips on how to gently break it to women that you don't want to fuck their flabby baby-faced husbands. You will find pointers on how to deflect advances made by their husbands in full view of the wives so you don't have to get involved in other people's weird relationship shit. You will read about the experiences of other men and women who bravely attended events without a plus-one and came out alive. Check out our special section on what to do when friends try to awkwardly set you up, and our newly added bonus chapter dedicated to those who want to be gay for a weekend.

Chapters include:
- NO ONE AS GREAT AS YOU SHOULD BE SINGLE
- IS IT HARD TO BE AT A WEDDING?
- YOU'VE NEVER LOOKED BETTER
- HAVE YOU SEEN MARK ANYWHERE? I CAN'T FIND HIM

5.

GOD IS IN THE DETAILS!

This book will help you navigate all the intimate details that people want to know and, frankly, have a right to know. This includes how did you break up and where you are living now and who wanted it more and how long did you know and what is going on with the kids and how did you tell the kids and was it sad and is he mad and are you sad and does everyone know and who have you told and who can I tell and when will you make an announcement and does Margaret know and is it okay for me to call her and what's going on with the house and who is getting the money and how much money is it, exactly, and does Margaret know because I feel like she needs to hear it from me and do you have a boyfriend and does he have a girlfriend and what are their names and how much do they weigh and are weekends lonely and are you happier and do you think you will ever get married again and are you going to have more kids and could you just tell me exactly every detail from the beginning especially the bad stuff?

6.

THE HOLIDAYS ARE RUINED!

This book is one page long and just contains that one sentence.

My hope is these manuals will help you navigate such a supremely shitty time. I promise you, someday happy couples won't make you cry anymore. Someday you may be in one again. Someday you will wake up feeling 51 percent happy and slowly, molecule by molecule, you will feel like yourself again. Or you will lose your mind and turn into a crazy person. Either way, let's just hope you avoided tattoos, because most are pretty stupid anyway.

NOT

HING

IS ANYONE'S BUSINESS.

talk to yourself like you're ninety

I SUPPOSE I AM PRE-PERI-MIDDLE-AGED. At forty-three, I feel right in the middle. I am no spring chicken but I am not an old lady. I know the names of all the members of Odd Future but I didn't have the Internet in college. I can party like a twenty-year-old but it takes me almost a week to recover. Sometimes I am a tired mother taking her kids to the park, and other times I am a petulant teenager giving the finger to a speeding FedEx truck. I idle right in the middle.

I don't know when middle age starts, exactly. According to my current edition of the *Oxford English Dictionary,* middle age is "the period of life between young adulthood and old age, now usually regarded as between about forty-five and sixty." Sixty? Nice try, *Oxford.*

I think middle age begins once you start looking forward to eating dinner before six thirty, or when you call the cops when your next-door neighbor has a party. I know my body feels older. I recently hurt myself on a treadmill and it wasn't even on. I was adjusting my speed and stepped wrong and twisted my ankle. I felt a moment of frustration filled with immediate relief. I didn't have to actually work out, but I still got credit for trying. It was a gym snow day. You know those exercise pools where the water comes at you strong and you have to swim against it to build up your strength? That's what the social pressure of staying young feels like. You can either exhaust yourself thrashing against it or turn around and let the pressure of it massage out your kinks. Fighting aging is like the War on Drugs. It's expensive, does more harm than good, and has been proven to never end.

Hopefully I have another forty to fifty years of living ahead of me before I pass from this earth either in my sleep or during a daring rescue caught on tape. Ideally my penultimate day would be spent attending a giant beach party thrown in my honor. Everyone would gather around me at sunset, and the golden light would make my skin and hair beautiful as I told hilarious stories and gave away my extensive collection of moon art to my ex-lovers. I and all of my still-alive friends (which, let's face it, will mostly be women) would sing and dance late into the night. My sons would be grown and happy. I would be frail but adorable. I would still have my own teeth, and I would be tended to by handsome and kind gay men who pruned me like a bonsai tree. Once the party ended, everyone would fall asleep except for me. I would spend the rest of the night watching the stars under a nice blanket my granddaughter made with her Knit-Bot 5000. As the sun began to rise, an unexpected guest would wake and put the coffee on. My last words would be something banal and beautiful. "Are you warm enough?" my guest would ask. "Just right," I would answer. My funeral would be huge

———

but incredibly intimate. I would instruct people to throw firecrackers on my funeral pyre and play *Purple Rain* on a loop.

It wasn't until I turned thirty that I started to feel like my adult life was beginning. I had just been hired on *Saturday Night Live* and was about to attend my own surprise dance party; then September 11 came and the whole world went bananas. I had met Will and I knew I wanted to marry him and try to have children someday. I had paid off my student loans and I knew how to jump-start my own car battery. I had spent so much of my twenties in a state of delayed adolescence and so much of my teenage years wishing and praying that time would move faster. I remembered being five years old when my mother turned thirty. My dad threw a big party for her and the adults got drunk in the basement. I sat on the stairs in Holly Hobbie pajamas and listened to the clinking sound of ice in glasses. They all brought dirty presents from Spencer Gifts, a joke shop in our local mall that had boob mugs and fart machines and penis pasta. We would go in there as kids and sneak peeks at the dirty stuff, pretending to understand the bad sex jokes. Ten years later, for my mom's fortieth, my dad made a homemade "Buns" calendar that included relatives and friends. They all posed in various funny underwear. Some were in Speedos playing the piano and others were in saggy pants showing their butt crack while fixing the kitchen sink. All this was the kind of groovy, semi-lewd suburban stuff that in some instances led to "key parties." Thankfully, at least to my knowledge, there was no wife swapping in my childhood home. If there was, I don't want to know about it. Family, please remember this when you all write your inevitable and scathing memoirs.

At thirty I felt like I had about six or seven years of feeling like a real adult before my brain and society started to make me worry

———

———

about being old. There is the built-in baby stuff, plus the added fascination with the new. But here's the thing. Getting older is awesome, and not because you don't care as much about what people think. It's awesome because you develop secret superpowers. Behold:

Getting older makes you somewhat invisible. This can be exciting. Now that you are better at observing a situation, you can use your sharpened skills to scan a room and navigate it before anyone even notices you are there. This can lead to your finding a comfortable couch at a party, or to the realization that you are at a terrible party and need to leave immediately. Knowing when to exit is a great aspect of being older, and since you are invisible, no one will even notice you are gone. Not getting immediate attention can mean you decide how and when you want people to look at you. Remember all those goofy comedies in the eighties where men became invisible and hung out in women's locker rooms? Remember how the men got to watch pretty girls take showers and snap each other with towels? You can do this, but in a different way. You can witness young people embarrassing themselves and get a thrill that it's not you. You can watch them throw around their "alwayses" and "nevers" and "I'm the kind of person who's" and delight in the fact that you are past that point in your life. Feeling invisible means you can float. You can decide to travel without permission. You know secrets and hear opinions that weren't meant for you to hear. Plus, it's easier to steal things.

Getting older also helps you develop X-ray vision. The strange thing is that the moment people start looking at you less is when you start being able to see through people more. You get better at understanding what people mean and how it can be different from what they say. Finally the phrase "actions speak louder than words" starts to make sense. You can read people's energies better, and

———

this hopefully means you get stuck talking to less duds. You also may start to seek out duds, as some kind of weird emotional exercise to test your boundaries. You use the word "boundaries." You can witness bad behavior and watch it like you would watch someone else's child having a tantrum. Gone are the days (hopefully) when you take everything personally and internalize everyone's behavior. You get better at knowing what you want and need. You can tell what kind of underwear people are wearing.

Lastly, because you are a superhero, you are really good at putting together a good team. You can look around the room and notice the other superheroes because they are the ones noticing you. The friends you meet over forty are really juicy. They are highly emulsified and full of flavor. Now that you're starting to have a sense of who you are, you know better what kind of friend you want and need. My peers are crushing it right now and it's totally amazing and energizing to watch. I have made friends with older women whom I have admired for years who let me learn from their experience. I drink from their life well. They tell me about hormones and vacation spots and neck cream. I am interested in people who swim in the deep end. I want to have conversations about real things with people who have experienced real things. I'm tired of talking about movies and gossiping about friends. Life is crunchy and complicated and all the more delicious.

Now that I am older, I am rounder and softer, which isn't always a bad thing. I remember fewer names so I try to focus on someone's eyes instead. Sex is better and I'm better at it. I don't miss the frustration of youth, the anticipation of love and pain, the paralysis of choices still ahead. The pressure of "What are you going to do?" makes everybody feel like they haven't done anything yet. Young people can remind us to take chances and be angry and stop our patterns. Old people can remind us to laugh more and get focused and make friends with our patterns. Young and old need to relax in the moment and live where they are. Be Here Now, like the great book says.

I have work to do. I remain suspicious of men and women who don't want to work with their peers, comedy writers who only hire newbies, and people who only date someone younger or of lower status. Don't you want the tree you love or work with to have a similar number of rings? Sometimes I get scared that I have missed out or checked out. Occasionally I don't recognize myself in a store window. When this happens, I try to speak to myself from the future. This is possible since time travel is real and I have the proof (more on this later). Here's what my ninety-year-old self tells me.

* Get to the point, please.

* Talk slower and louder.

* You look great and you are beautiful.

* Can you walk? Stop complaining.

* Stopcomplainingstopcomplainingstopcomplaining.

* Stop whining about getting old. It's a privilege.
A lot of people who are dead wish they were still alive.

* Ignore what other people think. Most people aren't even paying attention to you.

* Find a nice boy who is nice to you.

* Isn't dancing fun?

* Let's not talk about people dying.

* Don't go too long without talking to your family.

* Forgive your parents for what they never gave you.

* Eat some nice soup and you will feel better.
Or take a walk.

* Relax and let her win. Who cares?

* Whocareswhocareswhocareswhocareswhocares?

* Make "No" a complete sentence.

* Kiss every baby and pet every dog.

* Walk slowly and lie down when you're tired.

* What's next?

* That next-door neighbor is too loud; that's it, I'm calling the cops.

DO
WHATEVER YOU LIKE

Inside Vladimir

how i fell in love with improv:

chicago

I STOOD ONSTAGE PRESSED UP AGAINST A BACK WALL WHILE MY PEERS SCREAMED AT ME TO "SELL IT!" It was a "midnight improv jam" at the ImprovOlympic theater in Chicago, the freezing city I now called home. I had been taking improv classes and this late-night show was an opportunity to finally get onstage. Getting onstage was a big deal. You could spend week after week in classes doing scenes and studying improv forms, but a half hour performance brought out the best and worst in you. I learned a lot about myself onstage. Sometimes I turned into a desperate joke machine. Other times, I got shy and passive. Once in a while I would get weirdly physical or sexual. When people are nervous and put on the spot, they tend to show you who they really are. That being said, long-form improvisation had terms and rules—and I was learning how to work within them. An improv jam usually consisted of a more experienced improviser encouraging students to get up before they were ready. A paying audience

107

was there to watch young students get better. If improvisation is like surfing, this would be akin to paddling out for the first time to catch a wave on your own.

For those of you who know nothing about improvisation, I suggest you read *The Upright Citizens Brigade Comedy Improvisation Manual*. I will wait....

Okay, great! So now you know that to be a good improviser you have to listen and say yes and support your partner and be specific and honest and find a game within the scene you can both play. Long-form improvisation (as you already know because you just read our great book) comes from a one-word suggestion that turns into a whole show filled with scenes and other various forms.

It was 1993 when I moved to Chicago. Bill Clinton had just been elected president, Rodney King had been beaten by the police, and "Whoomp! (There It Is)" was burning up the charts. Speaking of burning, federal agents would storm the Branch Davidian compound that same year and the place would go up in flames. A short time later, during a series of Second City Touring Company gigs across Texas, two women named Tina Fey and Amy Poehler would visit that compound on their way past Waco, Texas. More on that in a minute.

I moved to a new city already knowing my Boston College roommate Kara and our friend Martin Gobbee, and the three of us lived together in a cheap but beautiful Chicago apartment. Crown molding, wasted on the young. My dad drove Kara's jeep across the country loaded with our stuff and I settled quickly into a life of waitressing and taking classes. It was an awesome time. I was extremely poor and had little to do. I painted my tiny bedroom Van Gogh Starry Night Purple, and I smoked a lot of pot. I would ride my bike to shows while listening to the Beastie Boys. I was twenty-two and I had found what I loved.

Watching great people do what you love is a good way to start learning how to do it yourself. Chicago was swollen with talent at the time. The first Second City show I ever saw was Amy Sedaris's last. The entire cast was saying good-bye to her and she was doing all of her best sketches. Amy Sedaris is the Cindy Sherman of comedy. When it comes to sketch, I don't think I have ever seen anyone funnier. That night she was onstage with her cast, which included the two Steves: Colbert and Carell. I remember watching them all with a mixture of awe and excitement. Some of them were about to head off to New York to shoot their sketch show *Exit 57*. I remember thinking, "You are all so good and I wish I were better. Now get out of here because I want to be where you are."

Over at the ImprovOlympic theater the talent was just as fierce. The "house team" there was a group called the Family. It was Matt Besser, Ian Roberts, Adam McKay, Neil Flynn, Ali Farahnakian, and Miles Stroth. They were improv giants, literally. Everyone was over six feet tall and imposing, physical, and hilarious. The Midwest grows its actors big. I would sneak into their packed shows using my student discount and sit in the light booth to watch what great improv looked like. The members of the Family were my rock stars.

They were my Chicago Bulls. I would get food with other amateur improvisers and talk about the different moves I had seen the giants pull. I would marvel at how easy they made it look. I would go home and write in my journal: "Amy, take more risks!" "Get better at object work!" "Don't be afraid to sing!"

ImprovOlympic had a mommy and a daddy, and Charna Halpern was the mommy. She is the Stevie Nicks of improvisation. She is feminine and witchy but does not take any shit. Charna was my first real improv teacher and she ran the place. She was responsible for putting groups together, deciding who could proceed to the next level, and making sure everyone was fed. She had the keys to the place—literally and figuratively—a responsibility I didn't truly understand until much later when I was running a theater of my own. It is incredibly hard to balance ego and opportunity as well as paychecks and liquor license boards. Being a small comedy theater owner is exciting and lonely. The shows are exhilarating, but few people stick around to help you sweep up. Charna took a liking to me, and me to her. She told me I was just as good as the big boys. She believed in me. She said there was another new improviser in another one of her classes whom she thought I would really like. Her name was Tina and she was like me but with brown hair. Yes, yes. I'm getting to it!

If Charna was the mommy, Del Close was the daddy. He was worshipped from afar and the man everyone was trying to please. He also had a beard, a tendency to be grumpy, and an amazing backstory. He was a comedy genius who had taught all of my heroes: Gilda Radner and Bill Murray and Chris Farley. He swallowed fire, toured with Lenny Bruce, named *SCTV*, and, according to him, was a good friend of Elaine May. He was a respected Chicago theater actor who believed improvisation was not an acting tool but a genuine performance form on its own. Del was also a Wiccan and a drug addict, and I was catching him in the last ten years of his too-short life. His story could fill many books. He is the most famous guy in comedy whom nobody knows. They weren't married, but Charna was Del's wife and emotional surrogate who encouraged his genius while running ImprovOlympic and keeping the lights on.

I took a class from a member of the Family, Matt Besser, and we started dating soon after. Matt was a talented Jewish boy from Arkansas who was effortlessly cool. He dressed like a punk rock soccer player. He had a fierceness about him that was exhilarating. He truly didn't care what people thought. He was also an artist and big thinker. I first saw him onstage playing a Southern female waitress in an improv scene. He paid such fine attention to detail. He played this woman with total grace, while still being really funny. Matt was the first of many men I've been attracted to because they know how to play women. He was antsy and cranky and had big plans. He encouraged me to write, create, and take risks. He introduced me to artists like Big Black and GG Allin and helped me film my first "reel," or excerpts of my best stuff for talent agents. Matt asked me to join the Upright Citizens Brigade, a relatively young sketch group. They needed a girl. I had heard of their shows around town, which seemed like a mixture of improvisation and performance art. They had done a show where each member sat on a street corner and had a Thanksgiving dinner. They did a show where they pretended a member was committing suicide. They did a show where they took an audience member for a virtual-reality tour out into the streets of Chicago. Most of their stuff was about getting the audience out of their chairs and out of their comfort zone. The Upright Citizens Brigade name came from a fake big bad corporation that was mentioned in one of their shows. The idea was this group had co-opted the name and was causing chaos on purpose—picture Occupy Wall Street if they renamed themselves "Halliburton Inc." Like I said, Matt had big ideas. He had a big plan for the UCB and I wanted to be part of it. I grabbed his coattails and held on tight.

Besser turned me on to Fugazi. He talked about the spirit of Ian MacKaye and how Fugazi never charged a lot for their shows. He wanted the Upright Citizens Brigade to feel like that—owned by the people. We had no plans for a school or theater or television show, but we all felt an itch. I scratched mine reading Daniel Clowes comic books and shopping at thrift stores for old Doc Martens. I went to bars and saw Liz Phair. I lived in a scary part of Chicago and watched police shoot a dog in our backyard. I started improvising with people better than me and got better myself. I started to call myself an artist.

The audience was staring at me as veteran improviser and all-around captain Dave Koechner pointed and yelled, "Sell it!" I had bailed on a scene. That meant I had started a scene with someone and either failed to commit, laughed, or negated that person's choice. Improvisation is like the military. You leave no man behind. It's your job to make your partner look good and if you are afraid to look stupid you should probably go home. Improvisation was about not being cool. Nobody stood outside of improv theaters in tiny leather jackets smoking cigarettes. Being "clever" wasn't rewarded. It was about being in the moment and listening and not being afraid. I had let my partner down and I was being told to "sell it!" This was a way to shame young improvisers. It was a rolled-up-newspaper-swat approach. When Dave Koechner told you to "sell it," it meant you had to do the monkey dance. The monkey dance was really embarrassing.

I was part of an improv team called Inside Vladimir. We'd named ourselves after a gay porn title we saw at JJ Peppers, a Chicago convenience store that sold only porn and food. Very convenient, indeed. Tina Fey was one of my team members. She was sharp, shy, and hilarious. We took classes together and sat in the back. She would whisper funny and harsh things about Del to me. When we did scenes together, they weren't particularly funny or interesting. There was absolutely nothing pointing to the fact that anyone on our team would be successful in any kind of comedy career. We were all just trying to keep up. Inside Vladimir performed frequently at Improv-Olympic, and the men on our team were great and supportive and totally fine with Tina and me taking over. Together we wrote a two-woman show that we performed one night only. It was called *Women of Color* and had a sketch about two policewomen named Powderkeg and Shortfuse. I think we did fifteen minutes of written material and then padded the rest with improv. Soon after, we performed the Del Close–invented long-form structure called "The Dream." In it, you interviewed a member of the audience about their day and performed what you thought their dream would look like at night. And the gentleman in the audience who raised his hand? A young Seth Meyers. I don't remember one thing about meeting him but I'm sure in Seth's memoir he will describe it as the night he saw god.

Soon after, Tina and I both auditioned for Second City's touring company. You had to do a bunch of characters and I have completely forgotten what I did. I'm sure Besser helped me. Here is a sheet someone recently found in an old drawer at Second City, from the day I auditioned.

Remember, kids, they can spell your name wrong and you can still get the job!

Tina and I were placed in a touring company called BlueCo, and I took the spot left behind by Rachel Dratch who had been hired for the Mainstage company. We traveled all over Chicago and the United States in a van with hilarious men and women. I think we were paid $65 a show. We would drive across Texas and perform three or four times and come back to Chicago deep in debt. Those van rides were tiny comedy labs. I remember a lot of beef jerky and bits. Tina taught me how to pluck my eyebrows. During our Texas tour we stopped at a Dallas S&M club and drank warm Diet Cokes as we watched a woman lazily whip a guy. Nothing is more depressing than a tired dominatrix. We did a show just outside of Waco and wondered if it was gauche to drive to the Branch Davidian compound. I complained to the manager at the Red Roof Inn about blood in my sink and then sheepishly asked him where the "bad stuff went down." He handed me typed-out directions. He had clearly been asked before. We arrived to find charred children's toys still littering the place. We noticed Jews for Jesus graffiti and many people still wandering around. An Australian woman with her arm in a sling was preaching on a burned-out school bus. She spoke of how handsome David Koresh was and how he was getting ready to return, while I stood fascinated by her wristwatch, which she had safety-pinned to her sling. It was weird, man. Especially since one of us was very stoned.

While I was touring with Second City, I continued to perform at ImprovOlympic and with the Upright Citizens Brigade. The group had morphed and now it was the fab four it remains today: Besser, Ian Roberts, Matt Walsh, and me. Ian was an intense and cerebral guy from New Jersey who was the best improviser I had ever seen. He was a great actor who looked like he wanted to wrestle you. I saw Matt Walsh for the first time when he played Captain Lunatic (Lou Natic), an over-the-top cop who chugged Pepto-Bismol and cursed God. I was in awe of his characters and his distinct voice. Adam McKay and Horatio Sanz were still performing with us on occasion, although both were being groomed to join *SNL*. Adam was good at everything. He was an unbelievable writer and bulletproof onstage. Horatio was sweet but fearless. He once walked through a sliding glass door on a dare.

The UCB4 started to write and perform our own shows, most of which included audience plants and fake gunplay. This included *Thunderball,* a sketch show conceived during the baseball strike. We dragged our audience to the entrance of Wrigley Field and declared baseball officially dead. We had the crowd light candles and chant "Baseball is dead, long live Thunderball." James Grace played a plant in the audience who supported baseball and we shot him. Horatio played the ghost of Babe Ruth, and he wept over James and shouted "No!!" up to the heavens. It started to rain and then cops made us disperse. James committed to lying in the rain for hours. We got big crowds and mixed reviews. Del liked to remind us that "no prophet is accepted in his hometown." He also liked to tell us to "fall, and then figure out what to do on your way down" and that "professionals work on New Year's Eve." People around us started becoming actual professionals. Adam and Horatio and Tim Meadows got hired at *SNL*. Andy Richter was on *Late Night with Conan O'Brien*. Big stars, like Mike Myers, Andy Dick, and Chris Farley, would come back and perform with us. I had coincidentally rented Farley's old Chicago apartment years after he had left. He was incredibly nice and painfully sensitive. He would stand back-stage and berate himself if he felt he didn't do a good job. It was almost like he couldn't hear how loud everyone was laughing.

We were rehearsing for a UCB show when the O.J. Simpson ver-dict came down and we watched it live. When O.J. was acquitted, Besser predicted O.J. would find himself back in jail not long after. Besser knew something about the future, it seemed. He was a time traveler and understood the long game. In addition to doing UCB, Matt performed as a stand-up comedian and had a manager. His name was Dave Becky, and Matt told Dave about this group with the funny name. Dave traveled to Chicago and saw something in the Upright Citizens Brigade, and seventeen years later Dave still represents me. The UCB had done a few showcases in New York and Los Angeles, and soon Besser decided it was time for us to leave Chicago. We sat in a booth at the Salt & Pepper Diner and charted our course.

No one thought this was a good idea. A casting director told me we would never make it as a group. Second City reminded me I was in line to get a spot in a Mainstage company—the big-time there. ImprovOlympic was a warm blanket we didn't want to crawl out from under. My choice was easy to make, though, because I was moving back east near my family and had wisely learned to do whatever Besser told me to do. Also, Ian and Walsh and Matt were the funniest people I knew and Ian had once punched a drunk guy wearing a sombrero who yelled gross stuff to me from across the street. I felt protected.

It's easier to be brave when you're not alone.

We were young and foolish and didn't know what we were up against. Thank god. We said good-bye to our friends and our cheap and beautiful apartment in the scary neighborhood. We packed all of our things and my yellow Lab, Suki, and pulled away in a U-Haul truck. We had no apartment or job or place to perform in New York City. I didn't really know who I was, but improv had taught me that I could be anyone. I didn't have to wait to be cast—I could give myself the part. I could be an old man or a teenage babysitter or a rodeo clown. In three short years Chicago had taught me that I could decide who I was. My only job was to surround myself with people who respected and supported that choice. Being foolish was the smartest thing to do.

I stood onstage and did the monkey dance. I put my two fingers up my nose and turned it into a pig nose. I took my other hand and put it up between my legs and grabbed my crotch. I danced and made monkey sounds as everyone clapped. These were the people I wanted to impress. They still are. Who needed a job? I was already my own boss! (Cue my parents gasping.) Money? Who needed money when I was already so rich? (I was very poor. I needed money badly. I borrowed a lot from my parents.)

New York, here I come!

SHORT PEOPLE

DO

NOT

LIKE TO BE PICKED UP.

the russians are coming

MY PARENTS STILL LIVE IN THE HOUSE WE MOVED INTO WHEN I WAS FIVE. In my old bedroom are the dried flowers from my prom and a street sign I stole when I hung out with some bad kids for a few months. I loved school. I loved new shoes and lunch boxes and sharp pencils. I would hold dance contests in tiny finished basements with my friends. I roller-skated in my driveway and walked home from the bus stop on my own. We never locked our door. I had a younger brother whom I loved and also liked. I thought my mother was the most beautiful mother in the world and my father was a superhero who would always protect me. I wish this feeling for every child on earth.

Because of this safe foundation, I had to create my own drama. I'm aware many children were not afforded that luxury. Some had houses filled with chaos and abuse, and they learned to keep their mouths shut and stay out of trouble. I was dealt two loving parents, and they encouraged me to be curious. This safety net combined with the small drumbeat inside of me meant I did a lot of silly things to try to make life seem exciting. Our little town of Burlington, Massachusetts, was quiet and homogenous, an endless series of small ranch houses on tree-lined streets littered with pine needles. The only thing we feared was the dreaded gypsy moth. Burlington was sleepy, and to a restless young girl like me it often felt like a ghost town. I yearned for adventure and spent a lot of my youth in my own head, creating elaborate fantasies that felt grown-up and life threatening.

The streets and woods around my house were a perfect setting for fake mischief. I would spend all afternoon pretending I had run away and had to live on my own. I would bring Toll House cookies and a sweatshirt and try to make a fire. I would sneak outside of our house at dusk with a pair of binoculars and search the streets for murderers. I created scenarios in my head that I always managed to escape from: kidnap fantasies where I would wriggle free from the ropes, fire fantasies where I would save my whole family and jump from my window into a snowbank, drugstore-robbery daydreams where I would find a way to connect with the troubled teen and get him to drop the gun. After school, I would eat ravenously and then hop on my pink Huffy bike. The bike read CACTUS FLOWER on the side, and as I coasted down the street, I would pretend I was being chased. Riding fast and helmetless, I would look over my shoulder and pick a random car and decide it was filled with Russians. I would pedal furiously up to the edge of the woods and jump off my bike, stashing it in the bushes. I would pile leaves on top of me and lie very still, imagining how ridiculous those bad guys would feel when they realized they had walked right past me. This was during the Gorbachev/Reagan years, and our enemies had thick-tongued accents and fur hats. "Do you see the girl?" the small and scary boss would say. "*Nyet,*" the big and dumb one would answer. I would pretend to wait

122

until they were gone and then jump out of the leaves to get to the business of delivering the microchip into the hands of Pat Benatar.

On long car trips, I would make my little brother, Greg, pretend he was deaf while we sat in the backseat. We would communicate in made-up sign language as we sped down the highway, in the hope that a passing car would see us and feel pity for the beautiful family with two deaf children. When you have a comfortable and loving middle-class family, sometimes you yearn for a dance on the edge. This can lead to an overactive imagination, but it is also the reason why kids in Montana do meth.

My best friend, Keri Downey, lived a block away. Her house was a much livelier version of mine. Keri and I met the first day of kindergarten. I was dressed in a cowgirl outfit, which says more about my mother's wonderful acceptance of my weirdness and less about my fashion choices at that time. Remember, this was still the 1970s, a time when my teachers wore leotards and corduroys and kissed their boyfriends in front of us. My mother was at home, but Keri's mom, Ginny, worked. Keri was a typical latchkey kid, and her house had that exciting *Lord of the Flies* feeling of being run by children. Keri had a list of chores and suffered consequences if she didn't do them. I came from a home where my mother would gently suggest that maybe I could pick up my room if I had the chance. Keri had a police officer dad who slept during the day and was not happy if we woke him up. I had a dad who would snore on the couch as we all stood around him and teased him loudly. Keri had fierce sisters who punched. I had a brother whom I occasionally argued with. The Downey sisters were a tiny gang. They fascinated me. They would fight hard, wrestling around and pulling hair. They would even challenge me to fight, occasionally pushing me into the scrum. One time Keri's sister threw a set of toenail clippers at her

———

eye and it drew blood. Blood! So exciting! They would torture each other with big emotional threats, and then they would cry and make up and eat a sandwich. They had each other's backs even when they were talking behind them. Keri would come to my house and luxuriate in the calm and the junk food, and I would head over to her house to watch her sisters in action. I would come back from Keri's house riled up, like I had witnessed some kind of dogfight. I would talk back to my mom and mess up Greg's baseball cards and act like I was a real tough piece of business. My parents would send me to my room and I would stomp up the stairs, excited to be such a troublemaker. I would knock over some books. I would kick the wall. I would put on my Jane Fonda workout and really feel the burn this time!

Even though we had such different families, Keri and I were a good pair, both freckled and Irish with a strong belief in justice. We would go out for recess and spend the whole time walking and talking. This is something I still love to do today. I call it "walking the beat." I often call my friends and tell them to meet me on a New York corner at a certain time. The physical act of walking combined with the opportunity to look out at the world while you are sharing your thoughts and feelings is very comforting to me. You are in charge of the route and the amount of eye contact. I guess those days with Keri were when this started. Anyway, Keri and I spent most of our fourth-grade recess time walking the beat and discussing the important issues of the day: the recent release of the Iranian hostages, the attempted assassination of Pope John Paul II, the fact that Luke technically raped Laura on the dance floor when they first met but now they were the best couple on *General Hospital.*

One day a student named Jamie brought a pair of handcuffs to school. I don't remember where he said he got them, but looking back now it was really odd. Where does a ten-year-old find a pair of handcuffs? This felt like an incident one would file under "having older brothers." This was by far the most dangerous thing anyone had ever brought to school besides the honeycomb full of bees that the beekeeper brought for career day. It's an indication of how truly safe and idyllic my childhood was that the handcuffs didn't scare me. They didn't remind me of one of my relatives being hauled away to jail or anything traumatic like that. They only reminded me of a terrific episode of *Hill Street Blues*. And they were a pair of handcuffs, not a gun, a homemade bomb, dynamite-infused bath salts, or whatever horrible shit kids have to deal with these days.

Keri and I immediately took them and then shared a look as we locked them on to our wrists. Keri discreetly dropped the key to the ground and then we pretended it was lost. We faked being upset while a small group of kids gathered around, excited about the idea of handcuffs and lost keys and people being stuck together. The general hubbub turned into real concern once we couldn't actually find the key we had dropped. The recess bell rang and Keri and I walked back into the building to find a teacher. We were wrist to wrist; I could feel our pulses quickening. I was thrilled. The other kids crowded around us as we told the teacher what had happened. "They are stuck together!" they cried. "They will never get free!" Attempts were made to pull us free, but we would yell out in fake pain and the pulling would stop. We were brought over to the sink. Paints and brushes were moved aside and thick liquid soap was poured on our hands. Our tiny wrists looked like they could easily slide out, but they refused. Teachers became irritated at the thought of sending us home in handcuffs. I loved the attention. I loved acting cool and calm about being handcuffed to my friend. We became instant celebrities.

Eventually, Keri got nervous about getting in trouble. I spoke quietly and evenly to her about how everything was going to be okay.

———

I made jokes about splitting up the week with each other's families. It was the beginning of what I now think is my natural instinct to try to bring levity and calm to stressful situations. I am an excellent person to be around if you're having a bad drug trip. You need a balance of humor and pathos mixed with some light massage and occasional distractions. I once helped a now very famous actor cross over while he was on ecstasy by speaking to him softly and then pretending to do magic tricks. I was also on ecstasy at the time. This may have helped my comedy, but it certainly didn't help with my magic.

Keri and I sat in class for what seemed like hours while the teachers huddled to figure out what to do. There was talk of going to the police station! There was even talk of getting a big machine to cut us apart! Then we went back outside to look again and found the key. Keri was happy because she didn't want her police officer dad to lecture her on handcuff etiquette, but I was so bummed. We rubbed our wrists and talked to everyone on the bus about how scared we had been. We dined out on the great handcuff incident for weeks. The school called us the Handcuff Girls, which will be my band's name when I become a rock star in my midsixties. It was the most exciting thing that had ever happened to me up to that point, and it was the perfect kind of scary story that only lasts a few hours and ends up well.

As we grew up, Keri's house remained my comfortable danger zone. We would pile up pillows for Fright Nights on Fridays, when we would watch scary movies and make popcorn in a giant and expensive microwave. We would sit through *Friday the 13th* and *The Thing* and *A Nightmare on Elm Street* while we folded laundry. I have fond memories of cranking up the air-conditioning in Keri's house and then lying under tons of blankets to watch those movies. Her scrappy sisters would snuggle together and her sweet mom, Ginny, would join us. I would mostly watch through the holes of an afghan, and Ginny would tap my shoulder just before each scary part. I vividly remember watching *Carrie* and tensing up at that last scene when Amy Irving lays flowers at the grave. Ginny gently sat tapping my shoulder and I prepared for the inevitable zombie hand bursting out of the dirt and the chorus of screams that followed.

Once middle school rolled around, Keri went to Catholic school while I stayed in our public school. She wore a uniform and became proficient with black eyeliner. Older kids meant more chaos, and my school suddenly had the energy and excitement I was looking for. It also started to teach me that there were kids who truly weren't loved or happy. Even though most of us lived in the same detached homes with wall-to-wall carpet, inside those homes were drunk moms and mean dads. The danger I was looking for started to become a little more real. There was a fight in our school every day. Students rushed to the parking lot or the hallway when a fight was starting. Cops broke up parties and boys got drunk and started to smash their bodies into each other. Steroids were a big drug for a lot of the high school boys in my town, and this produced a weird collection of rage-filled football players who were just as bored as I was. The difference is when I was bored I would listen to my Walkman and pretend I was in a music video. When they were bored they would beat someone up. Years later a few of these football players would be arrested for picking up a prostitute near their college campus and raping her. It would be a landmark case of an admitted prostitute and drug addict winning a conviction against a bunch of white men. I watched it on Court TV and thought about all those boys and the parties they attended in my house.

The girls were a tough bunch as well. I was pushed into a locker and punched by a cheerleader. One girl pulled my hair at lunch because she thought I was "stuck up." It was bad to be "stuck up."

It was also bad to be a "slut" or a "prude" or a "dexter" or a "fag." There were no openly gay kids in my high school. My school had a quiet hum of racism and homophobia that kept all of that disclosure far away. Every year the girls would have a football game called the Powder Puff. The girls would play tackle football on a cold high school field while the boys dressed as cheerleaders and shouted misogynist things at everybody. It was as wonderful as it sounds. I played safety and tried to talk my way out of getting beat up. I saw a girl hike the ball and then just go over and punch someone in the nose. There was so much hate and hair spray flying. Black eyes were common. I started to learn that as much as I chased adventure, I had little interest in the physical pain that came with it. I also realized I didn't like to be scared or out of control.

And then Keri's mom, Ginny, got cancer.

Suddenly the world was small and tight. Our parents could get sick and our pretend games felt a million miles away. The inevitability of death became a new nightmare. I don't remember when I first heard of Keri's mom getting sick, but it was in that way young children receive news, a watered-down fashion that is a combination of investigating and straight-up eavesdropping. I remember her children pleading with her to stop smoking, and stealing her cigarettes from her purse and throwing them in the garbage. I remember her daughters spending days lying in her bed with her as her cancer spread from her brain to the rest of her body. I remember their dad and her husband, Mike, seeming very lost but also very strong. I also remember my incredible paralysis through the whole thing. All of my practice chasing bad guys did not add up to much. Cancer was too scary and too real, and I wanted the whole thing to go away. I was in high school when Ginny died, and I didn't do a very good job of being there for my friend. I had little experience with death and did that classic thing of thinking I should just leave everyone alone and wait for the sad parties to reach out when they needed help.

Now that I am older life seems full of things to worry about. Sometimes I search for bad news as if reading the details will protect me somehow. I call it tragedy porn. I will fill myself up with every horrible detail about the latest horrible event and quote it back to people like some bad-news know-it-all. Remember that Austrian dad Josef Fritzl who raped his daughter and kept her and her kids in the basement for twenty-four years? I do, because I spent many nights reading every horrible specific fact about it and talking about it to everyone who would listen, until one day Seth Meyers gently reminded me that I worked at *Saturday Night Live* and it was a comedy show and maybe I was bumming everybody out. At the end of the year the "Update" team surprised me with a framed copy of an *Entertainment Weekly* cover Seth and I had posed for. They replaced Seth's face with Josef Fritzl's. I am smiling and pulling at his tie. This is what it is like to work in comedy. Hilarious and horrifying.

Speaking of horrifying, I still troll the Internet for terrible stories. I see an awful headline and try not to click it. I often can't believe how hard it is not to read. For a while I was obsessed with a cable show called *I Survived . . .* I was never very interested in the people who were attacked by mountain lions while hiking or the dummies who crashed their single-engine airplanes. Those stories seemed like foolish risk-taking scenarios I could successfully avoid by never going outside. No, I would watch the horrible pieces on women who had been assaulted and left for dead. First-person accounts of people being attacked by strangers or stabbed by boyfriends. This is the ultimate narcissistic white-girl game. I would picture how I would handle the attack differently. Or the same. Inevitably, I'd think about my own death, which next to staring at your

129

face in a magnifying mirror is probably the worst thing you can do for yourself. The ambulance-chasing aspect combined with the Monday-morning quarterbacking of it all is the luxury afforded to those of us left untouched by trauma. Sometimes I would use these tragedy-porn shows to unlock deep feelings or cut through the numbness. I would read terrible stories to punish myself for my lucky life. Some real deep Irish Catholic shit. Either way, it was all gross and all bad for my health. I remember being depressed after my second boy, Abel, was born. I couldn't lose weight and I couldn't stop working. One evening, Will tried to gently point out that drinking a bottle of wine by myself while I watched *Oprah* on DVR probably wasn't the best way to feel better. I remember arguing with him that these shows didn't make me feel sad. They were real. They were emotional. They were what I needed to feel better. Then Oprah's show came on and she announced the topic was African baby rape. I was forced to admit perhaps it was time for a break.

Let's not end on African baby rape (or start with it, for that matter). Let's end by pointing out all the positive ways you can scare yourself and feel alive. You can tell someone you love them first. You can try to speak only the truth for a whole week. You can jump out of an airplane or spend Christmas Day all by your lonesome. You can help people who need help and fight real bad guys. You can dance fast or take an improv class or do one of those Ironman things. Adventure and danger can be good for your heart and soul. Violence and desperation are brutal things to search out. Why search out the horror? It's around us in real ways every day. I'm talking to you, the people who made that movie *The Human Centipede*. No more *Human Centipede* movies please. No more movies about people's mouths being sewn onto people's butts. The whole idea of making and watching a movie like that makes me want to take a ten-year nap.

———

Having said all this I would like to pitch some taglines for the inevitable *Human Centipede 4* movie.

IT ALL MAKES SENSE IN THE END

FROM YOUR MOUTH TO GOD'S BUTT

RUN, DON'T WALK TO THIS MOVIE!

[UNLESS YOU ARE A HUMAN CENTIPEDE. IN THAT CASE, CRAWL.]

HUMAN CENTIPEDE?

[NO THANK YOU PLEASE.]

REASONS WE CRY ON AN AIRPLANE

1. We are a little drunk.

2. We are a little scared.

3. We feel lonely, which is different than being alone.

4. We are missing someone or have just left someone.

5. We are headed towards our family and can't stand our cousins.

6. We feel like time is suspended and therefore we can feel real emotion without consequence.

7. We look out the windows and see the sky and are reminded of how amazing it is to get in a giant steel bird and not have to die on the trail like our forefathers.

8. We have just watched a movie. ANY MOVIE. Recent movies I have cried to include 21 Jump Street, That's My Boy, The Taking of Pelham 123 and Jackass 2.

9. The pressure.

10. The pressure! (different)

humping justin timberlake

I WAS HIRED ON *SATURDAY NIGHT LIVE* IN AUGUST 2001. We were supposed to have our first read-through on 9/11. I turned thirty years old five days later. My first year was a total blur that consisted of my trying not to get fired and trying not to die. It was a tough time to join the show. It felt like America might not ever smile, never mind laugh, again. I hoped that the entire idea of comedy would not be canceled just as I was starting this dream job. I like to refer to the transition period of any new job as "finding out where the bathrooms are." Not only did I have to find the bathrooms, but I had to attempt to do comedy in a city that was battered and still on fire, while avoiding being killed by the ANTHRAX that had been sent to the floors below us. Talk about jitters.

Wonderful things happened my first year on *SNL*. Will and I decided to get married. I met Meredith Walker, who would become one of my best friends and help shepherd *Smart Girls at the Party* into the world with me. She was tall and from Texas and had already met Sting and Tupac. I got to see Tina Fey and Rachel Dratch every day. I met Seth Meyers in Mike Shoemaker's office and something clicked inside of me, like a broken locket completed. I got to work with Will Ferrell. It's tough for me to find a single story that would really explain to you what *SNL* felt like or what it meant to me. So I'm not going to try. I told you, writing is HARD. In lieu of that story, I present to you my bite-sized *SNL* memories, mixed in with some benign gossip about past hosts. Enjoy.

My first show was on September 29, 2001. I walked in the background during a "Wake Up, Wakefield" sketch but according to my parents, you couldn't see me. Paul Simon sang "The Boxer" and Lorne Michaels solemnly asked Mayor Giuliani, "Can we be funny?" The mayor paused and answered, "Why start now?" Lorne wrote that joke. We all drank hard with exhausted firefighters at the after-party, their uniforms still covered with dust.

The first time I appeared on air was the last sketch of the night, a week later. I wrote it and played a porn star on a date with Seann William Scott. Seconds before we went live, Lorne asked me if I wanted white or red wine in the prop wineglasses. I still don't know if he was genuinely asking or doing some Jedi mind trick to help me be less nervous.

In that same episode, Will Ferrell played an overzealous office worker who displays his patriotism by wearing an American flag Speedo. I watched him spread his legs and realized that America could and would laugh again. A few shows later, Will and I wrote a sketch where we played two background actors and I realized I wasn't going to be fired. Will Ferrell is one of the most naturally talented people I have ever met. He was our benevolent captain and will always be a hero in my eyes because: 1) he used his talent to heal me and the country in ways he will never know, and 2) he is a straight-up king.

Later in my first season, they pulled host Britney Spears out of a cold open because she didn't have time to change. I did her part with five minutes' prep. It was a skiing scene and I may have worn her clothes. I also think I said "Live from New York" for the first time. For some reason I feel like Dan Aykroyd was also in it? I'm not sure. I could fact-check this but I'm too lazy.

Britney Spears also signed a poster for me that hung in my office. I don't know where the poster is now. Here is a picture. Yes, I knit.

Molly Shannon, Kristen Wiig, and I all had that office at some point in our *SNL* careers. Each one of us carved her name in the desk.

One night Chris Parnell hid under that desk for an hour while I was writing. He kept gently hitting my drawer so it would spring open. I couldn't figure out what was going on and so I looked below to investigate. He was curled up in a ball and I screamed my head off. There was a lot of pranking. Horatio Sanz used to call me and pretend he was a weird gentleman named Gomez Vasquez Gomez. Writer Andrew Steele used to leave us notes from a pervert named Thurman, letting us know he was a big fan of "butts and boobs." Will Forte would call writer Emily Spivey and me to ask us to work on a sketch and we would come in to find him and his writer office-mates Leo Allen and Eric Slovin completely naked at their desks.

We were never fed and were left to our own devices when it came to meals. Interns would go on McDonald's runs and buy a shitload of horrible candy. A lot of time was spent ordering food and waiting for it to be delivered. The traffic around 30 Rock often meant that we were constantly starving and complaining. One time, Slovin was bitching about his food taking forever, and once it arrived, Forte grabbed it and threw it out the window.

I cried a lot in Mike Shoemaker's office. Once, a few years after 9/11, I did a 9/11-based joke on "Weekend Update" during rehearsal. It didn't go well and I came offstage and cried to producer Mike Shoemaker about how I was bad at telling jokes and how I wanted to quit.

I also cried a lot in Maya Rudolph's office and Spivey's office. And in elevators. Some of the crying was from exhaustion or stress, and some of it was just the bitter burn of rejection. A teeny tiny cleaning lady named Rosa had worked at *SNL* for over thirty years. She barely spoke English and we all loved her. Maya and I were both crying about something and Rosa came in to empty the wastebasket. She put her hand on Maya's shoulder and in a thick Spanish accent said, "Don't cry, sexy."

Tina wrote a sketch where Chris Kattan and I played a white trash couple. It was very physical and I blacked out during a show when I was flipped upside down into a Dumpster. I woke up to Kattan standing over me and yelling. John Goodman was the host that week and is probably still my favorite, because he was nice to me when no one knew my name.

Once, after a long after-party, I was outside smoking with "Weekend Update" writer and future *Parks and Recreation* creator Mike Schur. Seth Meyers was also there, as well as many other men whose opinion I cared about. Host Ashton Kutcher walked out of the party and headed to his limousine. He casually said good-bye to me and I loudly and sincerely shouted like a crazy fan, "Love you, Ashton. You're the best!!" It was very uncool. I was much too loud.

When Sir Ian McKellen hosted, he greeted us every day by booming out in his perfect voice, "Good morning, actors!" Colin Farrell was super hungover and super nice. Hugh Jackman was incredibly kind and sent everyone a case of Foster's beer. Jessica Simpson was the prettiest host I had ever seen without makeup. Bernie Mac was the sweetest and kindest.

Matthew McConaughey wore a sarong in Lorne's office, I danced at a club with Christina Aguilera, and Antonio Banderas smelled the best of any host.

I made a drink for James Gandolfini to settle his nerves before an "Update" piece he was doing. Once I asked Paul Giamatti during the show if he was having fun, and he smiled and said, "This is a fucking nightmare!"

When Ashlee Simpson's song screwed up, Dratch, Maya, and I were dressed in Halloween costumes for Parnell's "Merv the Perv" sketch. We screamed and ran into Tom Broecker's wardrobe department and hid under a table. Maya was dressed as a pregnant woman in a catsuit. I was Uma Thurman from *Kill Bill*. Dratch was Raggedy Ann. I remember us huddling together buzzing about the excitement of that weird live moment and then someone saying, "At least *60 Minutes* is here." For those who don't remember, *60 Minutes* was doing a profile on Lorne and happened to be there. Jackpot, Lesley Stahl!

Maya, Queen Latifah, and I were in a sketch where we had to sing a few songs as backup singers. Five seconds before we went live our stage manager, Gena, told us there was a problem with the track and we had to sing without music. We looked at each other wide-eyed and excited. When that sketch was over Latifah said, "That was crazy!" and we high-fived.

I sat in on Prince's sound check. He was the musical guest and Steve Martin was the host. He walked over to me after he was done. My musician friend and lifelong Prince fan Amy Miles burst into tears. I turned to Prince and awkwardly asked him, "How was your summer?"

When U2 performed, Bono came over to hug me. My whole body blushed and I almost died from excitement and fear. Years later I paid him back by making out with him during a bit at the Golden Globes, thus completing a circle and allowing myself to effectively time-travel.

Speaking of time travel, I did a sketch with Jon Bon Jovi where I was a fourteen-year-old version of myself and he stepped out of a poster. The set was designed like my actual bedroom as a child, and Spivey and I had a long discussion about what brand of hair spray should be on the dresser. I think White Rain won. Jon Bon Jovi went into his own archives and got out the actual outfit he had worn twenty years before during the Slippery When Wet Tour. It still fit. Jon Bon keeps it tight.

140

I wrote that scene and most of my favorite scenes with Emily Spivey. Spivey is an insanely talented writer and actor from the Groundlings via North Carolina. She has a sharp tongue and gifted sense of character, and we would huddle together on Tuesday writing nights and try to do a "jam out," which basically meant write something fast and fun. Out of that came Kaitlin, the hyperactive girl with a heart of gold. Kaitlin had boundless optimism, and she was a tribute to all latchkey kids who had to amuse themselves. It was also an homage to a Gilda Radner sketch called "The Judy Miller Show." Spivey and I would spend hours talking about the genius of Gilda, or Jan Hooks, or Phil Hartman. We were also obsessed with the song "I'm No Angel" by Gregg Allman for some reason. We spent our whole tenure at *SNL* trying to get that song into a sketch. It ended up being the soundtrack to a scene where the super-pregnant me hits on Josh Brolin in a honky-tonk bar. Spivey was also pregnant at the time. It might have been the only time two pregnant women wrote a scene about a pregnant woman on *SNL*.

141

Spivey and I wrote a sketch based on a real moment we had with the handsome and talented Justin Timberlake. He was hosting and came into the office one writing night. We both got very flummoxed, and it caused us to write a scene where I was attempting to give him notes backstage during a show. I was dressed as a leprechaun with a giant orange wig. I ended up getting tongue-tied and eventually just started humping on him. Justin had a lovely Southern woman who was his ex-teacher and "handler" at the time. She did not think it was a good idea for him to be shirtless during this sketch. I point to these boundaries as one reason why Justin has kept his shit together.

I once wrote a sketch where Steve Martin and I were two drunk people applying for a bank loan. It didn't make air, but he still asks me about it sometimes, which is better.

You could spend the whole night working on a sketch and arrive the next morning to see that it was not in the read-through packet. Spivey and I wrote a sketch once about two dumb girls in a car shouting out the window at an eighteen-wheeler semi. The girls kept telling the driver to "honk it!!" Shoemaker called us the next morning to tell us the sketch wasn't going to be read because there was no way to get a semi into Studio 8H. I'm sure he pulled it because he was trying to save us from embarrassment.

Read-through day was always exhausting and fun. I sat next to Seth and scribbled notes. Fred Armisen would write end-of-the-year diatribes where he pretended to be angry at everyone. They worked because we all loved Fred and we knew he loved us. One day before a Wednesday read-through, Rachel Dratch threw her back out and had to lie down on the floor. Host Johnny Knoxville offered to help and pulled ten loose pills out of his pocket before realizing none of them were painkillers. A hot NBC doctor came upstairs and all the single guys started hitting on her. Rachel did the entire first half of the read-through from the floor.

We had a sexual harassment meeting once and I spent the whole time sitting next to Will Forte drawing penises. At the end of the meeting I was asked to hand in the sign-in sheet and I gave the guy the penis paper by accident. Tracy Morgan used to tell us, "Don't peak at dress," and "Don't let the pages jinx your shit." Paula Pell was usually the funniest person in the room. Or Fred Armisen. Unless Baldwin was there.

"Debbie Downer" was one of the few sketches where I broke, and I remember watching Horatio Sanz laugh so hard that tears squirted out of his eyes. I still believe that sketch may be a cure for low-level depression if watched regularly.

Jim Downey ignored the fact that I never did a good impression of Hillary Clinton and used to sit with me between dress and air going over his notes for the scenes he had written. It took me a while to find a real "take" on her. We used to use videotapes to help with impressions, and I would take my tapes into Darrell Hammond's room where he would give me tips on how to sound like Hillary. I gave her a crazy laugh, which she didn't have in real life. As the election year progressed I loved getting to play her as this highly focused and slightly angry woman who was tired of being the smartest person in the room. I secretly hoped she watched some of my sketches and could live vicariously through the things I got to say.

The memories I have with Seth could fill a whole book. When I left *SNL,* I gave Seth a badge of courage, like Dorothy gives to the Cowardly Lion. The props department helped me make it. He kept it in his pocket during "Update" until he didn't need it anymore. Now it sits in a box on his desk at *Late Night.*

———

When Tina left, I gave her dog tags that read "Pleasant Tomorrow." Recently she gave them back to me while I was going through a tough time. I like to think we will give them back and forth to each other whenever needed.

"Bronx Beat" was a sketch that was a dream to write and perform. Maya and Spivey and I would just improvise for hours in their office. We named those characters after Jodi Mancuso and Betty Rogers in the *SNL* hair department. Jodi had that accent and attitude. Maya and I would sit on set a few minutes before our scene went on the air and just talk to each other in character.

I spent many nights sitting in Spivey's office, smoking out the window and staring at the Empire State Building.

I spent many nights in Tina's office, watching her write and pretending to help her.

I spent many nights in Seth's office, watching him write and adjusting his temperature and lighting.

I watched the Rockefeller Center Christmas tree lighting from Lorne's office and all I remember thinking is "I am so tired." Most of the bigger moments in my career happened in that office. Steve Higgins brought me in there to tell me I was hired. Lorne called me in to tell me I was doing "Update." He told me that once I said my name everything would change. He was right. Lorne once told me he was "never nervous when [I was] out there." He never scared me and often made me laugh. He handed me a rope and it was up to me whether I would climb it or use it to hang myself. He gave kind advice and expected the best from me. He loves his kids and paid for me to fix my teeth. One Saturday morning I bit into a bagel and the veneer Lorne had bought me popped off my front tooth. I had an emergency appointment at the dentist and spent an entire "Weekend Update" living a real-life stress dream that my tooth was going to fall out. Lorne is my friend and I love him and will always be grateful for the huge opportunities he gave me and continues to give me. I hope one of his assistants will print this out for him because otherwise he will probably never read this.

Every single time I heard Don Pardo announce my name I would bow my head in gratitude. Don kept his voice-over booth warm and stocked with goodies. He told me he used to drive to 30 Rock in the 1950s and park right out front. He would record for NBC and then use the two dollars he'd brought with him to buy a sandwich and a cup of coffee. He was one of many nonagenarians who still worked on the show. Another was lighting designer Phil Hymes. One time Kenan Thompson was testing with me as a possible "Weekend Update" replacement for Tina. Phil took a look at Kenan sitting next to me and said, "Kenan, I hope you don't get this because there is no way I can light the two of you next to each other."

Once Dratch and I played Michael Jackson and Elizabeth Taylor, respectively, in a sketch where we sat in a tree twenty feet in the air. I looked out over Studio 8H and for the millionth time laughed at my crazy life. Tina and I used to look at each other before "Update" and also laugh at our crazy lives. We would whisper, "We fooled them!" Sometimes I would pat her knee. One time I ran into Mick Jagger, Tom Petty, and Eric Idle in the hallway and I was legitimately mad that they were in my way, but the gratitude never left me. Comedy had not died. Someone was still letting me do it.

145

NOBODY LOOKS STUPID
WHEN THEY ARE HAVING

F U

N.

every mother needs a wife

I HAVE ALWAYS HAD A JOB, SO WHEN I HAD MY TWO CHILDREN I DIDN'T ASSUME I WOULD STOP WORKING. I slowed down, which I was happy to do. I was grateful that I could. Most can't. However, I had no plans of being a full-time stay-at-home mother. This is not to say I think being a stay-at-home mother is not a job. It certainly is. It's just not for me. Remember my motto, "Good for you, not for me."

The whole business of working mothers and stay-at-home mothers is so touchy (or tetchy, if you're a Brit). The subject inherently sucks. Not a week goes by without annoying and bullshit articles claiming "breast milk makes kids better liars" or "you should have only one child unless you live on a farm." We torture ourselves and we torture each other, and all of it leads to a lot of women-on-women crime. Here are some examples:

1. A stay-at-home mother is introduced to someone as "Aiden's mom" rather than her own name, which apparently doesn't matter.

2. A working mother is out at a function and people say, "What are you doing out? Don't you have little kids? Who's watching them?"

3. A new mother talks about how she is breast-feeding her baby because she "just wants [her] baby to be healthy."

4. A working mother sees a woman breast-feeding and asks her, "Are you still doing that?"

5. A working mother acts like she is too busy to answer e-mails.

6. A stay-at-home mother acts like she is too busy to answer e-mails.

7. A stay-at-home mother talks about how she doesn't work because "they are only young once" and she doesn't "want to miss a thing."

8. A working mother talks about how "it's not quantity, it's quality."

9. A stay-at-home mother needs a nanny, can afford one, and refuses to hire one, and in doing so denies her kids another caring and nurturing adult and denies herself some much-needed personal time and self-care.

10. A working mother relies too heavily on her nannies and feels defensive about it, so she overcompensates by talking nonstop about some weird music class she took her kid to once.

11. A stay-at-home mother approaches a working mother and grills her about how many hours she works. She gets really interested in what time the working mother leaves in the

morning and comes home at night. Then she comments, "I honestly don't know how you do it."

I've gotten the last one a lot. The "I don't know how you do it" statement used to get my blood boiling. When I heard those words I didn't hear "I don't know HOW you do it." I just heard "I don't know how you COULD do it." I would be feeling overworked and guilty and overwhelmed and suddenly I would be struck over the head by what felt like someone else's bullshit. It was an emotional drive-by. A random act of woman-on-woman violence. In my fantasy I would answer, "What do you mean how do I do it? Do you really want to know the ins and outs of my nanny schedule? Do you want to know how I balance child care with my husband and the different ways I manipulate and negotiate work to help me put my kids first when needed?" Sometimes I would fantasize about answering the question "How do you do it?" with quick one-word answers: "Ambivalence." "Drugs." "Robots."

Of course, the ultimate comeback would be "Obviously you don't know how I do it. Because you don't do it. You couldn't. What do you do, again?"

See what I did there? Crime!

There is an unspoken pact that women are supposed to follow. I am supposed to act like I constantly feel guilty about being away from my kids. (I don't. I love my job.) Mothers who stay at home are supposed to pretend they are bored and wish they were doing more corporate things. (They don't. They love their job.) If we all stick to the plan there will be less blood in the streets.

But let me try to answer the question for real.

Do you want to know how I do it? I can do it because I have a wife. Every mother needs a wife. My wife's name is Dawa Chodon.

Sometimes it is Mercy Caballero. It used to be Jackie Johnson. Dawa is from Tibet and Mercy is from the Philippines. Jackie is from Trinidad. Over the past five years they have helped me and Will take care of our children. We are lucky. Some people cannot afford this option and have little family support. Every mother needs a wife. Some mothers' wives are their mothers. Some mothers' wives are their husbands. Some mothers' wives are their friends and neighbors. Every working person needs someone to come home to and someone to come get them out of the home. Someone who asks questions about their day and maybe fixes them something to eat. Every mother needs a wife who takes care of her and helps her become a better mother. The women who have helped me have stood in my kitchen and shared their lives. They have made me feel better about working so hard because they work hard too. They are wonderful teachers and caretakers and my children's lives are richer because they are part of our family. The biggest lie and biggest crime is that we all do this alone and look down on people who don't.

Can't we all agree that more eyes on a kid is ultimately better? Doesn't that at least lower the chances of him running into the street?

Now let me tell you about the music class I took my kid to once.

my world-famous sex advice

I THINK SEX IS GREAT. I love it and I am here to say I am good at it. Here is my World-Famous Sex Advice. Please follow it to the letter and don't challenge me on any of it. Note that all of this advice is meant for older people (strictly eighty-plus). This advice works for both straight and gay couples but you'll have to do your own work with switching the pronouns. All sex, in this instance and every instance, should be between consenting adults. Thank you in advance.

Ladies, listen up.

1. **Try not to fake it.** I know you are tired/nervous/eager to please/unsure of how to get there. Just remember to allow yourself real pleasure and not worry about how long it takes. If it makes you feel better, set a time frame. Say to your partner, "I think you are going to have to work on me for close to

forty-five minutes and then we can see how it's going and regroup." God punished us with the gift of being able to fake it. Show God who the real boss is by getting off and getting yours.

2. **Stop being so goal oriented when it comes to sex.** You might not make it to the finish line every time. Don't worry about it. Each part of the journey can be great.

3. **Keep your virginity for as long as you can,** until it starts to feel weird to you. Then just get it over with. Try not to have your first time be in a car.

4. **Don't have sex with people you don't want to have sex with.** Remember that no matter how old you are, every time you see that person the first thing you will think of is "I had sex with you."

5. **Don't get undressed and start pointing out your flaws or apologizing for things you think are wrong with your body.** Men don't notice or care. They are about to get laid! They are so psyched. Men are very visual, so if you don't want them to look at your stomach just put fake mustaches on your breasts to distract them.

6. **Get better at dirty talk.** Act like a bossy lady ordering at a deli. "I want the ham on rye and make sure you toast it!" If your guy is bad at dirty talk tell him to shut up. He might like that. If you don't like dirty talk, don't worry about it. It's pretty hot if done well but it may not be up your alley. Also, try not to stick things up your alley.

7. **Don't let your kids sleep in your bed.**

8. **You have to have sex with your husband occasionally** even though you are exhausted. Sorry.

9. **Don't make fun of men.** Don't be mean to them or hurt their feelings. Try not to crush their dreams or their balls.

10. **Stay away from pics and videos.** They last forever and you don't want a snooping babysitter (me) to find them.

11. **Laugh a lot and try new things with someone you love.**

Gentlemen, rules for you. Eyes up here, please.

1. **We don't need it to last as long as you think.** Hurry up. We are so tired.

2. **We don't want to remember your penis.** We want to remember everything else but hopefully your penis is just a wonderful blur of goodness. If your penis is too big or too small or goes to the side or has a weird thing, we will remember it. If you have something very weird, tell us right away so we aren't wondering if you know. Then we can laugh and get back to doing it.

3. **You can't fall asleep right after.** You have to stay awake for at least a few minutes. Remember, if you fall asleep we will stare at you and evaluate you. This is a very vulnerable time when we may decide we don't want to have sex with you again.

4. **Keep it sexy.** Don't believe what you see in movies. It really isn't cute when you stick out your gut.

5. **Cool it on the porn and jerking off.** We think porn is great and so is jerking off, but if we are going to have sex it may cause some problems. If you depend too heavily on the technical or visual then you may not notice the real flesh-and-blood person in your bed.

6. **Be nice, tell your woman she is hot, never shame her, and never hurt her.**

7. **Work on your dirty talk too.** Try different things but keep trying. Avoid the words "climax," "moist," and "mom." Don't speak in a fake accent. Or blaccent.

8. **If you don't get an erection, we know it's usually not because of us.** We look concerned because we are wondering if it will keep happening.

9. **Stay away from orgies.** They just take so much organizing and I feel like your time could be better spent.

10. **Open up** and try new things with someone you love.

11. **If you don't eat pussy, keep walking.**

gimme that pudding

I HAVE BEEN NOMINATED FOR SOME AWARDS. This is very cool. I have hosted a few award shows, which is also cool. My first was the High Times Stony Awards in 2000, and the last was the Golden Globes in 2014. The Upright Citizens Brigade had a strong and early relationship with *High Times,* which was then a magazine filled with Jerry Garcia conspiracy theories and sexy centerfold pictures of weed. For you young readers, the term "magazine" used to mean a collection of printed papers that you would hold in your hand and read by turning the pages. Still confused? Try this . . . picture folding your MacBook and sticking it in your pocket. Oh, you kids don't use MacBooks anymore? You use eyelid screens and mind cameras? Bully for you. I digress.

Let's all just agree that acting awards are strange. They are based on the idea that a committee of a select few puts a bunch of very different performances next to each other and then decides who gets the pudding. Don't get me wrong—to be in the company of other great actors and valued for your work is a whole lot better than being ignored. Nothing is worse than being ignored. Glenn Close said it best when she told Michael Douglas in the romantic comedy *Fatal Attraction,* "I WILL NOT BE IGNORED, DAN." She was so upset about being ignored she cooked a bunny on the stove. You don't even want to find out what I would do. A lot of people don't know I am always thisfuckingclose to doing some crazy shit.

Getting nominated for an award is very exciting. Anyone who says it is not is either lying or on a very strong beta blocker. You have a one-in-five chance of getting the pudding! That being said, I have not won very often. Always a bridesmaid, I guess. By that I mean people are always mistaking me for someone from *Bridesmaids.* I have also been mistaken for "that girl from *MADtv,*" and Chris Rock once called me Rachel Dratch, proving once and for all that Chris Rock is horribly racist.

The worst part of being nominated for any award is that despite your best efforts, you start to want the pudding. You spend weeks thinking about how it doesn't matter and it's all just an honor and then seconds before the name of the winner is announced everything inside you screams . . . "GIMME THAT PUDDING!!" Then comes the adrenaline dump, followed by shame. You didn't even want the pudding and here you are upset that you didn't get it. You think about all the interviews you did talking about the pudding or all the interviews you passed on because you didn't want people to think you wanted that pudding too much. You leave the awards show hungry and confused. To combat this, I decided to distract myself in that awkward and vulnerable moment the "winner" was announced. I decided to focus my attention on something I could control.

Bits! Bits! Bits!

The first time I was nominated for an Emmy it was for Best On-Screen Orgasm in a Dramatic Civil War Reenactment. Just kidding, it was for Outstanding Supporting Actress in a Comedy, for *SNL*. As would become the norm, I was included in a great group of women whose work I admire. I had an idea that we should all wear mustaches when our names were announced as nominees. Then I heard Sarah Silverman, who was nominated for Outstanding Lead Actress, was planning on doing the same thing. She had even brought her own mustache with her. I chalk it up to great minds. A quick scramble ensued and I collected a series of props in hopes they would work. If I remember correctly, they consisted of some crazy glasses, an eye patch, and a monocle. You know, the things every girl must have in her purse when on the red carpet. I remember how fun it was asking the women if they wanted in on it and how quickly everyone said yes. Jane Krakowski, Kristen Wiig, Kristin Chenoweth, Elizabeth Perkins, and Vanessa Williams were all game. Since Vanessa's name was announced last I thought it would be funny if we all did something stupid and then Vanessa just shook her head like "Hell no, I am not doing this stupid bit." I called her from the car on the way to the show and started to feel better. First, because I had a secret, and that always feels exciting. Second, because my brain was focusing on something besides the pudding. We all did the bit, but because we didn't let the producers know we were doing it and it was the first award of the night, they didn't put our faces on the screen inside the auditorium, so it all kind of played to silence. This only goes to show the commitment of all those women to stick with the plan no matter what. Julia Louis-Dreyfus wanted very badly to join in even though she was in a different category, which shows you how much power distraction can hold. I ended up having a very fun night and coming to the realization that the less seriously I take these things, the better. I honestly don't even remember who won that year. (Kristin Chenoweth.)

The following year I was breast-feeding a six-week-old Abel. I was too tired to think of bits but my hormones were telling me to just jump onstage and grab the award before they announced the winner. Luckily I had enough oxytocin floating around in my body that I didn't care or notice who won. (Edie Falco.) Jimmy Fallon hosted and crushed. I sat in the front row and heckled like any good friend should. I then dragged my new-mama ass to the after-party with what Tina referred to as my impressive "temporary rack." I broke my toe on the banquette I was dancing on. That's right. ON. I acted like the blue-collar party machine I had been raised to be. Jon Hamm and I held Emmys that weren't ours. We called ourselves losers all night and years later threw a losers party where winners had to donate money to charity to get in.

The next day this mother of two woke up with a swollen foot and hobbled to the airport. Lucky for me and deeply unlucky for him, I ran into my old friend Bradley Cooper, who was on the same flight that morning. I asked him to "escort me to my seat." I imagined the paparazzi photos the next day lauding Cooper for helping an old and confused lady find her way.

Then came 2011, the best pudding quest yet.

A few weeks before the Emmys I was having dinner with Martha Plimpton, Andy Richter, and his wife, writer Sarah Thyre. Andy and Sarah were some of the first people I met and hung out with when I came to New York in the mid-1990s. They were already married then and had a duplex apartment where they threw great parties that brilliant writers like David Sedaris and David Rakoff attended. They were real adults at a time when I was still a struggling kid and were always generous and kind to me. At dinner, we all discussed a fun bit that could keep my mind off the pudding again. I was reminiscing about the great old bits done by Harvey Korman and Tim Conway. I had loved one particular moment when as soon as their names were called each man just immediately got out of his seat as if he had won. They stood onstage together and when the "winner" was announced they both shook Chevy Chase's hand and sat back down. It was simple and funny and supportive and stupid—all great things. We decided that this year Martha and I, along with our fellow nominees, should do something similar, but add in a beauty pageant element. I e-mailed my fellow nominees for Outstanding Lead Actress in a Comedy Laura Linney, Edie Falco, and Melissa McCarthy, and they were all in, of course. I knew my girl Tina was down to clown, because she herself was breast-feeding at the time, and as history has shown, this is when a bitch is most likely to go OFF.

I gave the producers just the right amount of info so they could shoot our bit properly this time. We had someone buy a crown and flowers, and slowly my craving for pudding vanished again. I desperately wanted to go up onstage first because I thought the person who went up first would get the biggest laugh. But Edie Falco was first alphabetically and it seemed too grabby to ask her to switch. As luck would have it, Edie Falco e-mailed me a few days before and asked me if I would like to go onstage first. I pretended like I was doing her a favor but I was super psyched about it. Rob Lowe and Sofia Vergara read my name and

161

I just got out of my seat and pretended I had won. Standing up there, I could feel the audience's delight and confusion, followed by pure joy when Melissa and the other women followed suit. Everyone added her own twist. Martha Plimpton screamed like she was Miss Virginia, Laura Linney pretended to wipe lipstick off her teeth, and Tina tried to kiss Jack McBrayer. We all came up onstage and held hands like we were in the final moments of the Miss America pageant. I felt like I might die from happiness. When Melissa won, we all genuinely screamed with joy. Standing onstage being funny with those ladies was so much better than winning. I can only assume. I didn't win. Melissa did. It doesn't matter.

In 2012, I felt a little pressure to do something better, which isn't helpful because there is nothing worse than being the sweaty one in the group leading the charge. Plus I was going to the Emmys for the first time without my husband of ten years and I kind of just wanted to hide. Instead, I sat next to Louis CK. Louie really doesn't care about the pudding, which is one of the many things I love about him. I also love that he is really honest, gives great advice, and knows how to drive a boat.

To combat my nerves, I picked a dress that made my boobs hang out so people would be too distracted to ask me about my personal life. It was very "eyes down here, guys." Because of our fun bit the year before, people had started asking me if I had "something planned" and this made me sad and self-conscious. Then Julia Louis-Dreyfus called me. It was two hours before the Emmys and I was already seven hours into my pregame. There is an insane amount of industrial light and magic required to make me look like a pretty lady at an awards show, and I won't say the process is enjoyable. Julia said something to the effect of "I think one of us will win. If I do, will you do this bit with me? And if you win can I do it with you?" Suddenly I was focused on something active and alive instead of worrying about my boob tape. Julia had the idea that we should hug and "switch speeches" so that the winner read the other woman's speech by mistake. I was so excited about doing the bit that I was hoping I wouldn't win. And I didn't! And I didn't care. **Ultimate pudding switch**

Hosting the Golden Globes in 2013 with my life partner, Tina, was so fun. Sometimes Tina is like a very talented bungee-jumping expert. All it takes is for Tina to softly say, "We can do this, right?" and I suddenly feel like I can jump off a bridge. Two things also helped me in my preparation for this year. I spent the first day of 2013 touring orphanages in Haiti as the Ambassador of Arts for Worldwide Orphans. Nothing reminds you of what is important more than being face-to-face with children who lack basic love and care. My separation had given me a major case of the fuck-its. Ambivalence can be a powerful tool.

To get ready for our first Golden Globes together, Tina and I spent a lot of time procrastinating and sending texts about how terrible it was going to be. Deep down I wasn't worried, because Tina is the finest joke soldier you could ever go to war with. She also keenly understands the importance of good lighting. We enlisted the help of our great friend and former *SNL* producer Michael Shoemaker, as well as America's Sweetheart, Seth Meyers. We treated the whole thing like we were preparing for "Weekend Update," only without a desk and with an audience of thirty million. On the day of rehearsal we were told that jokes often leak before the live show, so we stood in our fancy jeans and sneakers and delivered our monologue with the setups only, no punch lines. It was thrilling. When I walked out onstage that night, I realized I was actually a little nervous because I do a weird thing when I am nervous where I tilt my head back like I am super confident. This is my attempt to fake it until I make it, or at the very least make it easier for someone to slit my throat.

The jokes went well. The show was fun. Tina and I had the idea to pretend to be fake actors in the audience. I believe we were there representing the smash hit *Dog President*. We also decided to sit in the audience when our own category was announced and cozy up to some grade-A celebrity meat. Of the many things I learned from working at *Saturday Night Live,* one of them is to not overwhelm people with requests. So on the day of the awards I simply asked George Clooney's people to check and make sure George was okay with my sitting next to him at some point during the broadcast. "Of course!" said George's people, after not asking him. I knew enough to not ask them to check with George and see if it was okay to sit on his lap. This was a request better saved for the last minute and in person. Or better yet, when the time came, I would just sit on his lap without even asking. As the old saying goes, "Don't ask for permission to sit on George Clooney's lap, beg for forgiveness once you do."

So I sat on George's lap, and ever the pro, George asked me what kind of bit I was cooking up. I told him when they cut to me in the audience after announcing my nomination for best comedy actress I was going to act totally engrossed in talking to him. I told him I thought it would be funny if we were just flirting and laughing. He understood immediately and handed me a glass of champagne. I told him if I won there was a very good chance I would kiss him hard on the mouth. He responded, "That's not a bad Sunday." As the camera cut to me he whispered in my ear, "The thing about making movies is . . ."

There is a reason why Clooney is considered the best. BECAUSE HE IS.

The lessons? Women are mighty. George Clooney loves bits. Doing something together is often more fun than doing it alone. And you don't always have to win to get the pudding.*†

---

* It is at this point that Julia Louis Dreyfus's lawyers would like me to point out that she won the Golden Globe in 2013.

† It is at this point that I would like to point out that once I won a Golden Globe, in 2014. I was sitting on Bono's lap this time and I was genuinely surprised. I am now forced to admit that PUDDING IS DELICIOUS.

---

great acceptance speech!
feel free to use!

I always assumed I would be smooth and prepared when I won something, but adrenaline is a crazy bitch. I stumbled through my speech when I won some pudding, and I was too embarrassed to ever watch it. I had written an acceptance speech but forgot all about it. It is below. I think it sums me up pretty well and I can't wait to use it one day, #godwilling.

(1)

```
            WINNER SPEECH


        Whaaaaaaaas up? How are you guys feeling tonight?
I SAID . . . How y'all feeling tonight??? How you guys
feeling over on this side?? Let me hear you on this
side!!! Not gonna forget you guys in the balcony!
I am here because of you. I share this win with you.
I believe it was Gandhi who said, "Winning is everything
and the only thing." Big ups to Gandhi. And Biggie.
Big ups to Biggie. Can't forget Biggie, y'all.
```

(2)

```
        Thank you first to God. And Buddha. Maybe these days
it's a little more Buddha than God. You know what? Screw
it. They are both dope. Honestly, most times I wish I was
Jewish. They kiss their kids on the head a lot and seem
to know how to argue better. Speaking of Jewish people,
I would like to thank my agents, managers, lawyers,
publicists, travel advisers, business managers, surgeons,
ob-gyns, trainers, and neighbors, and every producer
and writer I have ever worked with.
```

(3)

Now on to politics. What's the deal, guys? Seriously. I mean, come on. Get it together. It's like, when are we going to wake up? It's all crazy. Who's with me? Thanks for letting me get that off my chest.

What else? Oh, I am launching a jewelry line and my pieces are in the lobby and available for sale. Euros only! This is also a good time to mention my album is dropping. By dropping I mean someone is dropping it and I need someone else to pick it up and make it. Thank you in advance, Diplo.

(4)

To my fellow nominees, Lourdes Ciccone, Nancy Pelosi, Eddie Izzard, Animal from the Muppets, and the inimitable Maggie Smith. It is an honor.

To my stuntwoman, whose name I can't remember but whose violent death I will never forget. My deepest thanks.

To the love of my life, George Clooney, a man who wore me down with letters and phone calls until finally I gave in and let him have sex with me. You're welcome.

(5)

And finally, I would like to salute our troops by singing a slow and racially inappropriate version of "I Loves You Porgy" from the classic musical Porgy and Bess.

PEEEEAAAAAAACE.

IF IT'S NOT FUNNY, YOU DON'T HAVE TO

LAU

GH.

bad sleeper

SLEEP AND I DO NOT HAVE A GOOD RELATION-SHIP. We have never been friends. I am constantly chasing sleep and then pushing it away. A good night's sleep is my white whale. Like Ahab, I am also a total drama queen about it. I love to talk about how little sleep I get. I brag about it, as if it is a true indication of how hard I work. But I truly suffer at night. Bedtime is fraught with fear and disappointment. When it is just me alone with my restless body and mind, I feel like the whole world is asleep and gone. It's very lonely. I am tired of being tired and talking about how tired I am.

The phrase "going to sleep" has always given me great anxiety. I don't like doing things I am bad at, and I have been told since I was very young that I am a bad sleeper. As soon as I become prone, my head will begin to unpack. My mind will turn on and start to hum, which is the opposite of what you need when you begin to switch off. It is as if I were waiting the whole day for this moment.

Trying to go to sleep is often when I feel most engaged and alive. My brain starts to trick me into thinking this is the moment it should turn on and start working overtime. It is a problem. I need some rest. I have a lot to do.

Our parents surround us with origin stories that create deep grooves in the vinyl records of our lives. Mine included the simple fact of how little I slept as a baby. My mom and dad nicknamed me "Tweety Bird" because I was a tiny not-quite-six pounds, had big eyes, and was bald until I was two. I was told I resembled a cartoon chicken, which is still true, especially after a rough weekend. My parents tell stories about my staring at them from the crib at all hours of the night. Sounds pretty creepy, right? A pale, bald, and tiny baby bird peering out through the slats of its cage, challenging the adults to an all-night staring contest? By all accounts I came home and my parents didn't sleep again for another ten years. I was born in a different time. Women still smoked when pregnant and no one talked about folic acid. Kale wasn't even invented yet! My mother, who was constantly nauseous, was encouraged to keep her weight down by her doctors. She gained only eighteen pounds during her pregnancy with me, a fact she was very proud of and told me repeatedly while I was pregnant for the second time and forty pounds overweight. She may have stopped after I threatened to dropkick her into the neighbor's yard if she mentioned it again. My mother was also a tiny baby, and my grandmother (another petite flower) used to brag that she would put my mother to sleep inside a dresser drawer. It seems like in the olden times people loved to stick their babies in strange places and then brag about where they fit. My father also told me a story about using a warm baked potato as some kind of mitten. I don't know. Things were weird back then. Whatever the case, I was small and a bad sleeper and these labels have stuck.

At a young age I would grind my teeth and snore. I sleep-laughed and sleep-talked. I didn't sleepwalk, but I sleep-scared my brother, Greg. We would sleep in the same bed on Christmas Eve, too excited to be apart. He was three years younger and would easily fall asleep while I did my usual ritual of spending two to three hours going over lists in my head, worrying about my family, and then reading Nancy Drew books with a flashlight. One Christmas morning Greg, who was five at the time, woke me up to go downstairs. I looked at him and said, "Okay, let's go wake up Greg." He looked at me with his big kindergarten eyes and nervously said, "I am Greg!" From then on our family has used the phrase "I am Greg!" any time one of us is having an existential breakdown. One Christmas, when we were a bit older, Greg and I got up in the middle of the night and turned all the clocks in the house ahead a few hours. We woke up our parents and opened presents until they finally realized it was pitch-black even though the clocks read eight thirty A.M.

Sleepovers were a big thing when I was young. Sleepovers were girl summits—confabs where we all snuggled next to each other and decided who we were going to be. They were also stressful social experiments. I had two wonderful friends growing up whom I still consider my close friends. I met Kristin Umile in second grade. She was shorter than me, which was a big deal. She was half Italian and talked a mile a minute. She won the superlative "cutest" in both middle school and high school but was incredibly well liked, which gives you a sense of her wonderfulness. Andrea Mahoncy, whom I called Sis, was the social quarterback of the whole school. She came from a warm Irish family with lots of older brothers and sisters, and she was a pretty athlete who made everyone feel welcome wherever we were. I was lucky to be included in that sandwich. As we would line our Snoopy sleeping bags up next

———

to each other I would sink into the relief I felt from having friends like these girls. Smart. Patient. Good daughters and sisters. That's who I ran with. That being said, I still went through the young-girl rites of passage, including being kicked out of the group. Almost every girl goes through this weird living nightmare, where you show up at school and realize people have grown to hate you overnight. It's a *Twilight Zone* moment when you can't figure out what is real. It is a group mind-fuck of the highest kind, and it makes or breaks you. I got through it by keeping my head down, and a few weeks passed and all the girls liked me again. We all pretended it never happened. There should be manuals passed out to teach girls how to handle that inevitable one-week stretch when up is down and the best friend who just slept over at your house suddenly pulls your hair in front of everyone and laughs.

The nerves of suddenly being a social outcast would be enough to keep me up, as well as my terrible snoring and overall unattractive sleeping style. Ever since I was a young girl I've snored and drooled and slept with my mouth wide open. It wasn't pretty, and at eleven, pretty can be important. At sleepovers I would often be the last girl standing. Everyone would fall asleep while I stared at the ceiling. Sometimes I would tiptoe around and watch everyone sleep. After tossing and turning, I would lightly snoop around and then put on my coat and sneak outside. I watched more than one sunrise in a strange suburban driveway. Then I would sleep late and wake up to an empty house and a mother who would reluctantly mix up a new batch of pancakes.

My first-period class in high school started at seven thirty A.M. We lived in a ranch house with two bathrooms and my mom taught special ed at our high school, so Mom, Greg, and I would be angling for the shower at the same time. I would snooze until the last

174

possible second and then rush to get ready. My hair would still be wet and often frozen by the time I walked from my house to the car of whatever friend was driving me to school. I never rode with my mom. I generally preferred to ride with Rob, who played his U2 cassettes and wore acid-wash jeans. I would fight sleep in my first couple of classes, until lunch came at 10:20 A.M., when I would eat the ten thousand calories given to every American teenager. I would get home from school at 1:45 and crash hard on the couch, waking up only to watch my beloved *General Hospital* or do homework or sluggishly walk to softball practice. I was always tired. I am always tired. I now read articles about how great sleep is and how important it is and I cry because I want it so bad and I am so mad at how great everyone else seems to be at it.

I got some relief from my sleep problem once I started working at *SNL* (this sounds crazy, I realize that). It was truly a vampire life and one that suited my internal clock. At the time I did not have children, so I was able to stay up very late and sleep very late. I remember ten A.M. feeling incredibly early and three A.M. being my usual bedtime. This was my life for seven years. New York City is the perfect place to be awake in the middle of the night. I would rub shoulders with the nurses and truck drivers. I would watch newspapers being delivered and the workout maniacs getting in their first runs of the day. I would watch wired rich kids stumble out of clubs and old Italian men water down the sidewalks. Being awake and sober at four A.M. is a much different experience from being wasted and stumbling home. I have certainly done both. I remember a particularly awful night when I went to a club and stayed out all night, only to have to shoot a commercial parody the next morning. I was tired and wired as I shivered in a freezing trailer getting a spray tan to look like Fergie. The host that week was Jon Heder and we were supposed to be playing the Black Eyed Peas. We had to dance in the middle of a New Jersey highway at six A.M. I think Jon was the only one who had slept the previous night. Kenan Thompson kept pretending to take calls from himself asking why he had done this to himself. It was a long day.

But nothing during my *SNL* years prepared me for children.

The thing about little babies is that you are always afraid they are going to die. At least in the beginning. You are constantly checking to make sure they didn't die and you haven't killed them. Because of this, it's truly impossible to sleep when you are a new mother. The other thing about little babies is that you don't get the weekends off. You don't get a Saturday where you can catch up. The sleep deprivation after children is so real. I liken it to what it must feel like to walk on the moon and to cry the whole time because you had heard that the moon was supposed to be great but in truth it totally sucks. I started working on *Parks and Recreation* when my first child, Archie, was three months old, and I can remember a few times when I fell asleep standing up, with my eyes open. I slept wherever I could. Twenty minutes at lunch. During production meetings. In my car. I remember being filled with rage when childless people would talk about brunch. I had my second son, Abel, and aged a hundred years in his first year. I had a hard time getting my body back after baby number two. I am still excellent at sleeping in places that aren't my bed. I can sleep on an airplane like a boss. Sometimes I look forward to travel for just that reason.

My children forced me to realize the true value of sleep and made me want to conquer my inability to get any. I try to believe what Annie from *Annie* says, when she reminds us that tomorrow is only a day away. Sleep can completely change your entire outlook on life. One good night's sleep can help you realize that you shouldn't break up with someone, or you are being too hard on your friend, or you actually will win the race or the game or get the job. Sleep helps you win at life. So at the ripe old age of forty, I decided to go to a sleep center and see if I could get better at sleep. I was spending a lot of time in Beverly Hills, which is the strangest place in the world. It is also the capital of doctors. If you have never been to a doctor's office in Beverly Hills, you haven't lived. Every single waiting room looks like a gorgeous apartment owned by a Persian billionaire. I rolled up to a fancy sleep center at the assigned ten P.M. call time. I had spent the entire day not drinking caffeine, as instructed. I am a tea girl. Coffee smells so good but my stomach doesn't like it. Tea is what my mom and I would drink together in the afternoon, and what Archie and I sometimes sip when we want to have serious talks. I abstained from tea too, yet was still worried about my chances of falling asleep.

I knew I was going to be hooked up to wires so they could record my snoring and check me for sleep apnea, and I seriously doubted I would be able to go down. I wondered out loud if anyone had ever stayed up all night. The sweet and gentle technician shook his head no. He asked why I was sent to him and I tilted my head and in a very flirty way said to him, "I am told I snore."

What I should have said was "Throughout my life I have been told I snore so loudly that it sounds like I am dying or choking. I come from a family of snorers and we all used to record each other to show each other the damning evidence. I am convinced my body is trying to gently strangle me to death."

I was led into a small room that looked like the weirdest Holiday Inn you have ever seen. A bed and a lamp did not distract from the multiple pulleys, wires, clips and clamps. I was hooked up like a puppet while I continued to make small talk with the technician. He had a terrific bedside manner, which is extremely important when you are the only man on duty in a weird sleeping center. I cracked bad dirty jokes as he hooked me up with electrodes. I sheepishly asked him about his kids as he showed me a crazy breathing machine he would try on me later. He turned off the light and shut the door and I laughed out loud. "There is no way I can sleep here," I thought. And then I fell asleep. Eventually. The rest was all weird memories of being nudged, hooked up again, and turned over. I was gently woken up eight hours later and felt like shit, which was disappointing. I think I had expected to feel terrific, or at least pleasantly buffed and shined. He told me the doctor would read my results and come speak to me. I asked him if I had snored. He gently nodded and said, "A little."

The doctor sat me down in front of a neon green graph showing my sleep pattern. Even to the untrained eye it didn't look good. It looked like a bad polygraph. It looked like I had been constantly lying to someone as I slept. He asked me how many times a night I thought I woke up. "Four?" I said. "Sometimes five?" He told me I woke myself up twenty to thirty times a night. I had mild to moderate sleep apnea and I was only reaching REM sleep for a few minutes at a time over the course of a few hours. I nodded my head. This just confirmed what I had always known: I was a bad sleeper. In some ways I was disappointed. I had hoped he would pull me aside and say, "You are the worst case I have ever seen. It's a miracle you do all that you do. I am sending you to a Hawaiian sleep rehab immediately." Instead I was handed a CPAP machine, which stands for Compression Something Amy Poehler. I don't know. I'm sorry, I wasn't listening. I just stared at this crazy mask and accompanying gurgling device next to it and just couldn't wait for the instructions to be over. I looked at it the same way you look at a plate of vegetables. You know it's good for you but most of the time you don't feel like it.

I have a boyfriend who knows how to settle me. He puts his hand on my chest and tells me boring stories. He promises me we can stay up as late as I want. On one of our first nights together I woke up apologizing for my snoring and he pulled out the two earplugs he had worn to bed so that he could hear what I was saying. It was one of the most romantic gestures I have ever seen. I know I should wear my crazy breathing machine but I just can't pull the trigger. I wore it religiously for a short time and then stuck it in my closet to gather dust.

I know I should use it. I'm working on it. I'm a bad sleeper; I told you. Until I commit to the machine, I will try strips and mouth guards and special pillows. I want to sleep. I do. I want to go gentle into that good night, so help me God.

SYMMETRY IS PLEASING BUT NOT AS

SE

XY.

EINSTEIN IS COOL BUT PICASSO KNOWS WHAT I'M TALKING ABOUT.

BE

WHOEVER YOU ARE

COMEDY CENTRAL

UPRIGHT CITIZENS BRIGADE

how i fell in love with improv:

new york

I HELD A MICROPHONE AT LUNA LOUNGE AND REPEATED INSTRUCTIONS TO THE AUDIENCE. It was a warm summer night in 1997 and the New York street sounds bled through the doors and onto the stage. I was twenty-six years old and supporting myself doing comedy.

The UCB was guest-hosting a Monday evening show and the audience was stoned and happy. They were happy because they had seen great comedy with young talent: The State, Marc Maron, Janeane Garofalo, Zach Galifianakis, Louis CK, Jon Benjamin, Jon Glaser, and Sarah Silverman. They were stoned because we had brought weed for the entire audience and bullied people into getting high. We handed out joints and coaxed people into digging their own one-hitters out of their backpacks. Being asked to host a Luna Lounge show was a big deal. We had worked hard on our introductions and bits in between guests, which included handing out weed and potato chips. This was a pre-9/11 New York where no one had yet heard the words "Homeland Security," but it was also a Mayor Giuliani New York, where there was artistic push-back against the feeling that our rights were being slowly limited each day.

I had arrived in Manhattan in April 1996, a few months after a major blizzard that forced residents to ski down Fifth Avenue. We had come out to New York once to do a showcase while we were still living in Chicago, and performed at a cabaret bar in the West Village called the Duplex. I don't remember if anyone was in the audience, but the proprietor was not too thrilled with this loud Midwestern sketch group and their giant bag of props. More than once we were told "This is not Chicago!"

Besser and I found a street-level studio apartment listed in the *Village Voice* on the corner of Bleecker and Tenth Street. The West Village still had a tiny bit of edge, and our studio apartment was sandwiched between a store called Condomania and Kim's Video, a hipster record outlet that was notorious for its slow and grouchy employees. The apartment had bars on the windows and looked out onto garbage, and when we first arrived there were twenty people in line to rent it. We hustled to meet the horrible landlord and I called our parents to cosign from his cluttered and disgusting office. I have a vague memory of this millionaire slumlord standing up behind his mess of a desk and saying, "Let me take a look at you." I may have even spun around for him. Each evening Matt and I would roll our change and throw pennies at the rats outside our windows. We put bowls over our stove at night so the mice wouldn't come up through the burners. Once I pulled back the curtain and locked eyes with a masturbating Peeping Tom, and he just waved at me like someone saying farewell from the deck of a ship. It was the closest I have ever felt to Patti Smith. I loved it.

Much of our first year in the city was spent lugging props. New York was great for purchasing last-minute dildos, nitrous, and cap guns. UCB shows had evolved into a mix of sketch and improvisation, and we would roll out giant monitors to play our videotaped bits. This was before you could check out a person's entire career on YouTube. Important people had to come to see you live, and we would wait for network executives to show up, masking tape over their seats *Waiting for Guffman* style. We came to town with two shows we had already been performing in Chicago, humbly titled *Millennium Approaches* and *Perestroika*. These shows were made up of sketches and videos and improv. I was playing girl scouts and old men and everything in between.

The four of us (me and Ian and Besser and Walsh) performed sketch at black box theaters like KGB Bar and Tribeca Lab, and after paying a rental fee and buying props, we lost money on every show. Most of those early shows had an audience of ten: five nice friends, two strangers, one crazy person, and a set of parents. We started doing open mic nights at places like Surf Reality and Luna Lounge, where we met other performers like us. We would spend the day wearing giant cat heads or dinosaur masks, harassing people with bullhorns in Washington Square Park and handing out flyers to our show. We spent the nights performing and writing and dreaming and scheming. It was sketch and improv 24/7. We had no one to take care of but ourselves.

It was an interesting time to be doing comedy. Stand-ups had ruled the eighties, with some of them, like Roseanne Barr and Jerry Seinfeld, parlaying their success into eponymous television shows. The nineties were still a time when comedy could make you big bucks if a network wanted to give you a "development deal." But that was for the select few. For the rest of us, there was a movement happening in

187

New York and Los Angeles, a wave some were calling "alternative comedy." To some, we seemed like a bunch of green-apple performers reading half-baked ideas out of notebooks. But we knew it was something else. People were trying things out onstage and mixing everything together in an exciting soup. Stand-ups were incorporating music, performance artists told jokes, musicians wrote sketches. Small theaters were offering "alternative" nights, and audiences were treated to performers who were totally different yet tonally compatible. Anything seemed possible. Michael Portnoy (aka Soy Bomb) would contort his body to music and then Sarah Vowell would read a story and then Dave Chappelle would tell jokes. It felt like a language I understood and comedy I could participate in. My improvisational training had prepared me for this. I met Janeane Garofalo at a book club with Andy Richter's wife, Sarah Thyre. I loved Janeane's stand-up and her work on *The Ben Stiller Show* and in *Reality Bites*. We would walk all over New York and talk about life and art and politics. I would fight the urge to call her my idol and slowly we became close friends. Being in New York felt alive and weird and new.

"The show is not over!" I shouted into the microphone to the young and buzzed Luna Lounge crowd. We announced that we were all going to head across the street for the finale. Once again, the UCB was taking the audience outside. Cynthia True, our good friend and a comedy writer for *Time Out New York,* was going to stage an event. She would be walking down the street naked in an attempt to raise money and protest her rent increase. What had started as a gentle dare was now going to be a Lower East Side happening. We spilled out onto the sidewalk and I raced around the corner to help Cynthia prepare for her bold strut.

In those first few years in New York we had been lucky. Our second year in the city we found a small dance studio called Solo

Arts and made it our de-facto home. It was a five-story walk-up with a wonky floor, and my brother, Greg, served as our bartender. We programmed shows five nights a week and taught classes to pay the rent. At night we drew crowds with our free show, *Asssscat,* a completely improvised show where we would get an audience suggestion that would inspire a monologist to tell a story, and we would improvise off of those stories. The title *Asssscat* came from a scene where Horatio and Besser and McKay and others were bombing so badly that they started loudly saying "ass cat" in a sing-songy voice. The word represented a giant fuck-around; a night where anything goes. We did two shows every Sunday. It was the closest thing I had to church.

We supported ourselves with odd jobs and writing gigs. Conan O'Brien's show was speaking to a massive and young audience, and he would put us in weekly bits on *Late Night*. If you said more than six lines on air you made six hundred dollars, and comedy pieces like "Staring Contest" helped pay my rent. I once spent hours running around a hot track wearing the giant "Foam Rubber Andy" costume. Nipsey Russell was there that day and told me, "Hollywood has one typewriter and one thousand copy machines." I nodded my sweaty head as if I understood what he meant. Brian Stack, a former Chicago improviser and writer for Conan, wrote a character for me called Andy's Little Sister. Her name was Stacey and she wore headgear and was obsessed with Conan. I would sit in my tiny dressing room and memorize long monologues that often ended with my tackling Conan at his desk. It was another character to add to my repertoire of adolescent, lisping maniacs. Adam Sandler and Rob Schneider saw the bit when they were visiting and cast me in the film *Deuce Bigalow: Male Gigolo*. I was paid the basic daily rate the day I showed up on set in the summer of 1998. My first shot was with thousands of extras in Anaheim Stadium. It was my first big Hollywood movie but not the first time I had been on film. My film debut was *Tomorrow Night,* a 1998 New York indie from an up-and-coming auteur named Louis CK. I played "Woman Sprayed with Hose." Soon after, The State's Michael Showalter and David Wain would cast me in their cult classic *Wet Hot American Summer,* a film whose behind-the-scenes stories would make for a steamy beach read.

For a while we worked on a new Broadway Video online show called *This Is Not a Test.* We were all confused when the tech guys explained how in the future, everyone was going to eventually read articles on their computers. I scoffed at the idea. We spent our afternoons writing comedy and shaking our heads at white supremacist message boards. After weeks of writing, we watched the first demo and the slow flashing graphics looked like an old Lite-Brite. I was happy when we were eventually fired, because I was convinced this Internet thing was a passing fad.

This lack of technological foresight is why I am an actor.

Comedy Central took notice of us in 1998, due to our manager Dave Becky's persistence and network executive Kent Alterman's vision. We were offered a sketch show, and *Upright Citizens Brigade* aired on Wednesday nights after another brand-new show: *South Park.* One of us got great ratings. Besser and I broke up, and much to our mutual credit, we handled it smoothly. Matt met and fell in love with his now wife, Danielle Schneider, and UCB went to work writing, producing, and starring in our sketch show. It was all-consuming and totally exhilarating. Under the directorial genius of Phil Morrison, we were allowed to sit in an office (an office!) and think of sketch ideas (they would pay us!) and we would go to set (we had a set!) and it would get on television (my parents could

watch it!). When *UCB* premiered on Comedy Central, my parents threw a huge viewing party in their basement. My father got a UCB license plate soon after. The show was based on a long-form improvisational format our mentor Del Close had invented called "The Harold." Scenes were connected, characters lived in different worlds, and most shows were built around a theme. The premise was that a group called the Upright Citizens Brigade worked out of an underground bunker. We rarely used pop culture or parody, except for the always popular Unabomber, Harry Truman, Albert Einstein, and Jesus. RZA from the Wu-Tang Clan once played a neighbor who lived underground next to us and lent the UCB some sugar. The show ran for three seasons, and in those few short years I learned how to be in front of a camera, how to manage an incredibly long workday, and how truly awful it is to wear prosthetics.

191

We asked Del to record the voice-over for our opening titles.

"From the dawn of civilization, they have existed in order to undermine it. *Our only enemy is the status quo. Our only friend is chaos.* They have no government ties and unlimited resources. *If something goes wrong, we are the cause.* Every corner of the earth is under their surveillance. *If you do it, we see it. Always. We believe the powerful should be made less powerful. We have heard the voice of society, begging us to destabilize it. Antoine. Colby. Trotter. Adair. We are the Upright Citizens Brigade.*"

Hardly anyone watched. I wonder why, with that incredibly accessible opening. But it gave us a place to be seen. The show fed the theater and the theater fed the show. We outgrew Solo Arts. We needed our own space. We found it at the old Harmony Theater on Twenty-Second Street in Chelsea. The space had been a burlesque house, and after taking it over we spent days dismantling stages and smashing mirrors. The greenroom was lined with lockers, and those lockers were filled with old bikinis and Prince mix tapes.

I stupidly volunteered to clean the bathrooms, and I pulled at least a dozen condoms out of the horrible toilets. Even years after we opened in 1999 as a comedy theater, we would get confused men entering in the middle of the day. Well-dressed businessmen and Hasidic shopkeepers would saunter into the lobby, feign interest in the comedy flyers, and then quickly leave. The Twenty-Second Street space became a clubhouse for talented youngsters who are now your favorites. I celebrated the end of the millennium at that theater, saw amazing shows at that theater, fought, cried, and made out at that theater. After 9/11, we all gathered there, grateful that our lives in comedy meant we didn't work in a big building downtown. In 2002, our landlord was cited for a violation and the space was closed down. We panicked and then regrouped, and in the process learned that the theater was not the space, it was the people.

We opened our new 150-seat theater a year later and a few blocks away on Twenty-Sixth Street. It was a little fancier, but it was under a Gristedes supermarket and we had to contend with the sound of shopping carts being dragged and the threat of garbage water bursting through the floor and onto our heads. I continued to write and perform there while I was at *SNL*. During the big New York blackout in 2003, many of us spent the night sleeping onstage because our generator was working. During the writers' strike in 2007, we put on our own *SNL* episode there with old sketches. Michael Cera hosted, our musical guest was Yo La Tengo, and we gave Lorne a birthday cake as he sat in the audience. When I enter the theater and there is a show onstage, it makes me feel safe in the knowledge that the world keeps turning. It also feels like I have died and I am attending my own funeral, so it's good and bad.

Things have steadily moved along since. We opened our first theater in Los Angeles in 2005, the same year we shot a one-hour special for Bravo called *Asssscat*. It was an attempt to prove improvisation could work on TV, and it featured Tina and Dratch and

Andy Richter, among others. In 2006 we opened our Training Center facility in New York, which finally gave us a proper office and classrooms. In 2008 we launched the comedy website UCBComedy .com. In 2010 we became an accredited theater school. In 2014 we opened a new UCB Training Center in New York with fourteen classrooms and a picnic table, and a big new theater space in Los Angeles. At each theater we produce an average of four shows a night and twenty-five shows a week, all under ten dollars.

I will keep bragging.

Last year we sold over 400,000 tickets, produced over 4,000 shows, taught over 11,000 students, and employed 216 people. Del had died in 1999 after a long battle with emphysema. The day before he died, there was a Wiccan ceremony in his hospital room attended by Bill Murray and Harold Ramis (rest in peace). Del had drunk a chocolate martini and was gone the next day. Del always knew when to edit. His famous last words to Charna were "I'm tired of being the funniest person in the room." He donated his skull to be used in productions of *Hamlet* at Chicago's Goodman Theatre. Del filmed a message to the UCB with specific instructions on how to carry on. It was brilliant and touching and not especially lucid. He gave us our motto, "Don't think." In his honor we started the Del Close Marathon, an annual fifty-two-hour marathon of improvisation, which welcomes groups from all across the country. Fifteen years later, it now has fifty-six straight hours of improvisation on seven stages performed by over four hundred different groups. Our free improv show *Asssscat* has now been running for eighteen years.

My twenty years with the Upright Citizens Brigade could fill a book. Hopefully someone else will write it, because writing a book is awful and because most of my memories are drug fueled and rose colored. All I know is I will be quick to give photo approval, since I am very young and skinny in most of the pictures. But I will say this: New York can be a lonely place. I think we stuck together during hard times and provided a home for people to feel less alone. The UCB community is a collaborative and loving group, and it is filled with the funniest people I know. I am proud of the fact that Ian and Besser and Walsh and I never made money our motivating factor. We never took a salary, we never charged artists to perform, we never had a two-drink minimum. Artists could rehearse and perform and know they would be in front of an audience who spoke their language. This audience could pay very little to see great comedy, never knowing what famous people would show up, but always knowing that some of the people they were watching would one day be famous.

UCB's motto is "Don't think." It started as a directive from Del, transformed into a comment on corporate doublespeak, and now serves as the guiding principle for our school and theater. Don't think. Get out of your head. Stop planning and just go. The theater belongs to the people. It belongs to Alex Sidtis and Susan Hale, who run the spaces and keep the company strong. It belongs to the hundreds of people who have stood on the stage and the many more who have watched shows performed on the stage. It belongs to the students who are waiting to get time onstage, and the employees and interns who helped build the stage. Don't think. Just do. We did.

Cynthia took off her trench coat and slipped her naked and beautiful body into some sturdy rain boots. Janeane reminded her that she didn't need to go through with it if she didn't want to. We all laughed as I produced sparklers I had brought along for the occasion. A man approached us to ask for a light and didn't even react to the naked woman in front of him. New York had already seen it all, but I was just getting started. Everyone lined up to watch and cheer. We were all young and free and wide open. Cynthia walked the city block, and the camera in my mind panned to all the faces of people I loved and respected. It traveled over their heads up above the trees, dancing on rooftops and tilting up toward the moon. I had found my tribe. I had helped build a home for us to live in, by improvising. Making it up as I went along.

A.S.S.S.S.C.A.I.

long form comedy improvisation

Dec. 11 Friday 9:30pm
Dec. 13 Sunday 9:30pm

featuring the Upright Citizens Brigade

...OW! (but donation requested)

...d Broadway)

---

		walsh yells, "You son o'
CHRISTIAN COALITION #1	[cast]	Radio Head drives by
cranking out		
music - radio head "Creep"		
NAIL IN HAND	[besser, ian]	besser screams in agony
UCB #5 *SPANISH WORDS*	[amy]	amy says, "Mano."
music - midnight star "electricity"		
BUCKET OF TRUTH	[walsh, amy, ian]	walsh turns on tv
music - tv noise		walsh yells, "It's true."
UCB #6 *NATIONAL COCKFIGHT '95*	[amy, ian, besser]	besser and ian rooster
		walsh says, "...a golf course."
ASS PENNY	[ian, besser]	ian says, "...in my ass!"
		walsh shows penny collection
BROWNIE AND NUT #2	[cast]	besser picks up amy and runs
VIDEO #4		
FORTUNE COOKIE #3		
CHRISTIAN COALITION #2		
music - ministry "NWO"		
JUNGLE #3		

UPRIGHT CITIZENS BRIGADE

...comedy conspiracy for the next millennium

"Best Live Sketch In New York These Days!"
— TIME OUT NEW YORK

"Surreal, Edgy Originality!"
— NEW YORK POST

"Truly Spellbinding!"
— NEW YORK MAGAZINE

"A Group With Personalities And A
e So Strong They We
By Their Outlandi
— THE NEW YOR

"BIG DIRTY HANDS" — EVERY SA. Solo Arts 36 West 1

ASSSCAT improvisational comedy) — EVERY SU also at Sol

reservations for all shows, ca

1995 — 2000

TONY TURNS FIVE!

Week after week for the past five years, *Time Out New York*'s writers, photographers, editors and designers have strived to present the most informative, opinionated and lively coverage of everything that's happening in the world's most dynamic city. And so, to celebrate our birthday, we toast the New Yorkers who've left an indelible mark on NYC during *TONY*'s lifetime. On the following 17 pages are people —big and small— who, through their art, industry and vision, have changed the way we work and play.

1995 FIFTH ANNIVERSARY ISSUE 2000

Happy Birthday

CHAOS THEORY

Time Out New York

PHOTOGRAPHS BY ERIC OGDEN

3:00 – 5:00 PM N.O.R.M.L. SEMINARS "THE IMPACT OF MARIJUANA PROHIBITION ON CIVIL LIBERTIES, FAMILIES, AND RACIAL MINORITIES," LED BY DEBORAH SMALL (EXPERT ON RACE AND THE DRUG WAR)

OTHER PANELISTS INCLUDE: NANCY LORD JOHNSON (EXPERT ON FDA AND INTER-NATIONAL LAWS) AND MONICA PRATT & MIKKI NORRIS WILL TALK ABOUT FAMILIES AND THE DRUG WAR, USING SLIDE SHOW FROM HR95)

6:00 PM EXPO CLOSES

7:00 PM JUDGES LOUNGE CLOSES

7:30 PM LAST BUS TO MELKWEG

MELKWEG:THE MAX:OPENING CEREMONIES:HOSTED BY WATERMELON

8:00 PM DOORS OPEN

8:30-10:00 PM MUSIC BY DJ HEPCAT

10:00-10:15 PM VIDEO PRESENTATION OF "CANNABIS CASTAWAYS" FOOTA

10:15-10:45 PM STONER COMEDY BY "UPRIGHT CITIZENS BRIGADE"

10:45-12:30 AM SPECIAL MUSICAL PERFORMANCE BY PATTI SMITH

12:30-2:30 AM MUSIC BY DJ HEPCAT

MELKWEG:THE OLD ROOM:SMOKER'S REUNION PARTY "THE GRASS OF 2000"

8:00-10:00 PM MUSIC BY LOCAL DJ'S NOAH AND JEWLS

file://C:\WINDOWS\TEMP\HTML2\ELPD111.TMP   11/3/00

UPRIGHT CITIZENS BRIGADE

...the restructuring of society begins.

The days of h

MILLENIUM APPROACHES

Second City E.T.C.
1608 N. Wells
(312)-642-818

TUESDAYS 8:30

3HT CITIZENS BRIGADE:

PERESTRO

ImprovOlympic C
3541 N
(312)-88

SATURDA
OPENS

BIG DIRTY HANDS

ImprovOlympic Theater
3541 N. Clark Ave.
(312)880-0199

Saturdays 8:30pm
OPENS
MARCH 4TH

THE REAL REAL WORLD

...the *true* story that MTV tried to hide!

Anne Frank
The Diary of a Young Girl:
UNEXPURGATE

2 Scandals for the Price of ONE!!

a shocking account of yo...
love in a "secret anne...

DIRECTI...
JOE AUX...

SPAGHETTI JESUS

media web interruption
- The Standup Circus Act
- Hong Kong Dancer Duo
- Massage Volunteer
- Astronaut Prejudice
- Porkchop Doctor & Lil' Squirty
- The Tittle Brothers present "The Wom
- Gags In the Future
- Stage Combat
- Little Donny
- Alien Interruption
- The Improv (Abortion) Song
- UCB Focus Group: the Average American vs. the Alternative Ame
- Blue Man and STOMP guy
- Black Muslim Robot Rant
- Chef Therapy
- Gangsta Rap Audition
- The Wedding Present Party
- The Comedy Indicator: "Cunt Kills"
- Jesus vs. Jordon — the new religio
- Fans In The Background of News cas
- Rope Pitch and Movie Trailer
- The Candy Story with Marlboro Man
- Hootenanny + the Funbunch
  a. Dad's new idea   b. Nitrous Oxide

Failure

COMEDY CENTRAL

CHIEF ENGINEER OF SOUND AND LIGHT OPERATIONS
ERIC Escinozi

VIDEO/SOUND OPERATIVE
KAREN HERR

VIA FAX & MAIL   March 23, 1998

Ms. Amy Poehler
c/o William Morris Agency
1325 Avenue of the Americas
New York, NY 10019
Attn: Mike August

Re: The Upright Citizens Brigade

Dear Amy:

This is to confirm that Comedy Partners is exercising its first option pursuant to paragraphs 4 and 5 of the agreement dated as of May 1, 1997 between you and Aardvark Productions for ten (10) episodes based on the Pilot you submitted to us.

Congratulations!

Yours truly,

Joan S. Aceste

cc: E. Katz
      K. Alterman

UPRIGHT CITIZENS BRIGADE

JOAN S. ACESTE *Vice President, Legal & Business Affairs*
CENTRAL

jaceste@comcentral.com
Comedy Partners

UPRIGHT CITIZENS BRIGADE

A BUCKET OF TRUTH

BIG BLACK "KEROSENE" JEFF RICHMOND "E.P. Song" "MOGY PG"
MIDNIGHT STAR "Electricity" "HURRICANE" "NewYoDo"
Lyle Lovett "All My Love Is Gone" FAREWELL MY CONCUBINE
SUICIDAL TENDENCIES "don't give a fuck" DISNEY etc. Cool 10 N
MINISTRY "NWO" BOREDOMS "THALIDOMIDE CAR" therapy "Phoenix"
MEDICINE "AFRICA" SOUSA MARCH

BEST CITIZEN
Kathy mahaffey
dave koenig
charna halpern
del close
andrew alexander
second city, Anon
improv olympic
Karen Herr
just heard
the family, Inside
Vladimir, Armando
Daz experience
the Tribe, Stone
A Lot Things
Kermit Ruiz
squad 3 hrs
AUGUST-DION-STEIN
ADAM McKAY
WHITE HORSE
EXPERIMENT
DAVE KOECHNER
TOM GIANAS
MICHEAL O'BRIAN
GEORGE BARDEGI
DAVID BOCK
BILL CHOTT

PUNCH YOUR FRIEND IN THE FACE

SHELLAC "My Black Ass" "A Minute" "Song of the Minerals"
Altered States Led Zeppelin "Whole Lotta Love" Chrome
Kansas Midnight Cowboy JESUS LIZARD "Word Out"
Alan Parson's Project "Sirius" DEVO "Mechanical Man"
Sir Mix-A-Lot "Monster Mack" Flaming Lips "God Walks Among Us"
Bongwater THE Good, the Bad, and the Ugly

ADAIR	ANTOINE	COLBY	TROTTER
Matt Besser	Ian Roberts	Amy Poehler	MATT WALSH

additional material: ERIC ZICKLIN
PUNCH YOUR FRIEND IN THE FACE directed by Ned Crowley
A BUCKET OF TRUTH directed by Joe Auxilary
VIDEO: (GREEK N...

Mother is nice
My mother is nice.
My father is too.

Don't you think so too.
I love them so
I would't whant them to go
I like them so.
Don't you think so too.
THE END

parents just do understand

EILEEN FRANCES MILMORE WAS BORN FEBRUARY 7, 1947, IN WATERTOWN, MASSACHUSETTS. She was the oldest of three children. Her mother, Helen, worked as a secretary at St. Patrick's High School and her father, Stephen, was a firefighter and World War II veteran. She went to Boston State College and was an excellent student. She met my dad on a school bus on the way to a basketball game. She was head cheerleader and he was the best player on the team. She tapped him on the head and asked to sit with him. She was twenty-three when she got married, twenty-four when I was born, and forty-one when she got her master's degree in special education. She taught for thirty-one years, starting in elementary and ending in high school special ed. One of her most exciting moments was sharing an elevator with Sally Field. During a recent trip to Amsterdam, she sent me a picture of her smoking marijuana for the first time just because I asked her to. She is kind, she is chatty, and she writes beautiful poetry.

———

WILLIAM GRINSTEAD POEHLER WAS BORN SEPTEMBER 21, 1946, IN WAYNESBORO, VIRGINIA. His mother, Anna, was first married to William, his father, who left right after he was born. For the first five years of his life, my father lived in a foster home. Anna remarried and her new husband, Carl Poehler, adopted my father and his sister and moved them all to Massachusetts. Anna and Carl had two more sons. The first day my father met my mother he came home and told my grandmother, "I have met the girl I am going to marry." He was an elementary school teacher and also a financial planner. One of his most exciting moments was sharing an elevator with Boston Celtics Robert Parish and Kevin McHale. For my wedding, my father, his friends, and my uncles performed a surprise tap-dance number with top hats and canes. He is generous, nosy, and good at arm wrestling.

They have been married almost forty-five years. Here are some things they have taught me.

MOM
- Make sure he's grateful to be with you.
- Your boobs won't be as big as mine but you will be happy about that as you get older.
- Always tell people when they do a good job.
- Always have a messy purse.
- Guilt works.
- You are the smartest and best.
- *Monty Python* is funny.
- Be nice to your brother.
- Be a light sleeper, and every time your kid wakes you up, scream like you are being attacked.

poem & story

Parents ~~Mother~~ Parents

Although sometimes
mad they get. I would
always bet. That they
do it from love. If so
happens they punish
you. And you wish you
could punish them too.
They do it out of love,
They may yell at you
and make you mad,
But when they yell
It makes them sad
(I think) That why Parents
are the best. Mine
are better than all
the rest. THE END

- Have fun dancing.
- Have male friends.
- Have more female friends.
- Your female friends will outlast every man in your life.
- Love your husband and don't belittle him.
- Love your kids and hope they do better than you did.
- You don't want to be the sexy mom.
- Dye your hair constantly.
- There's not much we can do about our Irish eyebrows.
- Postpartum depression, anxiety, and skin cancer run in our family.
- Ask your kids how they are doing but sometimes ignore them when they say, "Not great."
- Love your work.
- Study hard and know how to write and read well.
- Memorize poems.
- Be nice to teachers. Teachers don't like kids who don't like teachers.
- Always bring wine.
- A home-cooked meal isn't so important.
- TV in your bedroom is okay.
- Follow sports and leave the room if you're a jinx.
- Be careful.

DAD
- Ask for what you want.
- Know how to shoot a free throw and field a ground ball.
- There are ways around things that aren't always legal.
- Hide cash in your house.
- Always overtip but make a big deal out of paying the check.

- Eat whatever you want.
- Keep trying.
- Never remember anyone's name.
- Girls can do anything boys can do.
- Street smarts are as important as book smarts.
- "Your mother is smarter than me and I am fine with it."
- Don't work too hard.
- You can have a chaotic childhood and still provide a stable home.
- Ask everyone how much money they make.
- Keep the TV loud and all the lights on in the house.
- You don't want to be the creepy dad.
- It's okay to cry.
- It's okay to argue.
- Tell everyone you meet what your daughter does until your daughter asks you to stop.
- Our family has a history of bad stomachs, heart problems, and a loss of hearing we will deny.
- Don't hit your kids, except that one time.
- Love your wife's family.
- Don't listen to experts.
- Everything in moderation.

don't forget to tip your waitresses

THE TOWN WHERE I GREW UP WAS DECIDEDLY BLUE-COLLAR, FILLED WITH TEACHERS AND NURSES AND THE OCCASIONAL SALES MANAGER. My friends and I fell asleep to the sound of our parents arguing about car payments and tuition. It was our soundtrack, this din of worry. If you were old enough, you were expected to have a part-time job.

When I was sixteen, I got one. I was a junior secretary in a podiatrist's office near my house in Burlington. I had to wear a short white skirt, a tight blouse, and high-heeled shoes. This outfit made me look like a teenage nurse, which sounds hot but I promise you was not. I was a teenager during a period of truly awful style. It made sense that my friends and I all had part-time jobs, because we dressed like Melanie Griffith in *Working Girl* during a long subway commute. Hair spray was king, and the eighties silhouette in Burlington was big hair, giant shoulder pads, chunky earrings, thick belts, and form-fitting stretch pants. My silhouette was an upside-down triangle. Add in my round potato face and hearty eyebrows and you've got yourself a grade-A boner killer, so remember that before you try to jerk it to my teenage-nurse story.

Anyway, this other nurse and I used to jump around in our underwear and kiss each other for fun.

Oh wait, what I meant to say was that I answered phones and filed things. The best part of my job was leaning into the waiting room and whispering, "The doctor will see you now." It always felt like such a WASPy phrase. Right up there with "It truly is my pleasure" and "We just got back from the country." Every once in a while we would get an exciting sprained ankle or a flat-feet emergency, but usually the patients were just old people who couldn't cut their own toenails anymore.

I was a really good waitress. Waitressing takes a certain gusto. You need a good memory and an ability to connect with people fast. You have to learn how to treat the kitchen as well as you treat the customers. You have to figure out which crazy people to listen to and which crazy people to ignore. I loved waiting tables because when you cashed out at the end of the night your job was truly over. You wiped down your section and paid out your busboy and you knew your work was done. I didn't take my job home with me, except for the occasional nightmare where I would wake up in a cold sweat and remember I never brought table 14 their Diet Coke.

My first waitressing job was in the summer of 1989, a few months before I left for college. I was seventeen and sticky. I earned the extra money I needed for textbooks scooping ice cream at Chadwick's, a local parlor that specialized in sundaes and giant steak fries. Chadwick's was in Lexington, Massachusetts, the rich town next door (the Eagleton to our Pawnee). Lexington was the famous home of the "Shot Heard 'Round the World." Burlington was the home of the mall. Lexington, as it turns out, is also Rachel Dratch's hometown, and much later I would learn that she also worked at the same sticky emporium a few years before I did. Imagine if our paths had crossed! Imagine how hilarious we would have been while we shoved toothpicks in the club sandwiches! Think of all the jokes about "marrying the ketchups." Such a waste. Lexington High still plays Burlington High on Thanksgiving Day, and Dratch and I trash-text each other. She calls me Burlington garbage and I tell her to go drive her Mercedes into a lake. In my town, the best way to insult someone was to call them rich and smart, which, looking back, was maybe a little shortsighted of us.

You know what? Who cares. Burlington rules! GO RED DEVILS!!

Summer jobs are often romantic; the time frame creates a perfect parentheses. Chadwick's was not. Hard and physical, the job consisted of stacking and wiping and scooping and lifting. At the end of my shift, every removable piece of the restaurant would be carted off and washed. Vinyl booths were searched and scrubbed. This routine seemed Sisyphean at first, but I soon learned the satisfaction of working at a place that truly closed. I took great joy in watching people stroll in after hours, thinking they could grab a late-night sundae. I would point to the dimmed lights and stacked chairs as proof that we were shut. It was deliciously obvious and final.

Chadwick's was one of those fake old-timey restaurants. The menus were written in swoopy cursive. The staff wore Styrofoam boaters and ruffled white shirts with bow ties. Jangly music blared from a player piano as children climbed on counters. If the style of the restaurant was old-fashioned, the parenting that went on there was distinctly modern. Moms and dads would patiently recite every item on the menu to their squirming five-year-olds, as if the many flavors of ice cream represented all the unique ways they were loved.

There was a performance element to the job that I found appealing. Every time a customer was celebrating a birthday, an employee had to bang a drum that hung from the ceiling, and play the kazoo, and encourage the entire restaurant to join him or her in a sing-along. Other employees would ring cowbells and blow noisemakers. I would stand on a chair and loudly announce, "Ladies and gentlemen, we are so happy to have you at Chadwick's today, but we are especially happy to have Kevin! Because it's Kevin's birthday today! So, at the sound of the drum, please join me in singing Kevin a very happy birthday!"

The appeal didn't last long. I'm not sure when the worm turned. Maybe it was during one of the many times we announced the Belly-Buster. The BellyBuster consisted of mounds of ice cream in a giant silver bowl carried in on a stretcher. The busboys would have to pretend to struggle under the weight of this giant sundae as they lifted it onto the table and handed a giant spoon to the maniac who had ordered it. I would ease my pain by exchanging looks with one busboy who was always slightly drunk and the ex-junkie cook, who was always slightly grouchy. The cook spoke in bumper stickers when describing his disposition: "Of course I'm mean. It's hard to be happy when you are standing this close to the fire."

But the teenagers were the worst. Teenage boys, especially. They would file in, Adam's apples bouncing, and announce it was their birthdays. Since Chadwick's operated on an honor system, I would have to look into their sweaty, lying faces and smile like a flight attendant. Some of them would order their sundaes while asking me to hold their nuts. I was relieved when I had to leave and head to college. It was time. Besides, I had started forgetting to charge for whipped cream. I was failing to use the ice scoop. A customer told me I was banging the drum "too hard." She was right. I was angry; I wanted to be gone. It's important to know when it's time to turn in your kazoo. The nights would end with the waitstaff in the parking lot, sitting on a car and drinking beer as we counted our tips. The boys would undo their bow ties and suddenly look weary and handsome. I would change into soft jeans and throw pennies at the Dumpster. I was aching for what came next. I felt my whole life stretched out before me like an invisible buffet.

I learned many things banging that drum at Chadwick's. I learned that a good tip is what a decent person leaves. I learned that how a person treats their waitress is a great indication of their character. I learned that chocolate chip ice cream is a bitch to scoop. I learned almost all the people in a working kitchen are having sex with each other. Except for the Bangladeshi busboys, who are supporting three kids back home and trying not to strangle the awful white teenagers complaining about their summer job.

My next restaurant job was in Boston during college at a place called Papa Razzi. I was immediately drawn to it because it was a step up from ice cream, and also because I LOVE the paparazzi!! I don't care what anyone says. I think the paparazzi are awesome and they are all great people and I should be allowed to see pictures of anyone I want anytime. Papa Razzi introduced me to the world of bread sticks and olive oil. We wore all white like professionals and talked about "cavatappi pasta." I had an affair with the bartender and attended wine tastings. I had great abs and listened to The The as we cleaned up. I knew the bartender was fucking someone else at the same time and I DIDN'T CARE. I felt very adult. At Papa Razzi I learned that I was actually a great waitress and it was easy money and everyone was doing cocaine and that maybe I actually *did* care about the bartender fucking someone else.

Carlucci was a joint in Chicago and my first foray into the big leagues. My uniform was a smart burgundy vest and floral tie. I looked like a serious waitress who was also capable of performing some light magic. Fine Italian dining was hitting its peak, and Carlucci was a way for upper-middle-class people to spend their Wall Street money. This place was no ice-cream joint; it catered to businessmen with fat ties and fatter wallets. We had banquet halls and *mise en place*. We had a mean Italian chef who gave seminars on homemade grappa. I opened my first bottle of two-hundred-dollar wine. I catered an off-site party for D'arcy from the Smashing Pumpkins and smoked with James Iha. Billy Corgan sang in D'arcy's living room and I listened from a closet. Once I heard a familiar voice in the restaurant and I turned to see Oprah at a table with what looked like a gaggle of producers. If my memory serves me correctly, she was giving them presents. I feel like it was diamond earrings. I want that to be true. I feel like Oprah pays all of her employees in diamonds and cashmere pajamas. While I was at Carlucci I learned how to dust a tiramisu and pair cordials. I learned having a pocket filled with cash is a dangerous thing. I learned that I was getting way too good at a job that was not my life's passion. I learned that I was the only one not doing cocaine.

My last big gig was at a real classy joint called Aquagrill in New York City. It was 1996 and I had just moved to New York. I needed a job so I walked around SoHo looking for "Help Wanted" signs in the windows. I was called a "server" by then and I knew how to navigate the fancier places. I walked into Aquagrill and began my experience of trying to help a new restaurant get off the ground. The owners were talented and lovely, but I felt like an imposter in all of our pre-opening meetings. I wanted to earn a living as an actor, and I wanted to pay off my student loans and maybe get some health insurance. It would be a long time before those things happened, but they felt close enough to see. Aquagrill is a beautiful little place with yellow walls and fresh seafood. I finally learned how to save a little money. I learned how to tell the difference between East Coast and West Coast oysters. I waited on people like Ellen Barkin and David Byrne and Lou Reed. I was getting closer to Lou Reed, one step at a time. I waited on restaurant critic Ruth Reichl. She would come in wearing wigs and using a pseudonym. The restaurant got a great review and she said this:

"In New York City, home of the fabulous, the chic, the loud and the exotic, a nice restaurant is a rare thing. So rare that when I encountered the pleasant staff at Aquagrill I was acutely uncomfortable. Don't those people ever stop smiling?"

She was uncomfortable with my smiling! I didn't care. I had made the *New York Times*! The restaurant opened and I left soon after, praying that my bimonthly *Conan* appearances and piecemeal Comedy Central gigs would sustain me. I was out of the restaurant business but I still had my appetite.

I turned toward my future, mouth watering.

OTHER

PEO

PLE

ARE NOT MEDICINE.

treat your career like a bad boyfriend

ONCE I WAS SLEEPING ON AN AMTRAK TRAIN TO NEW YORK AND WAS STARTLED BY A THUD. Someone had dumped a script in my lap as they prepared to get off the train. I woke to a kind-faced businessman smiling at me apologetically. He looked at me like we were friends. I was immediately enraged.

The script was for a movie called *I Don't Know Because I Threw It Away*. I was angry for a few reasons. I don't like it when people wake me up. Being a bad sleeper, I have a hard time opening my eyes. I am amazed at people who wake up and talk like normal humans. These are the same people who don't thrash around when they sleep and have never been told that they snore "like a dragon." I was also angry because I don't like to be solicited. My years of living in New York City make me very sensitive to the random encounter. When I walk down the street and someone asks me, "Excuse me, can I ask you a question?" I immediately put my hand up and firmly say, "No!" No one needs to ask me a question. There is no reason to talk to strangers. I do not want you to hand me your homemade CD or talk to me on an airplane or try to upsell me on drink specials. As I get older I get a real pleasure from maintaining boundaries with strangers. I have come to enjoy telling the cheese guy at the farmers' market that he does not value my time. I like letting my massage therapist know that she is putting her needs before my own. It may be difficult to tell my family I feel pressure to entertain them, but it's easy to tell the UPS guy that he needs to respect my personal space.

When someone randomly hands me a script it means I have already disappointed them. I don't like disappointing people. Some would say this is "codependent behavior," which I have discovered is a term that explains how most everyone acts all of the time unless one is a sociopath or a Russian computer that plays chess. PLUS, when someone hands me a script it only reminds me of how I should write more scripts and get my shit together and stop sleeping on trains. I don't care that you add an attached note that says, "My wife and I are lawyers by day but screenwriters by night and we think you could act in/produce/direct/rewrite this with us." I am not impressed when you assure me the story has "lots of twists and turns." I doubt it does and how dare you.

See? I am not as nice as you think I am.

Being a working actor whom people recognize sometimes means you occasionally get the young up-and-comer who thinks that meeting you is their chance to break in. The good version of this meeting is when someone tells you they are inspired by you and are hoping to follow in your footsteps. This makes your heart warm. It also gives you just enough of an inflated sense of self to justify eating an entire bag of Doritos later that evening and eventually falling asleep with your hands down your pants. The bad version of this meeting is when someone hands you something. Or asks you to do something for them. Or announces loudly that you better remember their name because they are going to be famous one day.

Good or bad, the reality is most people become "famous" or get "great jobs" after a very, very long tenure shoveling shit and not because they handed their script to someone on the street. People still think they will be discovered in the malt shop, even though no one can tell you what a malt is anymore. Everyone wants to believe they will be the regular guy from Sioux City who becomes a reluctant movie star despite his best attempts to remain a sensitive tattoo artist. People don't want to hear about the fifteen years of waiting tables and doing small shows with your friends until one of them gets a little more famous and they convince people to hire you and then you get paid and you work hard and spend time getting better and making more connections and friends. Booooring. It's much more interesting to believe that every person who makes it in show business just wrote a check to their mother when they were eighteen for a million dollars with an instruction to "cash in a year."

I was never great in auditions. When I was nervous I would often underprepare and act too cool for school. I would try to reject them before they rejected me, which was confusing since I had decided to audition and acted angry to be there. I remember one particular time I auditioned for the Coen brothers. I realized I was doing a pretty shitty job and I overcompensated by also acting like a dick. The Coen brothers were very nice. I think. I have blocked it all out.

It took me awhile to step out of my comfort zone and put my neck out to audition for something. College was filled with small parts in big musical productions. What's-her-name in *Brigadoon*. Who's-her-face in *A Midsummer Night's Dream*. That lady in that other play. All small and usually comical. All satisfying in their low level of risk. I surfed in a very cool and confident zone and my ego was snuggly and warm in a sleeping bag of safe choices. Then I moved to Chicago and the shit hit the fan.

I started going on cold auditions, the kind where your agent sends you in and you have no idea why. The worst auditions were what we called "bite-and-smiles." This is when you go in for a Wendy's spot and have to pretend to eat something and smile. No words, just the simple fact of presenting your face to the camera and hoping someone likes it. I had the presence of mind even then to know I would never book one of these. One, my teeth were kind of jacked up, and that never bodes well in close-ups. Two, I don't have symmetrical good looks and therefore I like to think that my personality is my currency. I remember the Chicago casting director asking me to pretend to bite into something and then smile. I did my best and was about to leave when the casting director asked me to stay and put something on tape. I got excited. Maybe she saw potential in me. Maybe I would finally get to play the blue-collar white-girl arsonist on my favorite show of all time, *Law & Order*.

Instead, she asked me to sit on a stool and tell her my "most embarrassing moment." I asked why. She said she just wanted to have some tape of me talking. I asked her if I could talk about something else and she shook her head and said, "Tell me your MOST EMBARRASSING MOMENT." And I said no. She never called me again.

Quick note here: Everybody wants you to share your MOST EMBARRASSING MOMENT all the time, and I am here to tell you that you don't have to. You don't have to tell it or tweet it or Instagram it. You don't have to put it in a book or share it with anyone who doesn't feel safe and protective of your heart.

More cold auditions followed and none amounted to much. Almost every job I have ever gotten was due to someone knowing my work or seeing me in something else. I was in UCB and Andy Richter suggested I do stuff for *Conan*. Being on *Conan* helped me land a part in *Deuce Bigalow*. My *UCB* television show and friends helped me get an audition for *SNL*; my *SNL* connections resulted in *Parks and Recreation*. See, years and years of hard work and little bits of progress isn't nearly as entertaining as imagining me telling a joke in a Boston food court when suddenly Lorne Michaels walks up and says, "I must have you for a little show I do."

I once was having dinner with an old friend back when I was on *SNL*. *Baby Mama* was coming out and I was in the middle of one of those weird press pushes where your face is on taxis and you are doing talk shows all the time. My friend, who was as funny and talented as me but chose not to be an actor, was talking about how he was seeing my face everywhere. He went on and on about how weird that was. He pointed out that people were really starting to know my name and asked me if I "could believe it." "Yes," I said. I had worked for over a decade to get to this moment. I hadn't just dropped my script into someone's lap on a train. "Can you?" I asked him.

But I was lucky. Your career and your passion don't always match up. Plenty of talented people don't have the careers they want. Plenty of untalented people make millions and make movies. There is a difference between determination and talent. Hard work

221

doesn't always matter. You can be the best at making contacts and going after jobs, but then suddenly you want it too much. Suddenly everybody feels how bad you want it and they don't want to give it to you. Even at six years old Archie is learning to stop paying attention to the toy he wants. He knows that if he lets on how bad he wants it his four-year-old brother will snatch that shizz up in a hot second. Pretending to not want something can work. Really not caring if you get it takes a lifetime of practice.

I guess the Buddhists would call this idea healthy detachment. Too often we are told to visualize what we want and cut out pictures of it and repeat it like a mantra over and over again. Books and magazines tell us to create vision boards. Late-night commercials remind us that "anything is possible." Positive affirmations are written on our tea bags. I am introducing a new idea. Try to care less. Practice ambivalence. Learn to let go of wanting it. Treat your career like a bad boyfriend.

Here's the thing. Your career won't take care of you. It won't call you back or introduce you to its parents. Your career will openly flirt with other people while you are around. It will forget your birthday and wreck your car. Your career will blow you off if you call it too much. It's never going to leave its wife. Your career is fucking other people and everyone knows but you.

Your career will never marry you.

Now, before I extend this metaphor, let me make a distinction between career and creativity. Creativity is connected to your passion, that light inside you that drives you. That joy that comes when you do something you love. That small voice that tells you, "I like this. Do this again. You are good at it. Keep going." That is the juicy stuff that lubricates our lives and helps us feel less alone in the world. Your creativity is not a bad boyfriend. It is a really warm older Hispanic lady who has a beautiful laugh and loves to hug. If you are even a little bit nice to her she will make you feel great and maybe cook you delicious food.

Career is different. Career is the stringing together of opportunities and jobs. Mix in public opinion and past regrets. Add a dash of future panic and a whole lot of financial uncertainty. Career is something that fools you into thinking you are in control and then takes pleasure in reminding you that you aren't. Career is the thing that will not fill you up and never make you truly whole. Depending on your career is like eating cake for breakfast and wondering why you start crying an hour later.

I was on a panel once with the genius writer David Simon. I think *The Wire* is the best-written show in recent memory. I have watched each episode of all five seasons twice. For Mother's Day one year, Aziz Ansari got me a signed and framed picture of Omar Little with the inscription "Amy, You come at the King You Best Not Miss. Omar."

Next to my children and my blood diamonds this is the only thing I would grab in a fire. A nice young person stood up at the panel and asked David and me how we found the "courage" to do what we do. We both bristled a bit at the idea of our work being "courageous." We both admitted that we often think about how if everything went away tomorrow we would still have a trade and a skill to depend on. He could go back to reporting, a career he started in, and I could go teach improvisation at the UCB theater or choreograph dance for child pageants. (A path I am interested in pursuing at a later date.) Either way, we both agreed that ambivalence is key to success.

I will say it again. Ambivalence is key.

You have to care about your work but not about the result. You have to care about how good you are and how good you feel,

Any you come at THE King you Best
Don't Miss
Mi[...]
"Omar"

but not about how good people think you are or how good people think you look.

I realize this is extremely difficult. I am not saying I am particularly good at it. I'm like you. Or maybe you're better at this than I am.

You will never climb Career Mountain and get to the top and shout, "I made it!" You will rarely feel done or complete or even successful. Most people I know struggle with that complicated soup of feeling slighted on one hand and like a total fraud on the other. Our ego is a monster that loves to sit at the head of the table, and I have learned that my ego is just as rude and loud and hungry as everyone else's. It doesn't matter how much you get; you are left wanting more. Success is filled with MSG.

Ambivalence can help tame the beast. Remember, your career is a bad boyfriend. It likes it when you don't depend on it. It will reward you every time you don't act needy. It will chase you if you act like other things (passion, friendship, family, longevity) are more important to you. If your career is a bad boyfriend, it is healthy to remember you can always leave and go sleep with somebody else.

EVERYBODY IS

SCA

RED

MOST OF THE TIME.

partner in crime

TINA FEY IS MY COMEDY WIFE. I have known her for almost a double decade. We met each other when we were poor and single. Now we are both rich as shit and have husbands all over the world. People think of us as a "comedy team" and I am not quick to correct them. Why wouldn't I want to connect myself to the fiercest and most talented voice in the comedy world?

I am mistaken for Tina all the time. I recently renewed my license at the DMV and the African American woman asked me to do my Sarah Palin. She was confused and perhaps racist, but it only made me happy. I'm happy that people call me Tina because she is my friend and she happens to be crushing it.

Tina helped me get on *Saturday Night Live* and asked me to join her on "Update" as one of the first two women coanchors. It was as fun as it looked. We have performed in front of our parents and the whole world, and each time we've looked at each other and laughed at what we get to do. Tina reminds me of how far I have come. She knew me when. When we are together I feel strong and powerful. Maybe too powerful. (I tend to show off and run my mouth a little bit.)

We don't compete against each other, we compete against ourselves.

Often there is only one other person in the world who understands the very specific thing I am dealing with, and it's Tina. Well, Tina and Judge Judy, actually, but I only have Tina's phone number. It is intense to have little kids and a television show and be a woman in general, and I am lucky to have someone to walk through this weird life with.

Tina shows her love for you by writing for you. I can't tell you how many times she wrote something special and wonderful for me. Most of my memories of her at *SNL* involve Tina sitting at her computer, working on something for someone else. Tina wrote a lovely chapter about me in her book, and boy have I dined out on that for a while. In an attempt to return the favor, I will honor Tina with an acrostic poem, arguably the laziest form of writing.

T — TWENTY YEARS AGO WE MET AND BECAME INSTANT FRIENDS. OUR RELATIONSHIP IS THE SAME AGE AS LOURDES CICCONE, AND LIKE LOURDES, WE THINK OF OURSELVES AS "MADONNA'S DAUGHTERS."

I — IMPROVISATION IS WHERE TINA SHINES. WE HAVE DONE HUNDREDS OF IMPROV SHOWS TOGETHER AND PERHAPS TEN WERE VERY GOOD. ←

THIS IS AN EXCELLENT RATIO.

N — NEVER BEEN ATTRACTED TO THE SAME GUY. IMPORTANT.

A — ABLE TO DO ALL THINGS WELL.

F — FAMILY. TINA IS A GREAT MOM.

E — ELIZABETH IS HER REAL NAME BUT I CALL HER BETTY.

Y — YOLO! (YOU ONLY LIVE ONCE) *

* Tina, please punch this up. Thank you in advance.

We host ALL the shit and RUN THIS TOWN cuz we COME CORRECT and NOBODY gonna stop us FUCK ALL Y'ALL HATERS!!!

i'm so proud
of you

ONCE A WOMAN TURNS FORTY SHE HAS TO START DEALING WITH TWO THINGS: YOUNGER MEN TELLING HER THEY ARE PROUD OF HER AND OLDER MEN LETTING HER KNOW THEY WOULD HAVE SEX WITH HER. Both of these things are supposed to be compliments but can often end up making this particular woman angry. I don't think a man who is fifteen years younger than me should tell me he is proud of me unless he is my sober coach or my time-travel dad. Older men can be sexy and powerful, but when a thrice-divorced entertainment attorney puts his bony hand on my knee, I want to whisper in his ear, "You're crazy, old man."

I'm not sure if you have heard about this new theory that men and women are different, but it's really starting to catch on. Most of my life has been spent in a room full of men, and I have learned the different ways they communicate. I find that, in general, the amount of sharing men do with each other in one year is about the same as what I share with my female friends while we wait for our cars at the valet. I was once part of an *Asssscat* show that included a young comedian doing monologues. In one of his stories he briefly mentioned his failed marriage. After the show, the comedian, ten other guys, and I were all hanging out in the greenroom drinking beers. This ratio is not uncommon in comedy. If you're a woman, you are often the only one, or one of two, in a room full of men. This is certainly the case in most writers' rooms, except for *SNL* and *Parks and Rec,* which both had more women writers than many other shows because Seth Meyers and Mike Schur (the head writers on each of these shows, respectively) are real men who love women. Anyway, back to the greenroom. One guy said to the comedian, "Hey, I didn't know you used to be married." The comedian said, "Yeah." Another guy said, "Huh." The comedian said, "Yeah." There was a moment of silence and then the comedian breathed deep and said, "Thanks for letting me talk about it, guys." He actually felt like he had shared something. This is how men talk to each other. It's amazing to see up close.

On the other hand, men are sometimes wildly inappropriate in the way they share with women. By a show of hands, how many of you have seen a strange penis on the street? On the subway? At a sleepover? I was once walking with my friend Keri in the middle of the day and some guy asked us for the time. When we looked down at our watches, his dick was in his hands. We giggled and screamed and ran away. We were probably ten. I have been really drunk in high school and had a guy try to fool around with me. I have been called a bitch and a lesbian when I rejected a guy in college. I have locked eyes with various subway masturbators. I have been mugged but not raped, pushed and spit on by someone I knew, and forced to pull over in a road-rage incident where a man stuck his head into my car and told me he was going to "cum in my face." And I count myself very lucky. That is what "very lucky" feels like. Oof.

Many women, and even some men, have their own version of how they have been lucky or unlucky. It can make it hard not to be on high alert for people using power to manipulate you. Which leads me to this story. I share it because it's an example of a shady use of power and how I attempted to push back. Also, it is a story that shows no matter where or who you are, it can sometimes be hard to get a creep to stop hugging you.

I was asked to perform at an event honoring someone. I had worked on my bit and was excited to be a part of a special night for this person whom I admire. Usually, leading up to an event you are asked to run your ideas past some producers. I have learned that with these events I need to conserve the amount of real estate I let people take up in my heart and brain. Most people like to talk about things too much and too often, especially producers. When you are dealing with nervous producers hoping for a great show, you can be asked to take on their energy and be responsible for their feelings. I try to combat this by ignoring e-mails and hoping the whole situation just goes away. When that doesn't work I spend an hour or so getting angry at myself for saying yes to the thing in the first place when I am much too busy! I am so busy! Why won't people understand that! After I have stomped around a bit more I usually call or e-mail the producer late in the game and speak as vaguely and as quickly as I can.

So I talked to the producers about my speech (briefly; see above) and prepared to head to the event. I was ushered in to do a little rehearsal. It all went well. We went over my bit, and it got a bunch of laughs. The producer was a pleasant older gentleman in

235

his sixties who thanked me for joining and assured me I would be in great hands. I cursed myself for having been so grumpy with the production team.

Right before I walked out onstage for the actual performance, the sound guy made some last-minute adjustments to my microphone. Then I walked out and started my section. My bit went fine. I would give it a B-minus. I'm at the point in my life now where delivering a B-minus performance on a televised show with some of my comedy heroes doesn't ruin my week. I don't know if that is the most inspiring or most depressing sentence I have ever typed, but there you have it. But right as I was building to the climax, the lights went down too early and I was cut off from delivering the ending that I was excited about and that had gone so well in rehearsal. At *SNL* we always wished for bad rehearsals. There was nothing worse than performing live and waiting for the laugh that came in rehearsals, and never getting it. I coined it "phantom laugh syndrome." A hot dress audience was met with some head shaking because usually there was nowhere to go but down. My hot dress had morphed into me not really delivering and being cut off too early. I semi-stormed offstage and headed right into the path of one of the producers.

"Great job," he said.

"You guys missed my cue," I said.

"No one noticed."

"I did."

"Relax, it was great."

"Relax" is a real tough one for me. Another tough one is "smile." "Smile" doesn't really work either. Telling me to relax or smile when I'm angry is like bringing a birthday cake into an ape sanctuary. You're just asking to get your nose and genitals bitten off.

"This is the part where you apologize to me," I said, getting angry. "You guys screwed up and this is where you make me feel better about it."

I like to use this tactic on people. It can work. When someone is being rude, abusing their power, or not respecting you, just call them out in a really obvious way. Say, "I can't understand why you are being rude because you are the concierge and this is the part of the evening where the concierge helps me." Act like they are an actor who has forgotten what part they are playing. It brings the attention back to them and gives you a minute to calm down so you don't do something silly like burst into tears or break their stupid fucking glasses. Not that there is anything wrong with crying. It was Marlo Thomas and the *Free to Be . . . You and Me* gang who reminded us that "crying gets the sad out." It's just that sometimes anger should just stay anger and tears can change anger to something else. However, if you do start crying in an argument and someone asks why, you can always say, "I'm just crying because of how wrong you are."

So, I tell this producer to apologize to me and he kind of slinks away like "Yeesh, she's a handful." Luckily, that doesn't bother me the way it used to. That kind of feeling would have been hard to hold in my heart and stomach when I was in my twenties. It was hard to feel like somebody didn't like me. It felt like such a failure. I don't care as much now. It's really great. It's like I can finally eat spicy food without the gut ache later, or something similar. I have a stomach for other people not stomaching me. Or at least I am working on it.

I stomped upstairs and felt angry for about five minutes, and then I watched the anger travel through my body like a wave and leave. Emotions are like passing storms, and you have to remind yourself that it won't rain forever. You just have to sit down and watch it pour outside and then peek your head out when it looks dry. I had all but gotten over the whole thing when I heard a gentle knocking on my dressing room door.

"Amy, can I talk to you?"

"He's coming to apologize," I thought. I instantly decided I was not upset. Not only that, I decided I was going to let him off the hook easy. I just wanted to go watch the rest of the show and have a drink and celebrate, so I opened the door with relaxed shoulders and a genuine smile of reconciliation. He came in and sat down without asking if that was okay with me. I noticed this.

"We have a problem."

"Oh?"

"Your audio wasn't good. Your mic wasn't working correctly."

"Oh."

So now I realized not only was he not coming to apologize, he was there to deliver more bad news. I practiced a few things I have learned from my therapist and other badass business bitches. I sat back. Actually, I leaned back. I thought about my second book, which will be a bestseller coauthored with Sheryl Sandberg titled *Lean Back*. I uncrossed my legs and I made eye contact. I immediately decided this was not my problem, and the relief of that decision spread across my chest like hot cocoa. Too often we women try to tackle chaos that is not ours to fix.

"Well, that is disappointing," I said.

"I don't know what to do," he said.

I practiced another new thing I've learned. I just sat there quietly. It was so hard. I once sat next to Christopher Walken as we were rehearsing a sketch for *SNL*. I had tried small talk with him a few times, and he was extremely pleasant, but I just felt like I was

———

bothering him. So as an experiment I tried to just sit next to him and be quiet. It was excruciating. I think I lasted for three minutes and then I had to pretend to read a bag of chips. Not talking can be hard for me. But I tried it.

"Hmm," I said. (I know, I know, I was *technically* talking.)

"Would you do it again? Without an audience? So we could make sure we have it for the broadcast?" he asked.

"I don't think so," I said, quietly but firmly.

"Well, I just don't know what to do," he said.

I sat in silence. I'm doing good so far, right?

"Maybe I can do ADR if you need it," I said. ADR is recording audio over a taped piece. Notice what I am doing? I am starting to offer ways to fix it even though a minute ago I felt great reminding myself it wasn't my problem to fix.

"That would be great," he said. "Are you sure you don't want to do it again, just so we can be sure we have it?"

So now he had heard my no and was still asking. Gavin de Becker talks about this in his wonderful book *The Gift of Fear*. He talks about how the word "no" should be the "end of the discussion, not the beginning of a negotiation." I am obsessed with *The Gift of Fear*. I quote it too much. My friends roll their eyes when they hear my *Gift of Fear* train coming. But how can you deny such hilarious gems as "Most men fear getting laughed at or humiliated by a romantic prospect while most women fear rape and death"? I mean, who doesn't want me spouting that kind of stuff at their Christmas party?

I said no again. I said that I didn't want to go back out and do my speech again in front of an empty room.

So that should have been it, right?

No.

———

Instead, the producer stood up and said, "I'm sorry. This has been stressful. Can I give you a hug?"

Now, I wish that I could tell you I said no. When I retold the story that night to my friends, I lied and told them I didn't let him hug me. I told them that I said something like "No. No, you can't." My friends all nodded their heads when I told them that. They all believed that I wouldn't let this guy give me a hug. I was a successful and independent woman! I was strong! I secretly disliked most new people!

But I did let him hug me. I let that creepy guy hug me. I stayed seated and he came over and hugged my stiff body while my arms stayed at my sides. All I was thinking at that moment was that if I let him hug me he would feel better and this would all be over soon.

Do you think he would have hugged a male performer?

Me neither. Either way, it never ends.

A little space.

Yes Please.

CALLING PEOPLE

SWEET

EART

MAKES MOST
PEOPLE ENRAGED.

let's build a park

PLAYING LESLIE KNOPE IS AS FUN AS IT LOOKS. I get to be the lead on a show I would actually watch. I've met friends whom I will treasure forever. I am allowed on a weekly basis to both crack jokes and cry. It's been hard to wrangle this chapter because I still feel too close to the job to step away and share it all with you. When this book goes to print we will be finishing our seventh and last season, and shooting our 125th show. My nose is still pressed up against the painting and I have little perspective. Because of this, I am going to do what I have been doing for the past six years, which is write something and ask *Parks and Recreation* creator Mike Schur to make it better. Let's continue . . .

Every acting job feels like the end of the road. If you're lucky, you get to peek at what is around the corner. It's a privilege if a clear path is laid out that will take you to another work environment. It's rare that someone builds a bridge to the next great thing. After

245

1 *Note from Mike:* My grandmother wanted me to be an engineer; being called a "bridge" is the closest I will ever get, and so I thank you.

2 *Note from Mike:* We didn't technically watch together—you were in New York and I was in L.A.— but you did call me after every game and scream things like "ORTIIIIIIIIIIIZ" into my voice mail.

3 *Note from Mike: Somebody Did Something: The Story of the 2004 Boston Red Sox.* It was every e-mail, text, and phone message our friends had sent me about the Red Sox from September 2003 to December 2004. I had it printed and bound and gave it out to my friends as a holiday gift. It totally made Seth Meyers cry.

4 *Note from Mike:* Whom I had not spoken with in two years, but who knew how important the victory would've been to me.

5 *Note from Mike:* Currently enjoying the fact that this took place before every human in the world had an HD video camera in their pocket.

6 *Note from Mike:* Two, really: compiling e-mails and "Baby Got Back"–related dance bits.

Saturday Night Live my bridge was Michael Schur. The next great thing was *Parks and Recreation.*[1]

Mike and I were friends and coworkers at *Saturday Night Live*. He was a writer before I got there and ran "Weekend Update" during the Tina Fey/Jimmy Fallon years. Mike is a whip-smart Harvard grad who manages to be as compassionate as he is funny. He is a lover of justice, the underdog, and the good fight. Never is this demonstrated more than in his love for the Boston Red Sox. I watched the Red Sox win the World Series with Mike and Seth Meyers and other Boston writers,[2] and Mike even turned all those e-mails into a book.[3] On the last page, Mike transcribed a phone message from his therapist[4] congratulating him on the Red Sox win.

Mike also knows all of the lyrics to "Baby Got Back" by Sir Mix-A-Lot. I know this because he sang them into his cell phone while pretending to take a call on the dance floor at my wedding.[5] Needless to say, he has a lot of skills.[6]

Before Mike left *SNL,* he, Seth, and I sat in his office and watched the brilliant Christmas finale of Ricky Gervais's UK version of *The Office*. We all wept in our hoodies.[7] I don't remember if Mike had already signed on to join producer Greg Daniels on the American reboot at that point.[8] I remember thinking that an American version of *The Office* was a terrible idea.[9] Then I heard that Greg Daniels, Mike Schur, and Steve Carell were involved and still thought it was dicey. Then I saw it and realized it was amazing.

In early 2008, Mike and Greg called me to ask if I'd be interested in working on a show they were creating once I left *SNL*. Greg now had a deal with NBC to develop a new series, rumored to be an *Office* spinoff, and had asked Mike to do it with him. We talked vaguely about ideas, but mostly just about how fun it would be to do something together. Greg's deal meant that the new show had been ordered straight to series with a thirteen-episode guarantee. Most shows start by making a pilot episode. When the pilot is done, a group of mysterious people gather in a room and weigh its merits, consult various oracles, and then send white papal smoke out of the holy chimney when it is decided it will become a series. Being ordered straight to series was great news because it meant we were able to skip that mysterious and painful pilot process, but on top of that, the first episode was slated to air after the Super Bowl, TV's most coveted slot. It was a remarkable and rare opportunity, a home-run decision for any actor. Then I got knocked up and figured the whole thing was a bust.

Mike and Greg started working on what would become *Parks and Recreation* and a few months later decided to ignore my "delicate condition" and pitch me the idea anyway.[10] Mike called me as he stood on the balcony of his house chain-smoking, a detail he has asked me to not put in my book.[11] He told me about a character he and Greg had created called Leslie Knope. She was an extremely low-level Parks and Recreation Department employee who had big dreams. She was

7 *Note from Mike:* The moment Dawn returned to the office and kissed Tim I jumped up out of my chair and involuntarily thrust my hands in the air, like my team had won the Super Bowl. Poehler clapped and cheered. Everyone in the room had a cathartic moment of pure joy. I remember thinking later that I wanted to write something someday that would make people feel that good. Many of the romantic and emotional story lines on *Parks and Rec* have been my attempt—my and the other writers' attempt, I should say—to reach that bar.

8 *Note from Mike:* I had not.

9 *Note from Mike:* So did I. So did everyone, except, thank God, Greg Daniels.

10 *Note from Mike:* By this point, with the idea pretty fleshed out, Greg's and my general feeling was: Poehler or bust, pregnancy be damned.

11 *Note from Mike:* Damn it, Poehler.

247

12 *Note from Mike:* It's so interesting to think about it this way, now, as we near the end—it was, at the beginning, really that simple: a woman who wanted to make something out of nothing.

13 *Note from Mike annotating previous note:* No, I'm not crying. Shut up.

inspired by the "Yes We Can" spirit of Obama's recent election. She believed that it only took one person to make a difference. She wanted to effect change, she wanted to someday be president, but most importantly, she wanted to turn an empty lot in her town into a park.[12, 13]

The show was going to be shot in the single-camera documentary style that was working so well for *The Office*. At this point I had no experience with this documentary/mockumentary-style format. Before *SNL,* I had done a few multicamera shows as a guest star or featured regular. On "multicam" shows, you shoot with three or four cameras in front of a studio audience, and you can hear people laughing—like *Cheers* or *Seinfeld.* Sometimes you shoot things without an audience, but at least once a week you have a "tape night" where an audience comes in and actors feed off the energy and laughs. My first television job was a tiny part in an episode of *Spin City*—which was a multicam show—in 1996. I didn't meet Michael J. Fox, but Richard Kind was kind. Two years later I had a part on a show called *Sick in the Head,* a pre–*Freaks and Geeks* Judd Apatow–produced pilot starring David Krumholtz, Kevin Corrigan, Andrea Martin, and Austin Pendleton. It was not picked up to series. The pilot process can be rough going.

I had a little more experience in shows that shot single-camera style. Single camera usually means using one camera and shooting each side of the scene separately—in other words, if two people are talking, you shoot over one of their shoulders and do a bunch of takes where only the person on camera is really performing. Then you stop, they adjust all the lights, and the cameras turn around and shoot the other person. It's extremely tedious and slow. It means long hours and lighting setups, and it feels like shooting a traditional movie. Years before, I had worked on a single-camera pilot called *North Hollywood,* which was also not picked up to series. Though looking back, it made sense that the show didn't go—it starred a bunch of losers named Kevin Hart, Jason Segel, and January Jones and was produced by the obviously talentless Judd Apatow. That's right. I am the common denominator in two failed Judd Apatow projects. Judd Apatow with me: zero dollars. Judd Apatow without me: two hundred trillion dollars.[14]

Mike and Greg explained their idea for a new mockumentary style. It seemed like a hybrid of *Spinal Tap,* the British *The Office,* and something entirely original. Scenes would be blocked and rehearsed almost like a play, with entire scenes performed top to bottom many times. Two or three cameras would find the action and just follow the actors as they moved around. Actors often didn't know when they were on camera or where the cameras were. "Spy shots" lent a sense of intimacy to moments. Actors were allowed to look into the camera to show their reactions to things and spoke directly to the camera with "talking heads," used to further the story or display another side of what a character was feeling.[15, 16] Camera operators were very close or very

14 *Note from Mike:* Roughly.

15 *Note from Mike:* Characters on mockumentary shows look at the camera for different reasons. For Michael Scott, it would be because he had just done something humiliating and then suddenly remembered that there were cameras there—his looks were often conveying: "Uh-oh." Ben Wyatt (like Jim Halpert from *The Office*) often looks to camera as a plea, like "Can you believe what I have to deal with?" Andy Dwyer looks to camera like it's his best friend and he wants to share how awesome something is. And so on. My point is that when we created the character of Leslie, we imagined that her relationship to the camera was one of guarded caution— she had political aspirations, and people with political aspirations both (a) like being on camera but are also (b) acutely aware that one slipup or inappropriate recorded moment can ruin their careers. In the beginning, Leslie had that cautious relationship with the cameras, but as time went on, Amy just kind of stopped looking at them. Amy and I never really discussed this, nor was it a conscious

decision on the part of the writing staff— it just kind of stopped happening. I thought about why it was happening toward the end of season 2, and I realized that Leslie had evolved into a character for whom there was no difference in her private and public thoughts, motives, or feelings. Amy had made her into a completely consistent, heart-on-her-sleeve character who was not embarrassed or ashamed by anything she ever said or did in any scenario. I remember thinking that was great, and from that moment on I used that as a North Star for writing Leslie—it became a mission statement that we would never write a story that involved her being ashamed of how she felt. It's a pretty badass character trait, I think, and it only works because of the supreme sincerity of the actress who embodies it. (Don't cut that part, Amy. I know you want to, because it seems braggy or something to have someone else's notes be about how awesome you are, but don't cut it, because it's true, and everyone else can just deal with it.)

16 *Note from Amy:* You're the boss.

far away but a dynamic part of the action. We would shoot eight or nine pages in a twelve-hour day, which is about double what one shoots on a feature film. There were very few makeup touch-ups or lighting adjustments.[17] Improvising was encouraged and accommodated, and if you tried something new the camera could swing and catch it.

Mike told me that once I shot a show like this, I would never want to shoot a TV show any other way again. This has proven correct. He sent me the script and it took me five minutes to realize Leslie Knope was the best character ever written for me.[18] My motto has always been "Do work that you are proud of with your talented friends." My other motto is "I need to keep working or the government will seize my boat." Both of these things helped me say "yes please."

I had a long discussion with my husband, Will, and I will be forever grateful that he agreed to move our family out to Los Angeles to allow me to give this show a try. We shot six episodes in a row instead of the usual method: shooting a pilot, then spending a month editing it, then thinking about stuff for a few months, then the oracle, then writing and shooting the next episodes months later. Also, due to the timing of my pregnancy, we became probably the only show to ever willingly give up the coveted post–Super Bowl slot. Before we started shooting, I was feeling dumpy and exhausted, overwhelmed and sad. I was still grieving not being at *SNL* and recovering from my rough delivery. And I was lost in Los Angeles, a city I still can't

250

quite figure out.[19] I spent a lot of time crying. I was scared I wasn't funny. I missed New York and my new baby at home. I wasn't being a good wife to my husband. I had a full face and round body. It had been a while since I had been asked to settle into one character for longer than a month, and I kept warning Mike and Greg that my performance might be too loud, like when you turn on your car and the radio is already going full blast.

Once we started to cast the show, what was fuzzy became sharper. Rashida Jones, Aubrey Plaza, and Aziz Ansari came on board early. Chris Pratt and Nick Offerman later. Retta, Jim O'Heir, and Paul Schneider rounded out our first mini-season of *Parks and Recreation*. Eventually we would be joined by Rob Lowe and Adam Scott and the circle would be complete. I don't remember much about those first shows. I started feeling my groove after a few episodes. I realized the cast was beyond talented and would eventually become like family. I constantly searched for Mike's face when I was nervous. But the thing I do remember clearly is a small scene I did in the pilot episode. It's raining and Leslie is standing and looking outside her office window. In voice-over, she speaks about how this park project is going to take a lot of work and last a long time, but it will be worth it.

17 *Note from Mike:* We told our excellent crew in the first week of shooting that we would be asking them to do things that would ordinarily get them fired. We told the makeup artists and hairstylists not to rush onto the set to fix minor problems. We told the director of photography and the grips and electricians to light the scenes as quickly as they could and not to worry about perfect shadow removal and things like that. The whole point of this style is to maximize the amount of time actors are in front of the camera, acting. This only works if you have a cast full of people who are willing to sacrifice Hollywood magic for maximal comedy—who are, in short, not vain, and who would rather be funny than look flawless and perfect. This is one of my favorite things about the entire cast— every single one of them was happy to make that deal.

18 *Note from Mike:* I think the best character ever written for you is Jeff Goldblum's part in *Independence Day*. Or maybe Fagin in *Oliver!* Is this helping?

19 *Note from Mike:* No one can. Don't even try. It's Chinatown, Poehler.

```
21 LESLIE TALKING HEAD

B-roll: Leslie staring out her office window at the
    small courtyard that serves as her "view."

              LESLIE

I've been in the Parks Department for six years, and
I've handled some things I'm proud of. For example,
last year I led the city-wide drive to disinfect the
sandbox sand after those problems with the cats. I
heard some testimony from mothers of toddlers that
would make you cry. But this pit! The chance to build
          a new park, from scratch . . .

            (she thinks)

        This is my Hoover Dam.
```

I remember standing and watching the props guys make it rain in our fake outside courtyard as we shot the B-roll part of that scene—the shot of Leslie from outside the window that the audience would see as she spoke those words. I listened to the words being read aloud by Greg and Mike, and realized this was my new job. A tiny whisper, no louder than the Who that Horton hears, told me we were going to make it. I believed.

We almost didn't make it. That first year was rough. Critics compared us to *The Office,* and not kindly. Our ratings were okay but not great. *Deadline Hollywood* decided to publish our pilot testing results, which was basically like having someone publish the worst parts of your diary.[20] According to testing, a lot of people liked it when "that Parks lady fell into the pit." It wasn't a good sign when people wanted the show's lead character to fall into a hole. We regrouped. We changed a little. We figured out what worked and soldiered on. Network presidents came and went as we hung on for dear life. Some liked us more than others. Some canceled us on airplanes, only to change their minds before landing. Critics started to watch the show again and notice new things.

We kept our heads down and did our jobs. We controlled the only thing we could, which was the show. We did the thing. Because remember, the talking about the thing isn't the thing. The doing of the thing is the thing.

In season 2 we started to gain momentum. Critics put us on lists and we were nominated for awards. Everyone realized we would never be a ratings juggernaut, but we just kept plugging along as we watched new NBC show after NBC show die on the table next to us. To be fair, we were often on life support ourselves. We would finish a season never really knowing if we would have another one, so Mike would always push the writers to take big swings and let characters evolve and change. Rob Lowe and Adam Scott joining us made us better and less likely to get canceled. We just kept doing it.

Mike would call me in July every summer and pitch me the upcoming season's story line for Leslie. I can't explain the joy and relief I felt, sitting on a porch in my Nantucket rental, swatting bugs and hearing

20 *Note from Mike:* Good analogy. I think of it more like a restaurant critic bursting into a kitchen, eating a half-cooked meal, and then writing a review. "The chicken was undercooked!" The only good thing about that cheap shot—both the leaking of it and the crummy decision to print it without even calling us for comment—is that Louis CK came to our defense in the comments section, and joined us as Leslie's boyfriend early in season 2.

21 *Note from Mike:* My grandfather really wanted me to be a deity, and this analogy is the closest I will ever get, and so for that I thank you.

22 *Note from Mike:* Your seven-year, real-life "will they, won't they" saga with Detlef Schrempf could fill a hundred volumes.

23 *Note from Mike annotating previous note:* This is a joke. He is married I think. Hi, Detlef! (He's definitely reading this right now.)

24 *Note from Mike:* So was I. Probably not in the same way.

about what was ahead. After spending years trying to generate my own material at *SNL,* this felt like someone was picking me up and carrying me Jesus/"Footprints" style.[21] Leslie got to run for office, fall in and out of love, fight for her town, and eat waffles with her friends. I got to write and direct episodic television for the first time. I got to work with people like Louis CK, Megan Mullally, Fred Armisen, Patricia Clarkson, Will Arnett, and Detlef Schrempf. I have sex stories about all of them but I am saving those for my next book.[22] [23]

In the middle of season 2, I got pregnant again. I was excited and surprised.[24] This meant that we had to sort of force NBC's hand and try to get them to agree to shoot more episodes before I really blew up. With its cameras-looking-everywhere shooting style, *Parks and Recreation* was not the kind of show where you could hide a pregnant belly behind a few bags of groceries. We got an early pickup for season 3, and as soon as season 2 ended we just kept rolling and shot some extra episodes that we would bank for the beginning of the next year. If you have any doubt as to what a great actor Adam Scott is, go back and watch him join a show and immediately figure out how to flirt with a tired pregnant lady. It's not easy. If I have learned anything from hip-hop, it's that there's nothing sexy about a baby that ain't yours.

Season 3 found us fighting for our right to party. We had been pushed to midseason, which is usually not exactly a vote of confidence from the network. The story line was all about a government shutdown, so both Amy and Leslie were frustrated about not getting back to work. The whole time Mike kept reminding me to keep my head down and control the only thing I could, which was the work. Somehow we survived.

Season 4 was all about Leslie's running for city council. The wonderful Paul Rudd and Kathryn Hahn joined us for a while. Leslie won. We all won. We soldiered on.

Seasons 5 and 6 were about the frustrations of Leslie Knope's new job. They also were about Ben and Leslie finally getting married and pregnant. They dealt with Ann and Chris leaving, Andy and April trying to figure out what they wanted, Donna finding love, and Tom entering a new business venture. I forget what happened with Jerry.

We had Sam Elliott, Michelle Obama, and Ginuwine on our show.

I can't believe we have done all these episodes and of course I can believe it because I always knew we would. (It's a miracle.)

In season 5, Leslie kicks off the season by visiting Washington, DC. Her boyfriend, Ben, decides to surprise her by setting up a meeting with her ultimate crush, Vice President Joe Biden. We shot that scene with Vice President Biden in his ceremonial office on the grounds of the White House, and he was charming and funny and a true pro—he didn't even flinch when Leslie slightly leaned in for a kiss. That's some old-school improv commitment right there. While we were walking out of the building, we learned that our show, which had been talked about as a front-runner for winning the Emmy for best comedy, did not even get nominated. We were upset, because as we know, no matter how much you think you don't want the pudding, once people start telling you that you might get the pudding it makes you want that pudding bad. Instead of being upset, Mike said, "I am going to go write the scene where Ben proposes to Leslie." He went back to his hotel room and wrote this.

255

INT. LESLIE AND BEN'S NEW HOUSE—NEXT DAY—DAY 3

Leslie and Martha the real estate lady.

MARTHA

Anything I can do to change your mind?

LESLIE

Sadly, no. My boyfriend might not be able to move
back for a while, so . . . I have to back out. I just
wanted to look at it one more time.

MARTHA

I can't give you your deposit back.

LESLIE

I know.

MARTHA

And there's a three hundred dollar penalty for—

LESLIE

All right, Martha. I get it.

She moves around the apartment, sadly.
Then turns around—

LESLIE (CONT'D)

Actually, is there any way—

Ben is standing there.

LESLIE (CONT'D)

What?! Hey! I didn't know you were—

He gets down on one knee. Looks up at her.
Takes her hand.

LESLIE (CONT'D)

Oh my God. What are you doing?

BEN

Thinking about my future.

He opens a ring box. Leslie GASPS.

BEN (CONT'D)

I am deeply, ridiculously in love with you.
Above everything else, I want to be with you,
forever. So, Leslie Knope, w—

LESLIE

<u>Wait!!!!!</u>

He freezes . . .

LESLIE (CONT'D)

Just . . . I need to remember this. Just wait a
second. Please.

He does.

BEN

. . . Leslie Knope, w—

LESLIE

No no no—hang on. One second longer. Please. I have
to remember everything. Every tiny little thing,
about how perfect my life is, right now, at this
exact moment.

She looks all around. Ben smiles. Waits.

BEN

You good?

LESLIE

I think I am good, yes.

BEN

So, I can . . . ?

LESLIE

Yes. I am ready.

BEN

Leslie Knope, will you—

LESLIE

Yes.

She attacks him and kisses him for a really long time.

BEN

—marry me. Okay good.

They kiss again.

He also wrote these vows in the wedding episode:

TOM

We are gathered here tonight to join Leslie
Barbara Knope and Benjamin Walker Wyatt in matrimony.
It's been a long and winding road for these two, and
they're so impatient to begin their lives together,
they moved their wedding date up by three months.
So I say, let's keep this short.

ANN

Hear, hear!

TOM

I assume—and hope—they have prepared their own vows.
We'll hear first from Ben.

BEN

In the ten years I worked for the state government,
my job sent me to more than fifty cities. I lived
in villages with eight people, rural farming
communities, college towns—I was sent to every corner
of Indiana. And then I came here. And I realized that
this whole time, that's what I was doing—I was just
wandering around, everywhere, looking for you.

She smiles and collects herself.

LESLIE

Oh boy. Okay. The first draft of my vows—which I wrote
the day after we got engaged—clocked in at around sixty
pages. But I don't have them with me right now.

259

There's a collective sigh of relief from the congregation.

LESLIE (CONT'D)

Wait! Maybe I have a copy in my office—

People wince . . .

LESLIE (CONT'D)

Nope. It's at home.

Relief again.

LESLIE (CONT'D)

So I will just say this. The things you have done for me—to help me, support me, surprise me, and make me happy—go above and beyond what any person deserves. You are all I need. I love you and I like you.

BEN

I love you and I like you.

Do you see the kind of maniac I am working with here? I have been shoulder to shoulder with a wonderful writer and excellent boss who loves big emotion as much as I do. Nightmare!

Maya Angelou said, "People will forget what you said, people will forget what you did, but people will never forget how you made them feel." I'm proud that Mike Schur and I rejected the idea that creativity needs to come from chaos. I like how we ran our writers' room and our set. People had a great time when they came to work on our show and that mattered to us. I like to think the spirit we had on set found its way onto the show. We used to leave enough time for "fun runs," improvised last takes where the actors could try out all the brilliant ideas they had been thinking about for the whole scene. Ninety-nine percent of the time these scenes were longer and less funny than what was written. But it made the actors feel funny. It kept the crew laughing and on their toes. It felt fun and alive and warm. Most days I was handed an amazing script that allowed me to stand in front of people I really loved and tell them how much I loved them. I got to work with the best writers and the best directors and the best producers. I won't miss memorizing those tongue-twisty "talking heads"[25] but I will miss everything else. This kind of job is magic. It comes around once or twice in a lifetime if you're lucky. And thank god, because it's all-consuming and sometimes work should just be work.

25 *Note from Mike:* I'll miss writing them and then watching you try to memorize them. Made for great blooper-reel material.

David Letterman liked the show and I received a steady paycheck for six years. That's about all you can ask for in life. Anyway, I've moved on. I'm working on a new HBO show called *Farts and Procreation* and it deals with some pretty dark stuff . . . whatever, no big deal.[26]

26 *Note from Mike:* I bet you win an Emmy for the role of Detective Janet Toughwoman, Special Ops, Fart Squad Delta.

MY CASTMATES AND FRIENDS

RASHIDA JONES (ANN PERKINS): Rashida is my old friend and chosen sister. She is my wife for life. I loved the scenes where it was just Ann and Leslie figuring out a problem. I would go sit on a fake apartment set and be friends with Ann and then go sit in my real trailer and be friends with Rashida. It was so easy to play being in love with Ann because next to my mom and my possible future daughter, Rashida Jones is the prettiest person I have ever met. She is also beautiful inside. We had so many deep conversations about our real lives in our fake offices. Rashida can speak on everything from Rodarte to Rodin to Rhodesia. I am so proud of the real friendship that Leslie and Ann had on-screen. It was important to both Rashida and me to show two women who supported each other and seemed like they would actually be friends.

- *My favorite moments on set:* Rashida and me singing and dancing between takes.
- *A lot of people don't know:* Rashida shares my obsession with miniature fake food.
- *I laughed the hardest:* The time Rashida and I (Ann and Leslie) had to try to pin Nick Offerman (Ron Swanson) down and feed him medicine in the "Hunting Trip" episode.

NICK OFFERMAN (RON SWANSON): I met Nick Offerman in Chicago in 1997. He had dyed his beard bright orange and his hair was shaped into two devil horns. He looked terrifying. He was doing a production of *A Clockwork Orange* with some cool theater company. Nick has real theater training and complete control over his instrument. This is why Ron Swanson is one of the best characters ever to be on television. He can do stillness like no other. He is incredibly professional but also giggly. We both talk about how much we love our jobs at least five times a day. He adores his wife and takes nothing for granted. He is someone I would run to when the zombies attack because he can build a boat and is great company.

- *My favorite moments on set:* Blocking scenes with Nick in Ron's office.
- *A lot of people don't know:* Nick is crazy for his two poodles.
- *I laughed the hardest:* The time Ron Swanson tried to push Leslie up onto a podium while the entire cast was slipping on ice in the episode "The Comeback Kid."

AZIZ ANSARI (TOM HAVERFORD): Aziz was a UCB wunderkind who had already had his own sketch show, *Human Giant,* before he joined *Parks.* He is a keen observer of the human condition and a lot sweeter and quieter than you would imagine. Like Tom Haverford, he is a total foodie and part-time culture vulture. Aziz and I spent a lot of time together building the world of Pawnee in those first couple of seasons. We stood together in a dusty pit and did our first television promos with a bunch of wild raccoons. We once shot a scene where Aziz had to run the length of a golf course and he barely broke a sweat. He has the stride and work ethic of a long-distance runner.

- *My favorite moments on set:* Hearing my kids call Aziz "turkey sandwich." I think it's because he was eating a turkey sandwich once? Either way they think he is hilarious.
- *A lot of people don't know:* Aziz went to business school.
- *I laughed the hardest:* The night Aziz and I spent shooting in a van during the episode "The Stakeout."

———

AUBREY PLAZA (APRIL LUDGATE): Aubrey is my devil child and my girlfriend in crime. She will do anything for me, and me for her. She was an NBC page and made up facts during her studio tours. She was an *SNL* intern and smoked cigarettes with the set painters. Her great work as April Ludgate turned what could have been a one-note performance into a deep character study. Both the character of April and person of Aubrey are secret softies. When I was going through my divorce and sad about coming back to Los Angeles, Aubrey dressed up as an alien and surprised me at the airport. She is a big-hearted warrior and a good and loyal friend. She speaks Spanish and gets the most sleep of anyone on our show.

- *My favorite moments on set:* Hugging Aubrey and asking her if she was eating enough.
- *A lot of people don't know:* Aubrey has a shrine to Judy Garland in her house.
- *I laughed the hardest:* The scene in the "Two Parties" episode where April discovers that the illuminated penis hat she is wearing is helping her as she digs to bury stolen artifacts.

CHRIS PRATT (ANDY DWYER): Chris had the best audition I had ever seen. No one knew his work and he came in and crushed. He is a comedy savant and a natural actor in a way I have never really seen. Each take is different and hilarious and completely unexpected. His character was only supposed to be on the show for six episodes, which seems ridiculous now. There are long discussions in the writers' room about how much Andy knows and doesn't know. Chris is exactly how you would expect him to be in person: friendly, open, and very strong. When we were going through tough times we would text each other, "How's the weather?" He also likes

———

hunting and country music. I've learned a lot from watching him. He constantly reminds me to stay loose and have fun.

- *My favorite moments on set:* Watching Pratt do physical comedy. Nobody falls like Pratt. Nobody does pratfalls like Pratt falls.
- *A lot of people don't know:* Chris actually plays the guitar and has helped write Mouse Rat songs.
- *I laughed the hardest:* Any time Andy got distracted in the middle of listening to important instructions, like in the episode "The Trial of Leslie Knope."

ROB LOWE (CHRIS TRAEGER): I can't believe I am Rob Lowe's coworker, let alone his friend. For the first few weeks after I met him I hounded him with questions about his movies. The scene when Sodapop comes out of the shower in *The Outsiders* was a very important moment in my adolescence. Rob gives wise advice and loves to talk about show business. He joined the show at a time when our status was very shaky and he helped keep us on the air. He is a committed father and has great wisdom about raising two boys. He delighted in the rigorous physical challenges we put him and his character through. He played Chris Traeger as a wide-eyed lunatic and loved every minute of it.

- *My favorite moments on set:* When Chris Traeger would have to go from standing still to a full sprint in less than five seconds.
- *A lot of people don't know:* We have a nickname for Rob. It's RoLo, and he loves it.
- *I laughed the hardest:* When Chris Traeger played "air banjo" in the backseat during the "Road Trip" episode.

RETTA SIRLEAF (DONNA MEAGLE): Retta can sing opera and cry on cue. She is a very warm person who does not suffer fools. The character of Donna Meagle has grown because Retta keeps adding small details in the fine work she does. I love how Donna is the only character who really holds her own against Ron Swanson. I love how she has nothing in common with Leslie Knope but tolerates her anyway. When we were rehearsing in the first few weeks of the show, Greg Daniels had me give a tour of the office and introduce everyone to camera. Retta, whom I barely knew, was sitting at Donna's station pretending to be on the phone. I came over and checked out the stuff on her desk and noticed a yellow leaf pinned up on a bulletin board behind her. I asked her where it came from and she deadpanned, "Outside."

- *My favorite moments on set:* Retta talking about anything she loves or hates.
- *A lot of people don't know:* Her aunt is the president of Liberia.
- *I laughed the hardest:* When Donna Meagle cried after a bullet hit her Benz in the "Hunting Trip" episode.

JIM O'HEIR (GARY/JERRY/LARRY/TERRY GERGICH): The character of Jerry is allowed to be such a loser because Jim the person is such a winner. He is sweet and funny and has the best timing of anyone on our show. He is a fine actor from Chicago who made what could have been a bad one-joke character into someone you root for and against. In real life, teasing him is okay because we all love him. In the show, Gary/Jerry/Larry/Terry is married to Christie Brinkley and has a gigantic penis. He is my parents' favorite.

- *My favorite moments on set:* Everybody making fun of Jerry.
- *A lot of people don't know:* Jim has a huge tongue.

- *I laughed the hardest:* When Jerry suffered a "fart attack" in "Halloween Surprise." Jim played it so real and it was ridiculous.

ADAM SCOTT (BEN WYATT): Adam is my TV husband and I couldn't ask for a better partner to fake come home to. The characters of Ben and Leslie have gone through so much together and I feel so lucky to have had Adam by my side. The fact that people cared about our TV love story is because Adam is a tremendous actor; he listens intently and always makes me better. Ben-and-Leslie scenes were exciting and nerve-racking to shoot because we all cared so much about making them work. Adam is a kind person who loves his family and cares about the people he works with. He also speaks slowly and tells really long and boring stories and someone needs to tell him to cut the shit. Adam always has fresh breath for kissing scenes and a very dry sense of humor.

- *My favorite moments on set:* Any time Leslie and Ben kiss.
- *A lot of people don't know:* Adam grew up in Santa Cruz and insists it's totally acceptable to drive barefoot.
- *I laughed the hardest:* When Ben had a kidney stone and lost his mind on morphine in the "Partridge" episode.
- *I cried the hardest:* When Ben got down on one knee and proposed to Leslie.

the
original brainstorm list

of possible character names for
what eventually became leslie knope,
thank god

Leslie Knope's name?

—by Mike Schur and Greg Daniels

Amy Poehler stars as Leslie Knope, Knopticut, Knoap, Knorbut, Knorrbet, Knorrer, Knoach, Knitch, Knill, Knonentity, Knobody, Knothing, Knottt, Knod, Knopf, Knoorshinty, Knoosince, Knebble, Knuteson, Knutesance, Knoose, Knuishience, Knupple, Sknapdragon, Knoble, Knoad, Knunt, Knerd, Knush, Knerscht, Knurk, Knopticalillusion, Knurch, Knasterson, Knob,

Knievel, Kune, Knack, Knacuck, Knapsick, Knapster, Knasterson, Knorsh, Knee, Kneep, Knunch, Knack,

Pfort, Pfrench, Pfrend, Pface, Pfunnyname, Pfinscheerr, Pfuctard,

Knrench, Knustache,

Knerch, Knurche

Leslie Knbross

Knrose

Knurine

Knude, Knabb, Knacke, Knacp

Knerst Knern Knormal

Leslie Knerm

Leslie Knute

Leslie Knoorstulmmlm

Leslie Broknet Borknust Borkdust Bornkt

Leslie Bornkvetch

Leslie Knooz

Leslie Knoop

Leslie Knornt

Leslie Knaint

Leslie Knabsolutyknot

Leslie Knay

Leslie Knough

Leslie Knotonmywatch

Leslie Knimbellety

Leslie Knazelle Leslie Kndawson-skreek

Amy Poehler plays Leslie Knuet, Knute, Knurch, Knerk, Knope

Inknert

Borrik

Borknt

Brunt Brulet knope

Leslie Knute-Gnorp

Leslie Gnope

Leslie Gknass

Leslie Gnass Gneiss Gauss Geisel Gnurstowicz Gnurch

Leslie Skreek

Leslie Knsklar

Leslie Sklorm

Leslie Krapf

Krafft

Knrunch

Knphillipsheadscrewdrivert

Kneugenic

Knuckl-jensen

things they don't tell you about the biz

THERE ARE LOTS OF TELEVISION SHOWS AND MOVIES ABOUT TELEVISION SHOWS AND MOVIES. Most people feel like they know what it is like to work in Hollywood. America has watched enough Billy Bush to know that Will Smith has a big trailer and the cast of *The Simpsons* are usually not in the same room when they record. Even in suburban Boston, my dad gets *Variety* delivered to his house every week and likes to call me up when a "Network Prexy Gets Axed." But take it from me, no one knows the biz like I know the biz. I love the biz. Hollywood is a crazy biz and I know the biz cuz the biz iz in my blood. Some say I am a biz whiz. Either way, show bizness is my business, so you better get busy with the bizness I know. Here are some inside thoughts and feelings from my years on set. I have had the privilege and the pleasure of wearing many hats, and because of that, my head is sweaty with all the knowledge I have about the biz. I may also have a fancy form of Hollywood lice. Anyway, here is what they won't tell you.

———

THE ACTOR

Acting is the best. When things go well, you get the most credit. If you are in a great film or play everyone just assumes you did it on your own. Your face becomes a symbol for all things good and cool. Athletes nod at you. People interview you and describe in great detail how you "entered a room." Acting lets you escape the real world and make out with people you are not married to. It lets you live in the skin of another person and run away from the person you actually are. Sometimes it heals old wounds and helps you discover something new about yourself. At its best, it's a true form of communication, and your performance changes lives and minds and gender roles and the core temperature of Mother Earth. But here's what no one in the biz will tell you. When you're the actor, you have little control. You audition for parts and deal with constant rejection. On set, everyone sits behind a monitor and whispers when you don't get it right. Your attractive yet interesting face better be shine-free and symmetrical as you try to remember your lines and blocking. Also, acting is embarrassing. I know this because Ted Danson told me. I was shooting a Beastie Boys music video with him and I spent an hour or so talking to Ted and his gently divine wife, Mary Steenburgen. The rest of the day was spent mentally high-fiving my teenage self for getting to talk to Sam Malone and the late, great MCA. Om mani padme hum MCA. (With the power of Buddha's compassion, may you be reborn swiftly into heaven's realm.) The scene required us to all pretend we were scared of the Beastie Boys as they crashed through the window, and one by one we mugged into the lens as the camera rolled. Ted leaned over to me and said, "Acting is so embarrassing, isn't it?" I knew what he meant. It ain't easy to get up in front of people and really go for it. Good actors make acting look easy, which means most people think they can do it. Most people can't. I tell this story because I want to be honest about the biz. I also tell this story because I am an actor and actors are allowed to take up everyone's time and tell long stories while other people stand around quietly fuming. Especially the writer.

THE WRITER

Writing is the best. The writer has the real power. You can create something and the world will be forever indebted to and dependent on you. You feel like the smartest person around, especially next to all those stupid actors. People quote your own lines back to you like a rock star. You invent stories and characters that will live on long after you are dead. When you are a writer you can work from home, live anywhere, and not have to lift things. The writer gets to decide who says what when and which way. But here's what no one in the biz will tell you. Writing can be thankless. People treat writing like it's some elegant act but it's usually lonely and isolating. You will struggle over a piece of writing and then get to set and some dumb actor will say it wrong or immediately want to change it. A writer needs to defend their words every day on set, especially since most of the people on set don't give a shit who the writer is. Except for one person. The head honcho. The director.

THE DIRECTOR

Directing rules. You answer questions and save the day. Everyone needs a captain, and a good director knows how to steady the ship. You can cast your friends and hold auditions while wearing comfortable shoes. Every department needs you in different ways. You get to wear headphones and drink coffee while you share dirty jokes with Eddie from props. You also get to talk to actors like you're their parent, coach, and lover. A good director knows how to clean up messes. They decide when the day is done and whether or not we "got it." Sometimes they get to have sex with an actor or actress, or at least their assistant. Directing is the most powerful job on any set. But here's what no one in the biz will tell you. Directing is a headache. You have to think of everything all the time. It's your fault if a stunt goes wrong. Directors are left cleaning up after the party, sitting around and editing the goddamn thing after everyone else has moved on. Actors can blame a director for not pulling a great performance out of them, but a director can only blame themselves if they cast the wrong actor. Most times the director is a gun for hire, uniquely beholden to one woman or man: the producer.

THE PRODUCER

Producing is the goal. Producing is the Shit. Producing is when you get to actually be in charge and apply all the things you know. The producer is above the fray. You get to visit the set, in your own expensive clothes, and then take everyone out to dinner. Then you don't have to visit again until the one hundredth episode, when you hold that knife and cut that cake. The producer creates, orchestrates, and, most importantly, makes that paper. Being a producer means you have the most connections and you have done your time in the trenches. It is the difference between staff sergeant and lieutenant general. But here is what they don't tell you. Producing is exhausting. If you are any good you have many projects going on at once and they are each on the verge of falling apart. You are the only one who knows how dangerously close all of them are to immolating, but you have to spend time on the phone making actors and writers and directors feel better. You have to hear every single one of those jerks tell you how they want to "make something really special." You are the only one who might lose money. You aren't as young and cute as the actor, and you have only met the writer once, so it's the director you depend on. And you didn't even want this stupid director in the first place, but he directed *Dog President* and it made a hundred mil domestic so the studio made a big push for him. Either way, the biz is amazing and Hollywood will live forever.

SOMETIMES I

WO

RRY

THAT NOT ENOUGH
PEOPLE HATE ME.

time travel

MY THOUGHTS ON TIME TRAVEL ARE SIMPLE: IT EXISTS AND WE ARE IN CONTROL OF IT. I am no scientist. I barely made it through my relatively easy college class entitled "Physics for the Curious." Our final was a multiple-choice test and the answers spelled out "Physics for the Curious." I didn't notice the pattern and got a C. Turns out I just wasn't curious enough.

The only thing we can depend on in life is that everything changes. The seasons, our partners, what we want and need. We hold hands with our high school friends and swear to never lose touch, and then we do. We scrape ice off our cars and feel like winter will never end, and it does. We stand in the bathroom and look at our face and say, "Stop getting old, face. I command you!" and it doesn't listen. Change is the only constant. Your ability to navigate and tolerate change and its painful uncomfortableness directly correlates to your happiness and general well-being. See what I

279

just did there? I saved you thousands of dollars on self-help books. If you can surf your life rather than plant your feet, you will be happier. Maybe I should have called this book *Surf Your Life*. The cover could feature a picture of me on a giant wave wearing a wizard hat. I wonder if it's too late. I'll make a call.

So change happens and time passes. If you hate your stupid boring town and can't wait to get outta there and show everybody what a kick-ass break-dancer you are, then this is good news. If you get really good at break dancing and then realize nobody gives a shit about break dancing anymore, this news is bad. Time moves too slow or too fast. But I know a secret. You can control time. You can stop it or stretch it or loop it around. You can travel back and forth by living in the moment and paying attention. Time can be your bitch if you just let go of the "next" and the "before."

I believe you can time-travel three different ways: with people, places, and things.

In the winter of 1997, the Upright Citizens Brigade was asked by *High Times* magazine to be judges at their world-famous Cannabis Cup. This was a high honor. (Perfect pun. You're welcome.) Before we took off for the Netherlands, a *High Times* interviewer sat down with us for a few hours and then realized he had never turned his tape recorder on. Heady days.

So we arrived in cold and wet Amsterdam, ready to sample marijuana from all over the world and finally settle the longstanding debate of whether or not Purple Kush is superior to White Rhino. As soon as we got to the venue people started giving us weed. Bags of it. Pillowcases filled with it. An amount that would have taken any man or woman down. We were much more concerned about rehearsing our sketches. Matt Besser had written out a running order with cues that the lighting technician should follow. We were going over it when we were told that UCB would be opening for Patti Smith. Totally great pairing.

Our show was pretty bad. A supremely stoned audience isn't the best audience for comedy, and our lighting technician lost our cue sheet before we went on. He literally lost it on the walk to the booth. Right before we were introduced he came up and said, "Bad news, guys. I lost that list you made for me." Then he handed us a sleeping bag full of pot. Patti Smith was amazing. She talked about politics and sang like a soldier. She was so cool and interesting. She stomped around and spit onstage. Spitting is disgusting, but when Patti spits it looks like ballet.

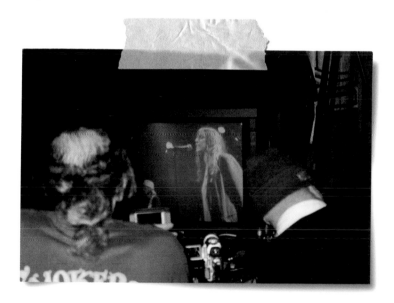

Fun fact: Seth Meyers was in the audience that night. He was living in Amsterdam and performing with a group called Boom Chicago. It would be four more years before we would officially meet and instantly become friends for life. Do you think it's a coincidence that Seth was in the audience again during another seminal night for me? I don't. People help you time-travel. People work around you and next to you and the universe waits for the perfect time to whisper in your ear, "Look this way." There is someone in your life right now who may end up being your enemy, your wife, or your boss. Lift up your head and you may notice.

As I watched Patti perform I took a mental picture of the moment. I looked around and thought about my life. I felt grateful. I noticed every detail. That is the key to time travel. You can only move if you are actually in the moment. You have to be where you are to get where you need to go.

Cut to 2013. I am at a restaurant in Los Angeles and Patti Smith comes out of the bathroom. I freeze and then I say, "Ms. Smith, my name is Amy Poehler and my group opened for you in Amsterdam in the late nineties." She was very nice and polite and pretended to remember. Maybe she did. It didn't matter. She said, "Right, Ann Demeulemeester was there." I nodded my head as if I understood what she was talking about and then I went home and Wikipedia'd Ann Demeulemeester. She is a beautiful fashion designer who lives in Antwerp and is currently doing design inspired by Jackson Pollock. Of course she and Patti are friends.

Patti Smith knew who I was. I shook her hand. Suddenly I was transported back to Amsterdam. Time stretched and bent and I went for a ride. I dare anyone to prove that I didn't.

Places also help you time-travel. My grandfather Steve Milmore was a wonderful man. We called him Gunka and he was a Watertown, Massachusetts, firefighter and served as a machine gunner in World War II. He married my grandmother Helen and went overseas for five years until he came back and put his uniform in the attic and never spoke of his service again. He had three wonderful children, including my wonderful mother. He died of a heart attack on my front porch on July 4, 1982, when he was only sixty-five. I was ten. He was the first important person in my life to die, and when he did, it was the first time I realized that life is not fair or safe or even ours to own. I miss him.

Gunka had a Wurlitzer organ, and he loved to play. His grandchildren would sit on his lap and he would play Bing Crosby or Nat King Cole. Lots of Christmas tunes. He wrote songs for us when we had the chicken pox. He went through his songbook and put numbers over the notes and then made a corresponding chart on cardboard that he laid over the keys so we could play songs ourselves. For a while I thought I was a genius and could totally play the organ. The reality was that I was the luckiest girl in the world because I had a grandfather who was a magic maker.

Sitting on the organ bench was important. Now that I think of it, benches are cool. Sacred by design. Benches are often a place where something special happens and important talks take place. Look at

Forrest Gump. Or *Hoosiers.* Or outside a brunch place. Brunch benches are where it all goes down. After my nana passed away in 2003, my family took Gunka's organ and put it in the basement of the house they shared. And it sat there for ten years, waiting for its chance to travel.

And now it lives in my apartment in New York City. My boys play it all the time. They sit on the same bench I sat on and feel the same good feelings of family and home. One night I was feeling lonely and stressed, and the organ started buzzing. I think Gunka was trying to talk to me. I sat on the bench and felt better. Inside the organ bench is old sheet music with my grandparents' handwriting. I also found a song that I wrote when I was seven. It is a poem that has numbers written above it, so it can be played the special way on my special organ. I wrote it in the past and put it in the sacred bench so I could pull it out at just the right time. Time is just time. Time travel, y'all.

Amy
Have a nice day
4 12 11 10
4 12 11 10
Hope you have a nice
8 6 4 5 67 ——— day

I hope you
arent sad
11 11 10 98
It make me
11 11 10 98 feel
good
To know that your not
3 4 5 dad
5t
So please have
a nice day
66 7 6 5 4
TODAY
10 ———   8

Finally, things can help us time-travel. A few summers ago I was feeling sad. I was in Atlanta and went shopping in a vintage store. I don't love shopping for clothes. I just wish I could wear a daily uniform. As previously noted, I had to look up Ann Demeulemeester on Wikipedia. In the shop, I found an old-timey bathing suit.

I brought the bathing suit home and looked at it. I thought about who might have owned it before. The bathing suit didn't fit into my life at that moment. I was too busy to go swimming. I felt disconnected from my body after having kids. And I was sad. I sat in the moment, looking at that bathing suit. I thought about how long my winter had felt. My brain fooled me into thinking the winter would never end. I closed my eyes and thought of what my life would look like when it did finally end—what six months from now might feel like. I put this bathing suit in a drawer and it waited for me to take it traveling. And then six months later I went to Palm Springs with a bunch of wonderful women. They were my beautiful friends who had helped me through a difficult year. We were going swimming and I reached into my bag to find a bathing suit. I had put this old-timey bathing suit in with the rest. I tried it on again and I felt beautiful. I thanked the bathing suit for waiting for me. I got into the pool with Rashida and Kathryn and Aubrey and thanked the women for holding me up when I couldn't hold myself. I thought about the woman who had worn that bathing suit before and realized she was another woman who had helped me. I thanked her too. I realized I had traveled again, this time into a happier future. I stood in the sun. I thanked the sun.

The more I time-travel the more I learn I am always just where I need to be.

obligatory drug stories,

or lessons i learned on mushrooms

GROWING UP, MY HOMETOWN WAS A DRINKING TOWN. We all sneaked into our parents' liquor cabinets at an early age and spiked our hot chocolate for our high school football games. Alcohol was accessible and drinking was slightly encouraged. Every family had a funny Polaroid of their five-year-old kid holding a beer. My parents weren't heavy drinkers, but they imbibed. I have fond memories of being ten and handing my dad Budweisers as he played slow-pitch softball. Summer sunsets were spent on a dusty field, as these men swung hard and spit in the dust and put us on their shoulders. It was a parade of mustaches and farmer tans. It was later that I realized those men were only in their early thirties and already married with children—a collection of young dads in their prime. My mother had her wine, which she didn't drink much of when we were young but now that she is sixty-seven and retired she allows herself a glass or three. I loved playing bartender behind the big bar we had in our finished basement. It was next to our giant record-player console and our faux-leather couch and shiny floral wallpaper. The wall-to-wall carpeting went all the way up the two concrete poles that supported the house. I spent hours down there pretending I was Michael Jackson or dancing as the Weather Girls told me it was "raining men." That basement was like my personal Copacabana, and when it was filled with my parents' friends I would sit on the stairs and listen to the clink of their glasses and their bursts of laughter. I would make an excuse to pad down in my Kristy McNichol nightgown and pretend I'd had a bad dream, all in an attempt to peep at the women with their shiny brown lipstick and the men packing their cigarettes against their hips.

Then there were the bad parts. Too many kids in our town died from drinking and driving. At least once a year there was a horribly sad funeral. Flowers would appear, tied up against some pole. Paper cups would spell out WE MISS YOU, KATIE in a chain-link fence at the entrance to our high school. I shudder to think of all the times I got into a car with someone who was wasted. Once I was with my best friend, Keri, and we were in the backseat of some ridiculous car, like an I-RAK or a Z-40 or a MIATI22 (I don't care about cars). Keri had a crush on the driver and he had brought his friend along. We were headed to Revere Beach to drive around and do nothing. The boy was a little drunk and driving really fast, and I was screaming at him to slow down. I was so angry. I kept thinking, "I can't believe I am going to die in this cheesy car with these two assholes with spray tans and names I don't even know."

I am ashamed of the few times I drove drunk. Drinking and driving is the absolute worst, because unlike doing coke in your basement while you teach yourself guitar, you could kill someone else. I think about the few times I drove drunk and I picture all of the beautiful families I passed in my car whose lives I could have taken. Please don't drive drunk, okay? Seriously. It's so fucked up. But by all means, walk drunk. That looks hilarious. Everyone loves to watch someone act like they are trying to make it to safety during a hurricane.

My town was good at supporting future drinking problems. Our parties consisted of kegs in the woods. The boys wore "drinking gloves" and we played quarters with cups of beer. Wine coolers made their debut just around this time, and the sugary concoctions made it easier for teenage girls to get drunk. Being young means you have no sense of your own limits, so we would all drink like it was our last night on earth. But even back then I fantasized about what it would be like to drink socially, like Sue Ellen on *Dallas*. I would pour grape juice into wineglasses and sit in our "fancy" dining room arguing with myself. This was the beginning of a long life of attempting to be much older than I was. I was on a search for the perfect amount of ennui. I would babysit while I watched *Thirtysomething*, clucking out loud when the characters were failing to communicate. I was sixteen. Why did I care if Hope and Michael had another baby?

I've tried most drugs but avoided the BIG BAD ONES. Meth never squirmed its way into my life, thank god. It is so evil and horrifying, but I am not going to pretend that I am not fascinated by the idea of staying up for days on end painting my basement. When I was twenty-five and living in Chicago, the building supers were two very polite and meticulous meth heads. Matt and I lived above them and listened to them constantly washing their floors. They also loved to vacuum. They often spent the night rearranging furniture and wiping down surfaces. More than once I woke to the sound of them sweeping the porch steps, moving the same pile of dirt around and around. They were tough to talk to, almost impossible to understand and make eye contact with, but I had a strange affection for their ability to channel their meth-taking into real apartment improvements. The problems began once they started knocking on our door claiming our sink was leaking. Then they would spend the whole day taking the sink apart. Then they would ask for twenty bucks to go find a special sink part and disappear for a week. Then one of them died. So all in all, meth seemed too risky.

Heroin was another drug that didn't catch my tail. I lived in New York's East Village in 1998, when heroin was making its forty-fifth comeback. The streets were filled with suburban junkies shooting up next to their pit bull puppies. My building was across from Tompkins Square Park, which had been suffering and/or improving due to gentrification, and the apartments were filled with a lot of musicians and models living alone in New York City for the first time. Most of the models took a real liking to me. Tall women are attracted to my littleness. I have a lot of tall female friends. They like how I am always looking up to them and I like having the option to jump into their pocket if I want to hide. One model, a Midwestern beauty I will call Hannah, met me at the mailboxes and told me she liked my sneakers. Not long after she confessed she was having an affair with a very famous professional basketball player and asked if I would like to go to a game with her. She wouldn't tell me his name, but she mentioned he was "the one you know." We sat courtside as the team warmed up, and this player made eye contact with us and nodded approvingly. "He likes when I bring girls to the game," she said. I didn't know exactly what that meant, but I did know that if that gentleman had put his penis inside me I surely would have died. I couldn't stop thinking about his giant penis, and every time I looked at tall Hannah I pictured the two of them having sex. A giant pale oak tree getting penetrated by a dark taller oak tree, their size-fifty feet rubbing up against each other on some special bed built to hold their enormous bodies. The player would come visit her at night while his driver waited outside, black SUV idling. Hannah lived above me, and I would picture them fucking and eventually breaking through the floor and crashing through my ceiling, killing us all with one giant official NBA penis. The fear of this encouraged me to move to a new apartment. That and the one freezing morning I had to step over a passed-out model who had nodded off while filling out a W-2 form, only to open the outside door to find a giant pile of human shit. I said good-bye to the East Village and moved over to the West Village, where we don't have those kinds of problems. In the West Village we just have tweaked-out gay hustlers who hit us over the heads with rocks, thank you very much.

I also didn't try heroin because I was told that everyone threw up the first time they did it, and I was never at a party where I felt like throwing up. When given the option to throw up or not throw up, I usually choose the latter. That being said, I am pretty good at making myself throw up, which I tried in high school when I watched my bulimic friends do it. I was lucky that habit didn't stick. Our school was riddled with beautiful girls who thought they were fat and ugly. Anorexic girls who cut peanut M&M's in half and climbed the stairs during lunch. Sometimes I think about those skinny girls and their rapid and hungry hearts and I just want to put my hands on their chests and cry chocolate tears that they can lick and swallow.

What else? I have never tried antidepressants. I probably should have after my first kid, when my postpartum blues felt deeper than I could handle. At the time I thought I was just tired and sad, and I remember the flat defeat I felt when my doctor suggested I "put on a dress and take in a Broadway show." I climbed out of that dark place, but rubbing shoulders with that depression made me keenly aware of the difference between being depressed and being DEPRESSED. Anxiety and depression are cousins and I have had a few panic attacks in my adult life that knocked me off my game. The best way I can explain a panic attack is that it's the feeling of someone inside my body stacking it with books. The books continue to pile up and they make me feel like I can't breathe. Meditation helps a lot. Sex does too. Calling someone equally as anxious on the phone makes you feel less alone. Sometimes the best thing to hear is not "Don't worry, it's going to be okay" but actually "Tell me about it! The whole world is going to explode and I haven't slept for weeks. Now let me tell you about my specific fears of small boats and big business!" As I have gotten older, my social anxiety has worsened. I am not great in a crowd. I don't see a lot of rock shows because sometimes I am afraid I won't get out. I used to squeeze my little self into the scrum and jump around and cause tiny trouble. Now I just want to sit down and have someone perform my five favorite songs while I eat a light dinner and receive a simultaneous pedicure. Is there some kind of awesome indie/alt/hip-hop/electronica music tour that can do that?

In my twenties I tried cocaine, which I instantly loved but eventually hated. Cocaine is terrific if you want to hang out with people you don't know very well and play Ping-Pong all night. It's bad for almost everything else. If you're wondering who is on coke it's probably the last people left at the bar talking loudly about their strained relationships with their dads while the bartender closes up and puts stools on the tables. The day after cocaine is rough. Same with ecstasy. I remember a wonderful UCB New Year's Eve party where we all danced and drank water and loved each other. I also remember the next day when I thought I had no friends and I was so sad I wanted to sink into the carpet and permanently live there. The next day is the thing I can't pull off anymore. How do you explain to a four- and six-year-old that you can't play Rescue Bots because you have to spend all day in bed eating Cape Cod potato chips and watching *The Bicycle Thief*?

We didn't take a lot of pills in my day, which was lucky. Those suckers are heart-stoppers. It's scary today to see all those downers find their way into young people's hands. Teenage bodies should be filled with Vonnegut and meatball subs, not opiates that create glassy-eyed party monsters. But the pills aren't just for teens. There are lots of middle-aged ladies who are thin and cranky hanging on to their slurring husbands who can't make a fist. It's all kind of a mess, isn't it?

But weed doesn't seem as bad.

I know there are people who get addicted to marijuana. I don't want my kids to smoke it. I plan on lying to my children about most of my drug use. I had a friend who told her adolescent son he was allergic to pot, and if he tried it he would break out into hives. This lasted for a while until one of his friends gently suggested maybe she had made that fact up. His whole world was blown. He came to her asking, "Did you make that up? How could you?" and she said, "Of course I did. Let me make you a BLT." I think this is a terrific idea. I think we don't lie to our children enough. We also don't bribe them enough. It's a wonderful day when your child gets old enough to be bribed. It's a whole new tool in your arsenal. I plan on telling my children I had a few drinks and a few joints but the whole thing just seemed like "it wasn't for me." Then I am going to hire private investigators to test their urine. It's not like they are going to read this book anytime soon. What's more boring than your own mother's take on her own life? Yawn. Also, I am counting on everyone living on the moon by the time my children are teenagers, and that they'll have really interesting space friends who are kind and good students and think drugs are lame and "totally, like, Earthish."

293

The first time I smelled pot was when I was a teenager and at a Bryan Adams concert. I thought to myself, "Hmm, that smells like my dad's car." I am aware that some of you may be wondering what I was doing at a Bryan Adams concert. Um, try rocking out and buying neon T-shirts, dude. Anyway, I went home and searched all of my father's pockets and drawers until I found some weed. The revelation that my dad was a pot smoker wasn't too shocking. He was always friendly and happy. He loved getting to places early to pick us up and sitting in his car, and he was always first to suggest we get ice cream in the middle of the day. I had some friends with alcoholic parents, and my memories of those houses always involved people being scared, afraid of what mood was around the corner. I never worried about my father and how he would act around my friends. He was generous and nice and didn't yell. He sort of whacked me once when I was being a straight-up biiiitch about wanting to wear my mom's coat. He surprised himself and I burst out crying and he apologized long into the night. I milked it for as long as I could, but I knew even at fifteen that he was under a lot of pressure and I was being a spoiled brat.

High school and college came and went and I smoked pot very rarely. Then I arrived in Chicago and lived the life of a stoner for a year. I would smoke in the morning and listen to Bob Marley. I would wear headphones and buy records and comic books. I would make mac and cheese while watching *Deep Space Nine*. I am not one of those people who smokes weed and suddenly has a burst of creativity. I am one of those people who smokes weed and spends an hour lightening my eyebrows. It slowed me down and helped with my Irish stomach and anxiety and the constant channel-changing that happened in my head. I can't perform, drive, or write stoned, and therefore I smoke pot a lot less than I used to. Gone are the days when I could walk to 7-Eleven and play the game of "buy the weirdest two things."

To sum up:

- Drugs suck. They ruin people's lives. They kill people too early. They destroy hopes and dreams and tear families apart.
- Drugs help. They pull people from despair. They balance our moods and minds and keep us from freaking out on airplanes.
- Drugs are fun. They expand our horizons. They create great memories and make folding our laundry bearable.

Addendum:

LESSONS I LEARNED ON MUSHROOMS

GOOD THINGS	BAD THINGS
1. Everyone needs love.	1. Your face will get old.
2. Never hurt a living thing.	2. We are all alone.
3. Don't worry about the choices you make because everything will be fun because life is a closet filled with pool toys.	3. Sometimes benches move.
4. Neil Young can read your mind.	4. Neil Young can read your mind.

STRANGERS SHOULD
BE A LITTLE

STRA

NGE.

I DON'T KNOW YOU, FOOL.

my boys

I AM A MOON JUNKIE. Every time I look at the moon, I feel less alone and less afraid. I tell my boys that moonlight is a magic blanket and the stars above us are campfires set by friendly aliens. I track lunar cycles on my iPhone and take my kids outside at night when a moon is new or full or blue. We call this "moon hunting" and we bring flashlights and moon candy along. The moon candy looks suspiciously like M&M's, but so far neither of my sons has noticed.

On moon-hunting nights, I give them a bath and rub both of my boys down with Aveeno lotion and comb their hair. I spread Aquaphor on my lips and try to kiss them. Sometimes I chase them around until I catch one and throw him on the bed like a bag of laundry. Most times I am too tired. Then we head outside. We wear pajamas, because going outside at night in your pajamas feels like breaking out of jail. I watch their little fat feet and their shiny cheeks as they jump into the backseat of the car. These boys, they

299

are delicious. I swear, if I could eat my children, I would. I'd consume them like some beast in a Hieronymus Bosch painting, but in a friendlier, more momlike way. Their little bodies make me salivate. It takes everything I have not to swallow them whole.

During one full moon, I announced my plans to drive to an open field and have us climb into our sleeping bags and howl at the night sky. As we drove to my preplanned spot, my boys once again reminded me to stay in the moment and stop overthinking. They kept pointing to the huge moon, shouting, "Mama, it's right there. We don't have to drive to the moon! It came to us!" We pulled over just a few blocks from our Los Angeles home and abandoned my previous plan. I spread out a blanket and we snuggled together, our bodies on the warm hood of the car. The car hood was slippery so we used our bare feet for traction. We all made wishes. I wished that my children would be kind and happy and I would wake up with a flatter stomach. Archie wished that "everyone in the world was a robot." Abel wished for "more Legos." They are boys, my boys. My Archie boy. My baby Abel.

My boy Archie has eyes the color of blueberries. He has a solid sense of design and is only months away from his first cartwheel. When he was just two weeks old, his dad and I took a picture of him in his crib with the *New York Times* draped over him like a blanket. The headline read OBAMA: RACIAL BARRIER FALLS IN DECISIVE VICTORY. He loves to run and strongly identifies with Luke Skywalker because they "have the same hair." He recently told me, "Mama, do you want to know something funny about me? I am afraid of little things and not afraid of big things." I think he was talking about bugs and elephants, but I understood what he meant in a very deep way. He deals primarily in poop and fart jokes, and insists these things will never fail to make him laugh. He is absolutely right. He is delighted when I laugh at him, but he is no ham. He is sensitive and stubborn, and as of this printing would like to be a police officer and a veterinarian and also Iron Man. He once asked me, "Are you sad that you don't have a penis?" I told him that I was happy with the parts that I had. I then reminded him that girls have vaginas and everyone is different and each body is like a snowflake. He nodded in agreement and then looked up at me with a serious face and asked, "But did you once have a penis and break it?" I was tempted to make a joke that would screw him up for life. "Yes, my son. Your mother once had a penis but it broke because you didn't love her enough." The bond between mothers and sons is powerful stuff. I firmly believe that every boy needs his mom to love him and every girl needs her dad to pay attention to her. Archie needed to figure out if I had ever owned and operated a penis. I get it. His penis is important to him. Anyway, he starts college next year. Just kidding, he's six. He recently asked if he could marry me and I said yes. I couldn't help it. I would marry him anytime.

My boy Abel has eyes the color of a pine forest. He is a red monkey who named himself. I went to a psychic before he was born and she told me I was having "another big boy. He wants to be called Abel." We agreed. As he was born, the song "Young Turks" played on the radio and Rod Stewart sang, "Young hearts be free tonight / Time is on your side." Abel has chocolate chip freckles and hair like a copper penny. He loves to dance and sing and recently composed a song called "I'm a Genius." He is a big hugger. He doesn't mind when I stick my head into his neck and smell him. He smells like a love cookie. He recently told me he "really like[s] it when girls wear nice blouses." He has a deep laugh and thinks Darth Vader is funny. He cries big tears and sweats in his sleep. He makes friends on airplanes. He is four. The first thing he does when he wakes up in the morning is look for Archie. He loves his big brother so intensely. His big brother protects him and tortures him. Abel feels like the wisest and oldest member of our family. When he was just starting to talk he used to ask me if I was happy. He has dreams that he is a different little boy with black hair and one eye. My beautiful Tibetan nanny, Dawa, believes he has been reincarnated many times.

When I was pregnant with Abel, Archie and I used to take naps together. We spent part of that summer in Nantucket and every afternoon we would snuggle together as the breeze blew in. I was holding one baby on the inside and one on the outside. I count those naps as some of the happiest times in my life. I imagined a peaceful and quiet life with my two boys. I pictured kissing their heads as they obediently put themselves to bed, as in a John Irving novel. I was so stupid. Everything is loud now. My guys need to touch each other all the time. They wrestle and bump and yank. They play like lion cubs, rolling around until one of them decides to bite. They jump off couches and buzz around on scooters. They swing sticks and tell people "food goes into your stomach and turns into poop." They love dinosaurs and superheroes and sounding like both. Everything is physical and visual and feelings are expressed by karate kicks.

I love my boys so much I fear my heart will explode. I wonder if this love will crack open my chest and split me in half. It is scary, this love.

I should point out here that I have a picture of them wearing underwear on their heads while simultaneously pooping. Archie is on the toilet and Abel is on a potty and they are facing each other and smiling like crazy people. I plan on using it for blackmail when they are teenagers and won't let me hug them in public anymore.

When your children arrive, the best you can hope for is that they break open everything about you. Your mind floods with oxygen. Your heart becomes a room with wide-open windows. You laugh hard every day. You think about the future and read about global warming. You realize how nice it feels to care about someone else more than yourself. And gradually, through this heart-heavy openness and these fresh eyes, you start to see the world a little more. Maybe you start to care a teeny tiny bit more about what happens to everyone in it. Then, if you're lucky, you meet someone who gently gestures for you to follow her down a path that allows you to feel a little less gross about how many advantages you've had in life. I was lucky. I met Jane.

Dr. Jane Aronson and I were at a fancy party thrown by *Glamour* magazine when we fell in love. We were both being given a *Glamour* Women of the Year Award. This type of award is really nice to win and also slightly embarrassing. It's hard to be surrounded by women who stood up against a totalitarian regime and talk to them about my experiences writing sketches where a girl farts a lot. Before the party, I Googled Dr. Jane and read all about her great work transforming the lives of orphaned children all over the world. As I sat in my seat and stared at Rihanna's gorgeous extraterrestrial face, I flipped through that evening's program and learned that Jane had founded the Worldwide Orphans Foundation, which addresses the medical, social, and educational needs of children living in orphanages in over eleven countries. But it wasn't until I heard Jane speak that the abstract idea of her work became real. She spoke plainly and openly about how every child in the world deserves the basic things in life: food, clothes, safety, shelter, and love. She was joined onstage by many orphans whose lives she had changed. She cried. I cried. We all cried. Then Bill Clinton introduced Maya Angelou and I thought to myself, "What the fuck am I doing here?"

After the event there was a loud party filled with famous people. This is going to sound like a real douche-bag thing to say, but I have been to a lot of parties with famous people and they aren't that great. Famous people are never as interesting as your friends. Parties with lots of famous people are usually crowded. I tend to feel plain and over- or underdressed. I get nervous. I don't like crowds because I am small and fear being trampled. My ideal night out is a dinner party in my backyard with a group of like-minded friends whom I boss around in a gentle and loving way.

Jane is bossy and socially uncomfortable in just the same way, and so naturally we started talking. Let me take a minute to say that I love bossy women. Some people hate the word, and I understand how "bossy" can seem like a shitty way to describe a woman with a determined point of view, but for me, a bossy woman is someone to search out and celebrate. A bossy woman is someone who cares and commits and is a natural leader. Also, even though I'm bossy, I like being told what to do by people who are smarter and more interesting than me. Jane asked me to host her next event. She spoke about her travels all over the world. I told her I would love to do that someday and she said, "Okay, then. We will." I hosted an event for her that next year and we became friends. Then she took me to Haiti a year after, as she'd promised.

At the end of 2012, I was in the middle of separating from my husband and preparing to host the Golden Globes for the first time. I felt completely sorry for myself while simultaneously believing I was hot shit. I spent a melancholy but sweet New Year's Eve with my wonderful friends Jon and Jen and Meredith and Tom and Rachel and Marco. We went to see *Sleep No More,* an epic NYC masquerade ball. I watched a beautiful dance piece as the clock struck midnight and was mesmerized by a young dancer who looked like Natalie Portman. At one point she touched my shoulder and I wondered if I should have sex with girls for a while. I was all over the place. My life was an open suitcase and my clothes were strewn all over the street. I was happy to be wearing a mask that night because I didn't have any idea who I was. Great things were happening in my career and my personal life had exploded. I was trapped in an awful spiral of insecure narcissism. I was nervous and excited to go to Haiti with Jane, if only for a change of scenery. When relationships end, it's hard at first to stay in a setting you used to share. No one wants to be the cat scratching at the door that won't open. And so, I boarded a plane bound for Haiti on New Year's Day 2013.

I was traveling with Jane and her colleague Noah Gonzalez, along with a few others. When asked if this was anyone's first visit to a third-world country, a fourteen-year-old girl named Grace and I raised our hands. I made note of this. On the flight, Jane spoke casually about Haiti and its challenges. It was a country filled with young people. Sixty-five percent of the country was under twenty years old and many Haitians died from diseases like hypertension and asthma. There are over 700 orphanages in Haiti. There are over 430,000 orphans. On top of all of that, the earthquake. A country with a battered and bruised infrastructure had just suffered a devastating earthquake. It sounded like there was so much to fix. It sounded overwhelming. I sat on the plane and listened to music.

I wondered if I was just doing this as some kind of ego trip. Then I decided I didn't care. Not enough is made of the fact that being of service makes you feel good. I think nonprofits should guarantee that giving your time and money makes your skin better and your ass smaller. Why not? There are so many people in the world with so little. Who cares why you decide to help?

We navigated the busy Port-au-Prince airport, and I felt very white and very tired. I felt like I was in a movie where the divorcée tries to turn her life around. I felt like a cliché, and I was angry that my head was filled with what felt like such self-indulgent bullshit. We met our driver, a young and handsome Haitian man. I thought about trying to have sex with him but did the math and figured the rest of the week would be too awkward once he had gently turned me down. Then I fantasized about him changing his mind and knocking on my door late at night. Then I realized I was in Haiti and was not paying attention. He leaned over, smiled, and said, "Welcome to Haiti. You might love it or you might hate it, but you will never forget it." I decided I would have sex with him if he so desired.

My first impression was of total chaos. The streets of Port-au-Prince were filled with dust and trash and babies. There was so much to look at. Everyone was busy carrying something. A man had a tray of hamburgers on his head. Women were trucking their laundry through the streets as young children pulled heavy pots of water. The roads were twisted and full of debris. It looked like someone had picked up Haiti, held it upside down, and shaken it. It felt unmoored. I understood the feeling. Now, don't get me wrong, I am not some crazy white girl who is comparing her divorce to the problems of the Haitian people. All I am saying is it felt totally chaotic and therefore familiar to my brain. We passed groups of handsome young boys hanging out on dirt bikes. I thought of the Sinéad O'Connor song "Black Boys on Mopeds." Then I thought of Sinéad O'Connor ripping up the picture of the pope. Then I thought about writing jokes for famous people. Then

I wondered if I should ask the Haitian driver to be my date at the Golden Globes. Then I snapped back to the present and remembered where I was.

Style is obviously important in Haiti. A lot of people wore bright colors and neatly pressed shirts. The taxis and billboards were beautiful. Haiti is not afraid of color. And texture. And depth. The young people looked fierce and bored. They looked like pure energy. There was a true aesthetic but also a palpable darkness. I mean, let's get real. Kids are slaves there. Kids are bought and sold and put to work. I saw Haitian boys with bodies the same sizes as Archie's and Abel's carrying huge jugs of water. In just a few minutes you could tell which kids had parents and which were on their own. I kept trying to connect the small children and the adults they were walking next to. I was looking for comfort. I was uncomfortable. You know that horrible feeling when you lose your kid for a minute in a mall and your heart pounds and your ears fill with blood? It was that feeling. When I drove the streets of Haiti it felt like many of the children I saw were lost and no one was looking for them. I kept peeking at Jane to see if she saw what I saw, but she was only concerned with what was ahead.

We visited one of WWO's toy libraries. They are rooms filled with donated toys that are organized according to developmental stage. All the toys were beautifully kept and displayed, and the room smelled like vinegar. We all sat in a circle and sang "Twinkle, Twinkle, Little Star." I held an adorable little girl and kept instinctually looking to hand her off to her mother, until I realized she didn't have one.

We drove up to Kenscoff, which is a mountainous and much greener part of Haiti. It reminded me of Haiti's rich and fancy cousin, the Dominican Republic, and how places so close could also be so far apart. We hiked up a hillside and I felt old. I sent e-mails to my assistant about the Golden Globes with subject headings like "Yes to the Fake Teeth." We arrived at an open field filled with young Haitian WWO volunteers. They wore matching shirts and led the kids in what looked like improv games. They sang and danced as each kid was encouraged to commit to looking ridiculous. Some of the boys were playing soccer, and Jane tied her long-sleeved shirt around her waist and joined them. I realized there was no getting out of physical activity, so I sashayed over to the small amplifier and started to DJ. A dance party broke out. The kids laughed at me at first until they realized I am a world-class dancer with moves of steel. I was exhausted in ten minutes. Some other children were painting bricks. I imagine the bricks were going to be used for something, but no one told me what. Most of these children were used to living in the moment. Thinking about the future was a luxury. They took turns with their paintbrushes. There was no crying about sharing. There was no pushing or saying they were bored. Everyone was used to waiting.

I met girls with names like Jenica and Suzenie. When I said their names out loud it felt like I had jewels in my mouth. One girl told me her nickname was Sexy. She couldn't have been twelve, and I worried about who had given her that name. A weird sandstorm kicked up and the dust swirled like a magic trick. We all paused together to watch, and I took a mental picture and time-traveled to the future. I thought about my boys being teenagers and playing soccer and dancing and sharing.

In Kenscoff we ate dinner and heard stories from WWO supervisors. Melissa was a soft-spoken blonde who knew perfect Creole and worked in West Africa with the Peace Corps. Her funny partner, Wendy, came from Michigan by way of Uganda and Kenya.

Wendy spoke with what I would call a "world accent," and she and Melissa told the story of meeting during the Haitian earthquake. Falling in love among the aftershocks . . . it sounded so romantic, and I wondered if Anderson Cooper had ever fallen in love during an earthquake. Then, for the hundredth time that week, I wished I were a lesbian. Melissa and Wendy told us a story about a woman in Haiti who used to dress up like a nun and collect donations for her "orphanage." She was not a sister of God, and the place she ran sounded like a jail. Melissa cozied up to her until she was finally allowed access inside. The children there were malnourished and dying. Some had rat bites. Girls were being sold into prostitution. WWO brought in toys and youth volunteers. They surreptitiously counted the children as they sang songs with them. They estimated there were at least sixty-five kids in danger in that horrible place. Melissa and Wendy spoke to anyone who listened about the terrible conditions, until the police and UNICEF intervened. The woman threatened them with voodoo, which is no joke in Haiti. Wendy and Melissa scrambled to find placement for all the kids, and on the day they were taken out of that nightmare there were WWO workers waiting in a line so each child had a lap to sit on. That evil woman went to jail. In just one month after he was rescued from her care, one little guy named Shashu went from being a nonverbal boy with a distended belly to being a butterball who loved to sing.

People are very bad and very good.

A little love goes a long way.

The hardest day in Haiti for me was when we visited a few orphanages. Some of these places were doing the best they could. Others had a long way to go. Jane's colleague Noah and I saw babies living in cribs that looked like cages. A little boy named Woosley jumped into Noah's arms and wouldn't let go. He was desperate for attachment, and men were especially scarce. Woosley held on to Noah like a bramble. We were filled with anxiety because we knew we would have to say good-bye. Noah had to drop him back off at his crowded room, and Woosley hung on and started to get upset. He finally got down and faced a corner as he cried. It was the loneliest thing I have ever seen. A teacher went to him, but it barely comforted him.

Those kids needed so much holding. Kisses and hugs and clothes and parents. They needed everything. The enormity of what they needed was so intense. We ended up talking in the street with Jane, and crying. Jane was agitated and passionate. She talked about all the work left to do and all the small changes that can improve children's lives. I was once again moved by her ability to steer into the curve. Jane was a big-wave rider. She didn't make the mistake that most of us make, which is to close our eyes and hope the waves will go away or miss us or hit someone else. She dove in, headfirst. That night, I read the deeply calm and at times sneakily funny Pema Chödrön, one of my favorite writers: "There are no promises. Look deeply at joy and sorrow, at laughing and crying, at hoping and fearing, at all that lives and dies. What truly heals is gratitude and tenderness." Pema reminded me to practice *tonglen,* which is this meditation breathing exercise where you breathe in all the pain and breathe out nothing but love. It felt like the opposite of what I had been doing for a year. I felt one tiny molecule in the bottom of my heart feel better. I heard dogs fucking outside my window and wondered if I should try to find my Haitian driver. I e-mailed Tina about her Mandy Patinkin bit.

On our last night we went to the Hotel Montana, which had started rebuilding after the earthquake. One of the owners, Gerthe, spoke of how she had survived and her sister Nadine had been pulled out of the rubble. I later read in the *Washington Post* that her sister was trapped for days and found by a beagle that caught her scent. The rescuers brought over her son, who called to her and said, "I think that is my mother down there." She was pulled out days later. In the same article, Gerthe says that Nadine had been kidnapped in Haiti a few years ago and held for fifteen days. "You have no idea what it takes to survive here," Gerthe said. I knew she had a very good idea.

311

Gerthe also talked about travel. She talked about living in Jamaica. She joked about her husband and her haircut, because she is more than the earthquake. A person's tragedy does not make up their entire life. A story carves deep grooves into our brains each time we tell it. But we aren't one story. We can change our stories. We can write our own. Melissa and Wendy and Jane and I joked about the Golden Globes and gave each other fake awards. I gave Melissa "Best Person in Charge." She gave me "Most Famous and Most Normal." This meant and means a great deal.

Later that night we talked about animals. Wendy shared a story about how her daughter was caught in a stampede of elephants and lived to tell about it because she ran left instead of right. And because she knew one simple fact: elephants leave the way they come in. This reminded me of something I read, that your divorce will be like your marriage. We all agreed that elephants win for coolest animal, and I showed off by reciting my elephant facts. Elephants have long pregnancies and purr like cats to communicate. They cry, pray, and laugh. They grieve. They have greeting ceremonies when one of them has been away for a long time.

I thought of this when I got back to my boys, the elephants and the greeting ceremonies. I told them about how one day we might ride an elephant and they climbed on each other to act it out, switching parts halfway through. I gave them a bath and put lotion on their skin. I realized how lucky my life is. And theirs. I lay in bed and thought about time and pain, and how many different people live under the same big, beautiful moon.

the robots will kill us all:

a conclusion

IN 1997, I PROUDLY DECLARED I WOULD NEVER OWN A CELL PHONE. I was on a New York City street corner and I was young, poor, and knee-deep in free time. A bunch of us were standing around smoking. A cigarette was my cell phone back then, a tiny social unit that helped me fill the day. Suddenly, we noticed Lou Reed walking our way. He strutted toward us like a grouchy mayor in a leather jacket. A Lou Reed sighting was like the first robin in spring; seeing him meant your life was opening up and you finally lived in New York City. He passed by us and we all exhaled. One of my friends took out his cell phone and pretended to call the *National Enquirer*. It was one of those "flip phones," a tiny pocket-sized clamshell that looked like a lady razor or a makeup compact. I held it and felt its weight.

"Nope," I said. "I just don't need it. Cell phones aren't for me. What am I going to do? Carry this thing around all day?"

When I was growing up, the Poehlers were the lower-middle-class family that had high-end gadgets. We had an amazing answering machine. It was as big as a toaster oven and used full-sized cassette tapes. I would come home and see the light blinking, excited that someone had tried to call us even when we weren't around. I would rewind the tape with a giant button and listen to a strange voice asking me to renew my subscription to *Seventeen* magazine. That answering machine was a big deal. We fought over who would leave the outgoing message, each one of us believing that we could find the right mixture of humor and gravitas beneath our excruciating Boston accents. The answering machine was my personal secretary. I would run home after school and change the outgoing message as needed. "Keri, I am going to the mall. Meet me at Brigham's and if you get there first order me a chocolate chip on a sugar cone with jimmies." Sometimes you went somewhere and people didn't show up. There was no way to instantly reach them unless you went to their house or called them on their home telephone number.

MTV arrived not long after. I would spend hours watching this incredibly cool and new station while thinking, "Finally, someone GETS ME." I was ten years old and receiving a crash course in adult life. MTV introduced me to punk music and gay people. I met Michael Jackson and his talent split me in half. I would dance all day in my basement listening to *Off the Wall*. You young people really don't understand how magical Michael Jackson was. No one thought he was strange. No one was laughing. We were all sitting in front of our TVs watching the "Thriller" video every hour on the hour. We were all staring, openmouthed, as he moonwalked for the first time on the Motown twenty-fifth anniversary show. When he floated backward like a funky astronaut, I screamed out loud. There was no rewinding or rewatching. No next-day memes or trends on Twitter or Facebook posts. We would call each other on our dial phones and stretch the cord down the hall, lying on our stomachs and discussing Michael Jackson's moves, George Michael's facial hair, and that scene in *Purple Rain* when Prince fingers Apollonia from behind. Moments came and went, and if you missed them, you were shit out of luck. That's why my parents went to a *M*A*S*H* party and watched the last episode in real time. There was no next-day *M*A*S*H* cast Google hangout. That's why my family all squeezed onto one couch and watched the USA hockey team win the gold against evil Russia! We all wept as my mother pointed out every team member from Boston. (Everyone from Boston likes to point out everyone from Boston. Same with Canadians.) We all chanted "USA!" and screamed "YES!" when Al Michaels asked us if we believed in miracles. Things happened in real time and you watched them together. There was no rewind.

HBO arrived in our house that same year. We had no business subscribing to HBO, with the little money we had, but Bill Poehler did not scrimp when it came to TV. I was a TV kid. There was no limit to how much I could watch. I even ate in front of the TV. (My parents will wince at this, but more than once we ate in the living room with TV trays or at the kitchen table with the kitchen TV on.) If we had the money we probably would have put a TV in every corner of our house. My parents didn't pay much attention to what I was watching because they were too busy working and remortgaging their house. I watched things on HBO that were much too scary and adult for my still-forming sponge brain. Seventies and eighties movies were obsessed with devil kids (*The Omen, The Exorcist*) and rapey revenge (*The Last House on the Left, Death Wish*). There were moments in those films that were just scary and sexy enough

315

to burn into my brain and haunt my subconscious for years. But mostly, HBO was about ADULT CONTENT, and that meant movies about Divorce and Intrigue and Betrayal. I learned how adults communicated from watching movies on HBO. I also learned what made me laugh. I watched every comedy I could find: *Annie Hall, Caddyshack, Fletch,* and *Airplane!* I sat next to the TV and transcribed *The Jerk* in blue composition notebooks. I thought about comedy. I thought about being a writer. Technology was creeping into my life in slow and manageable ways. The Future was Almost Now!

I spent my entire college career without a cell phone or e-mail. I typed my papers on a Brother word processor, which had a window that showed five sentences at a time and had a tendency to go on the fritz and make you lose all your work. I typed papers in my dorm and printed them out in my hallway, because I didn't want to bother my roommate with the loud mechanical noise of the Brother spooling out "Tiny Fists: The Use of Hands in the Early Poems of e. e. cummings." When I moved to Chicago, I used a paper map that folded in your lap to navigate the city. There was no Internet, no e-mail, no texting, no FaceTiming, no GPS-ing, no tweeting, no Facebooking, and no Instagramming. A few people in the late eighties had giant cell phones that lived in tiny suitcases, and I saw some in movies. I became aware of the existence of e-mail and considered checking out this company called America Online, but the film *WarGames* had taught me that the computers could start a nuclear war so I decided to wait and see. In the meantime, I wrote letters and maintained a healthy dose of eye contact. I still carried an address book.

And now? Now my phone sits in my pocket like a pack of cigarettes used to. I am obsessed and addicted and convinced that my phone is trying to kill me. I believe this to be true. By the way, when I say "my phone" I mean my phone and my iPad and my laptop and all technological devices in general. Look, I am glad we have electricity and anesthesia, but I think this Internet thing might be a bad idea. Sorry, guys. So far the only good things I have seen to come out of this recent technological renaissance are video-chatting with your grandparents, online dating, and being able to attend traffic school on your computer. The rest is a disaster. The robots will kill us all. Here's proof:

1. **My phone does not want me to finish this book or do any work in general.**

   After I wrote the first paragraph of this chapter, I checked my phone to see if anyone had e-mailed or texted. Then I Googled "flip phone" and "when did Lou Reed die?" (Rest in peace, Lou Reed.) That eventually led me to watching lovely Laurie Anderson videos and checking out a local place to learn Tai Chi. Then I went to Wikipedia and clicked on "Chinese Medicine." That reminded me of a healer I once met, which reminded me of a massage, which reminded me I needed my hair done, so I texted my hairdresser friend. She sent me a picture of herself from her recent trip and I put a filter on it with a funny caption and sent it back.

   I don't remember doing any of this. I am telling you, my phone wants me dead.

   It wants to sleep next to me and buzz at just the right intervals so I forget to eat or make deadlines.

2. **My phone does not want me to have friends.**

   I'm not on social media. It's just not my thing. There is an amount of self-disclosure and self-promotion involved that keeps me away. (Says the woman writing a book about herself.) But I've learned to never say never. Perhaps in a year there will be some amazing new way to be funny, humble, real, and accidentally sexy all at the same time, with a great filter option and a deep social message attached. I'm guessing it will be called SoulSpill™. Until then, I prefer to stick to group texting with my close friends. I love gathering four or five of the important folks in my life and forcing us to be our own tiny chat room. Remember those? I think if I have established anything in my book, it's that a key element of being my friend is being comfortable with my forced fun. I realize that a phone addict like me talking about how I don't do social media is like a heroin junkie bragging about how they would never touch meth. But I like to do things I am good at, and I am sure that having a bigger online presence would only get me in some shit, especially with my history of texting the wrong things to the wrong people.

Once I was wrapping Christmas gifts with an old assistant. She was a young and lovely girl whom I was thinking of firing. Let's call her Esmerelda (not her name). I texted my husband, Will, and said, "Not now, not today, but eventually we should think about getting rid of Esmerelda." I went back to wrapping my gifts and chitchatting about my upcoming schedule. Later that night, I received a call from Esmerelda. I had sent the text to her instead. I had sent it while we were together and she read it while I was humming Christmas carols right in front of her. She figured we should talk. She was right. I fired her. Then I threw my phone across the room and hid under my bed.

Another time, I spent an afternoon talking to a friend about a recent relationship she had been in. She had gone back and forth with a guy who was acting like an asshole. She had finally ended it and was processing her feelings. She left the room and I texted another friend and wrote, "Thank god they broke up. He is such an asshole." My friend came back into the room and asked why I had just texted her that weird sentence. She was upset that I hadn't even waited five minutes before reaching out to someone else and talking about her. I apologized. I threw my phone into the garbage and tried to run myself over with my car.

I wish I could tell you that those were the only times something like that happened, but it has happened over and over: an e-mail for the wrong eyes, a text to the wrong person, a picture sent with the wrong message underneath. My inability to keep my shit straight made me straighten out my shit. Now, as a rule, I try not to text anything that I wouldn't mind the whole world seeing. I try to use restraint of pen and tongue and thumb. It's a constant struggle. If my phone had its druthers, it would butt-dial my frenemies while I was in therapy.

3. **My phone wants me to feel bad about how I look.**
When I was younger we used to have these things called "parties." They were fun hangouts where young people would get together and talk and maybe dance. During these "parties" we would take pictures with things called "cameras." One week later, we would pick up those pictures from a strange man who lived in a tiny hut in the middle of town. By that time the party had become a distant memory,

something that I had experienced in real time with little regard as to how I looked. I would receive the hard copies of the pictures and throw away the ones I didn't like. No one would see those pictures but me. No one would be allowed to comment on those pictures until I decided to share them. They would be a reminder of a good time but not something that kept me distanced from the experience.

Now my phone lets college admission officers check to see if an applicant ever posed in a bra.

My phone also wants to constantly let me know what other people think of me. It lures me into reading about myself. At first, things seem really nice and great. My phone shows me lovely things the Internet made about my show or my work. But the phone doesn't turn off after I see the good things. It stays on, and in my hand, until I scrape further. Then I find out that some people think I have "a scary face" while other people think I'm "just not funny, period." My phone shows me that I didn't really get a lot of e-mails over the weekend. My phone directs me to news that is gossipy and awful. Which leads me to . . .

4. **My phone wants to show me things I shouldn't see.**
   I read in a book once the three things that shorten your life are smoking, artificial sweetener, and violent images. I believe this to be true. Violent images are not new, but the immediacy with which we see them is faster than ever. During the horrific Boston bombings, I reached out to my family in Watertown and prayed for those injured. I also went to news websites and was met with pictures of a man with his legs blown off. I was not ready for that. Who ever

would be? Certainly not that man, who must now live with the pain and struggle of losing his legs, and also live with the pain and struggle of his image being disseminated in perpetuity. Sure, these sorts of visuals have been around a long time. I saw the R-rated movies on HBO. War photographers documented horrors and published them in magazines and books. But one used to have to go to the library or one's personal book collection to see Nick Ut's photograph of the naked South Vietnamese girl running after being severely burned. That picture was accompanied by text. It had context. It was surrounded by other moving pictures that told a similar story. Now we can look at the grotesque while we wait in line at the bank.

Porn is everywhere. I am a fan of porn. It can be a very nice accompaniment to an evening of self-pleasure. It's as important as a good wine pairing. Lest you think I am using fancy language to avoid revealing intimate porn preferences, please know that I prefer straight porn with occasional threesome scenarios that preferably don't end in facials. I also like men who seem to like women, and women who seem to be on the top of their porn game. I basically like my porn like my comedy, done by professionals. But I am a forty-three-year-old woman, and so I can handle some of the images and feelings that porn conveys. I had a friend whose seven-year-old kid Googled the word "naked" once. The first picture he saw was a woman with asparagus in her vagina and up her butt. That's just too much to handle. How are we going to get him to eat his vegetables now?

The Dalai Lama has said that Hollywood is "very bad for [his] eyes and a waste of time." I understand. Most of what my phone shows me is bad for my eyes. My eyes need a rest, spiritually and literally. My eyes hurt from staring at my phone. But of course they do. My phone wants to kill me.

5. **My phone wants me to love it more than my children.**
Last summer I was sitting next to my youngest son, Abel, on the edge of a swimming pool. He slipped and went under. I jumped in and pulled him out right away. We were both a little scared but thankfully everyone was fine. My phone had been in my back pocket, and my first thought was total triumph that I had chosen my child over my phone. My second thought was complete devastation that my phone had been submerged. I couldn't Google what to do with a wet phone because my phone was wet, and so I quickly ripped it open and started to dry it with a hair dryer. I used my laptop to get on the Internet, where most sites told me to shove my wet phone in a bag of rice. I had just pulled my little guy out of a pool and I was sweating in my kitchen as I poured rice into a Ziploc bag. I spent the day without my phone, even though I had two other gadgets that allowed me to constantly check my e-mail and texts. I paced around hoping the rice would soak up the water. (It didn't.) I realized I might have to go out that night without a cell phone. I put my iPad in my purse just in case. I spent the entire dinner reaching for a phantom phone that I didn't have with me. This is the behavior of a crazy person. Don't you see what the phone is doing?

6. **People text and drive and die. People check their e-mails and get hit by trucks. People fall into shopping mall fountains**

while texting and the security footage is passed around on the Internet and that person dies of embarrassment.

Enough said.

7. **My phone won't let me go.**

It used to be that when we lost our phones we really did lose them. We had to rebuild our contacts list. We had to send out e-mails telling everyone to send us their contact information again. We didn't have everything saved and backed up. This gave us all a chance to reset. I am a firm believer that every few years one needs to shake one's life through a sieve, like a miner in the Yukon. The gold nuggets remain. The rest falls through like the soft earth it is. Losing your contacts was a chance to shake the sieve.

Now everything is backed up on the cloud and you can find your phone if you lose it in a taxi. Don't you realize it's only a matter of time before our phones can FIND US?

Our phones have somehow convinced us that they aren't trying to kill us; rather, they're trying to protect us. You are a ridiculous person if you are not reachable by phone or e-mail. As a parent you are expected to be constantly available at all times. You are encouraged to provide your children with their own devices. You are expected to monitor those devices, keep up with your children's technology, and have proper age-appropriate conversations about sexting and trolling, all while the super-nerds create apps that allow you to send a picture that disappears within seconds.

My phone has even gotten its grubby, technological hands on this book. This book is expected to have a big e-book presence. People don't buy books anymore, they buy e-books. Or maybe they buy both? Either way, it's very important that this sell as an electronic book. I am supposed to be excited about this. Gone are the days when you sat on your couch and turned pages with Dorito-stained fingers. Gone are the days when you took Henry James on the train and read it in front of cute guys to impress them. Gone are the books stuffed with pressed flowers and handwritten notes and hotel room receipts. For a minute, I wanted this book to be stuffed with things that fell out when you opened it, but my editors said no.

(They actually didn't, I just didn't get my shit together in time. It's a whole thing.)

So let's review.

My phone is trying to kill me. It is a battery-charged rectangle of disappointment and possibility. It is a technological pacifier. I keep it beside me to make me feel less alone, unless I feel like making myself feel lonely. It can make me feel connected and unloved, ugly and important, sad and vindicated.

So what do we do?

Well first, we go back to the Dalai Lama. He says, "I think technology has really increased human ability. But technology cannot produce compassion."

Man, that's good. That's why he's the Big Lama.

He goes on to say, "We are the controller of the technology. If we become a slave of technology, then [that's] not good."

So we must work hard to not be slaves. We must find a way to fight against complacency and mindless patterns. How do we do it? How does it work in movies when the good guys go up against the robots?

1. **We try to destroy them.**

   This is not happening. Technology is moving faster than ever and the Internet is here to stay. Plus, telling someone to not look at bad pictures or comments online is like telling a kid not to eat a cookie. And I'm here to tell you that any actor who says they don't search for their own name on occasion is a filthy liar.

2. **We beat them at their own game.**

   This theory was the impetus for *Smart Girls at the Party*, a Web series and website I created along with my friends Meredith Walker and Amy Miles. We wanted to build a brand that attempted to combat the deluge of shit young people see every day online. It actually all started with the idea of one simple show. It would be a *Charlie Rose*-type interview show for girls that ended in a spontaneous dance party. We wanted to celebrate the curious girl, the nonfamous, the everyday warrior. At first we only knew a few things: we wanted to make content we would have watched when we were younger, and we wanted to end our episodes with a dance party. Spontaneous dance parties are important in my life. I have one in the makeup trailer almost every afternoon on *Parks and Recreation*. Dancing is the great equalizer. It gets people out of their heads and into their bodies. I think if you can dance and be free and not embarrassed you can rule the world. *Smart Girls* is growing and changing, and Meredith and I have big plans to open up camps and create more content and connect with more and more young people. Our hope is to provide something for people who can't stand to look at another awful website highlighting some fame-obsessed garbage person.

3. **We believe in people, not machines.**

I will finish this book with a little story.

By the way, THANK YOU for reading *Yes Please* all the way to the end. I know how busy you are.

During my writing process, I struggled with my limited relationship with technology. I was forced to buy a new laptop, and I grew to love my tiny MacBook Air with my badass black cover and UCB sticker on the front. It has traveled with me for over a year and a half as I have pretended to work on this book all across America. Recently I flew to San Francisco, to shoot the finale of our sixth season of *Parks and Recreation*.

Life is endings and beginnings. Pema Chödrön says we are constantly being "thrown out of the nest."

It can be hard, this life. Beautiful too. Mine is beautiful, mostly. Lucky me.

I arrived in San Francisco with that rare combination of sadness and joy. There should be a name for that feeling. Maybe it's "intimacy." Either way, I had a wonderful time shooting the show and the shit with a cast of people I have grown to love like family. After two days, I reached into my bag to pull out my laptop and work on a piece for the book. The laptop was nowhere to be found. My heart sank. I assumed it had been stolen. Then I had the terrible memory of putting it in a separate tray in the security line. I was tired the morning I flew to San Francisco. I fly a lot, and it can wear you down. I opted out of the X-ray machine, because I was just getting tired of being zapped with rays that nobody could tell me were safe. I mean, if my phone is trying to kill me then that crazy X-ray machine at airport security is a straight-up assassin. I asked for a pat-down. It was nice, actually. A sweet woman and I chatted as she touched me. I didn't mind. It felt human. She told me she loved me in *Baby Mama*. I went on my way, but because of the small change in my routine, I had left my laptop at LAX security forty-eight hours before.

The first thing I did was cry. Because, see, I had a lot of writing on my laptop that I hadn't truly backed up, maybe forty or fifty pages. Technology can often feel like a club that didn't accept me, and so I punish it by ignoring it, which in turn often hurts me. Then I cried because I was tired, and worried about this book and getting it done while also being a good mom and a pleasant face on camera. Then I cried because I knew this was a first-world problem and I had no right to cry. Then I called TSA Lost and Found.

I spoke to a human. A man. He took my information. He was polite and he listened. He wasn't a machine. He put me on hold and took a quick look. He came back and said he didn't see anything matching that description. I started to cry again. He said, "Come on, Amy, you gotta stay positive." I thanked him. He took my e-mail and I considered my laptop gone for good. For like the millionth time during this process, I considered e-mailing my editors and asking them if I could give the money back and not write this book. The only difference was this time I had a real reason.

A day later I received this.

To: "Poehler, Amy"
From: "Fields, Sharita"
Date: March 5, 2014 at 8:51:04 AM PST
Subject: Recovered Laptop by LAX TSA Lost and Found

Hello Mrs. Poehler,
This is to inform you that your Laptop was located by the TSA at
LAX. Your TSA Tracking Item number is 14389 Report Number 192.

(TSA LAX Lost and Found only retains lost items for 30 days from
the date of this email.)

1. You can stop by our office in person with your Tracking Number
and photo ID. They will return your item after completing the
Release Form.

2. You may have someone claim your item on your behalf. On the
attached Form, please write in the upper margin: "I (your name)
authorized (name of person), to pick up my (items) on my behalf."

3. If you would like your item shipped to you, please complete
the Form and write your FedEx or UPS account number on Line
11 (described on the Return Information Instructions); and TSA
Tracking Number on Line 15. Please allow 5-7 business days from
the receipt of the Form.

Please let me know if you have any questions.

Sharita J. Fields
TSA Lost and Found
Airport Spectrum Building

Every book needs an angel. *Yes Please* had Sharita Fields.

I went straight to the LAX Lost and Found and recovered my laptop. I explained to Sharita that I was writing a book and I had been sure most of it was lost. I told her I would thank her in my book and send her a copy as soon as I finished. She was polite and professional. She let me take her picture. Look at how cute she is.

She also works with Homeland Security, so you know she knows people.

The only way we will survive is by being kind. The only way we can get by in this world is through the help we receive from others. No one can do it alone, no matter how great the machines are.

YES PLEASE THANK YOU SHARITA.

acknowledgments

First thanks go to my wonderful parents, Bill and Eileen Poehler. Thank you for contributing to *Yes Please*, and thank you for loving and supporting me. You always clapped for me when I roller-skated in our driveway. This book is all your fault.

Thanks to Carrie Thornton and Kate Cassaday, my badass editors. Your positive reinforcement and great ideas shaped this book. I'm sorry I constantly e-mailed you and told you I would never finish. It's very unlike me.

Thank you to Erin Malone, Dave Becky, and Sharon Jackson for believing I could do this and also for making me do this.

Thanks to Will Arnett for our amazing boys, Archie and Abel, and for your many years of love and support.

Thank you to Michael Schur and Seth Meyers for writing stuff for me. I know how busy you both are.

Thank you to Nick Kroll, who encourages me in all the right ways.

Thanks to my first friend, my brother, Greg Poehler, and his beautiful family. Thanks to Lewis Kay, Jeff Wolman, Warren Dern, Kate Arend, Charna Halpern, Del Close, Kelly Leonard, Rashida Jones, Aubrey Plaza, Keri Downey, Amy Miles, Rachel Dratch, Louis CK, Emily Spivey, Kristin (Umile) Haggerty, Andrea (Mahoney) Thomas, Susan Hale, Alex Sidtis, Kathy Dalton, Lorne Michaels,

Mike Shoemaker, Kemal Harris, Karla Welch, Chad Strahan, Robert Moulton, Kelly Campbell, Jeff Clampitt, Mary Ellen Matthews, Liezl Estipona, Anna Tendler, Kirston Mann, Tina Fey, and Lesley Arfin for the title. Special thanks to Meredith Walker, who is always on my side and likes to remind me I am from Boston and we finish our shit.

Thanks to Dr. Jane Aronson, Wendy Bovard, Melissa Willock, and everyone at Worldwide Orphans.

Thanks to Mercy Caballero, Dawa Chodon, and Jackie Johnson for taking such good care of my children.

Thanks to Anastasia Somoza, Spike Jonze, Marianne Leone, and Chris Cooper for letting me tell our story.

Thanks to the writers, cast, and crew of *Parks and Recreation*. Especially Morgan Sackett.

Thank you to the UCB theater community, and Ian Roberts, Matt Walsh, and Matt Besser. Special thanks to Besser, who sent me old flyers and remembered everything.

Finally, thank you, Dolly Parton. Just because.